LAYERS IN HUSSERL'S PHENOMENOLOGY

On Meaning and Intersubjectivity

New Studies in Phenomenology and Hermeneutics

Kenneth Maly, General Editor

New Studies in Phenomenology and Hermeneutics aims to open up new approaches to classical issues in phenomenology and hermeneutics. Thus its intentions are the following: to further the work of Edmund Husserl, Maurice Merleau-Ponty, and Martin Heidegger – as well as that of Paul Ricoeur, Hans-Georg Gadamer, and Emmanuel Levinas; to enhance phenomenological thinking today by means of insightful interpretations of texts in phenomenology as they inform current issues in philosophical study; to inquire into the role of interpretation in phenomenological thinking: to take seriously Husserl's term *phenomenology* as 'a science which is intended to supply the basic instrument for a rigorously scientific philosophy and, in its consequent application, to make possible a methodical reform of all the sciences'; to take up Heidegger's claim that 'what is own to phenomenology, as a philosophical "direction," does not rest in being *real*. Higher than reality stands *possibility*. Understanding phenomenology consists solely in grasping it as possibility'; and to practise *phenomenology* as 'underway,' as 'the *praxis* of the self-showing of the matter for thinking,' as 'entering into the movement of enactment-thinking.'

The commitment of this book series is also to provide English translations of significant works from other languages. In summary, **New Studies in Phenomenology and Hermeneutics** intends to provide a forum for a full and fresh thinking and rethinking of the way of phenomenology and interpretive phenomenology, that is, hermeneutics.

For a list of books published in the series, see page 226.

Layers in Husserl's Phenomenology

On Meaning and Intersubjectivity

PETER R. COSTELLO

UNIVERSITY OF TORONTO PRESS
Toronto Buffalo London

© University of Toronto Press 2012
Toronto Buffalo London
www.utppublishing.com
Printed in Canada

ISBN 978-1-4426-4462-5

Printed on acid-free, 100% post-consumer recycled paper with
vegetable-based inks.

Library and Archives Canada Cataloguing in Publication

Costello, Peter R., 1971–
Layers in Husserl's phenomenology : on meaning and intersubjectivity /
Peter R. Costello.

(New studies in phenomenology and hermeneutics)
Includes bibliographical references and index.
ISBN 978-1-4426-4462-5

1. Husserl, Edmund, 1859–1938. 2. Subjectivity. 3. Intersubjectivity.
4. Phenomenology. I. Title. II. Series: New studies in phenomenology
and hermeneutics (Toronto, Ont.)

B3279.H94C68 2012   193   C2012-905773-9

University of Toronto Press acknowledges the financial assistance to its
publishing program of the Canada Council for the Arts and the Ontario
Arts Council.

 Canada Council   Conseil des Arts    ONTARIO ARTS COUNCIL
for the Arts   du Canada   CONSEIL DES ARTS DE L'ONTARIO

University of Toronto Press acknowledges the financial support of the
Government of Canada through the Canada Book Fund for its publishing
activities.

This book is dedicated to my friend, Tim Mahoney, to my wife, Milena Radeva, and to our daughters, Anna and Laura. Tim, you are the image of the assimilation to God; thanks for all your help. Milena, I would never have written this book without your assistance and your love. Anna, I thought of you often while writing the examples. And, Laura, it was your impending arrival that most galvanized this book's completion.

This is also for you, Dad. I am sorry that you got to know medicine so intimately in your experience of cancer. I miss you.

But more often than not the idea of fusion or of coincidence serves as a substitute for these indications, which would call for a theory of the philosophical view or vision as a maximum of true proximity to a Being in dehiscence ... We should have to return to this idea of proximity through distance, of intuition as auscultation or palpation in depth, of a view which is a view of self, a torsion of self upon self, and which calls 'coincidence' in question.

Maurice Merleau-Ponty, 'Interrogation and Intuition'

Contents

Acknowledgments

Most of all, I would like to thank two people, Rene McGraw, OSB, and John Russon, whose teaching made Continental philosophy come alive for me in my undergraduate and graduate courses. Rene, you first imparted to me the sense that philosophy could connect careful textual reading to careful consideration of the people in the classroom. You were also instrumental in the development of my self-understanding. John, you have given me, in addition to your unparalleled teaching and support, a model of how to approach scholarship and its role in professional life. Your books, *Human Experience* and *Bearing Witness*, are ones that I strive to imitate and continue to read and to teach in my own classes. I am very grateful to have been your student.

I also wish to thank the many colleagues and students from Saint Peter's College and Providence College who helped me develop these insights. At Saint Peter's, I was privileged to develop contacts with Nina Shapiro, Richard Garrett, Patricia Santoro, Marysue Callan-Farley, Anna Brown, Larry Cassidy, SJ, and Gene Cornacchia. The students there were of great help to me as I developed ways of talking about Husserl. I will mention in particular Cory Gillyard, Jeff Engelhardt, Mohammad Riaz, Tomas Santos, Charlie Lassiter, and Daniel Rosenthal. At Providence College, I am greatly indebted to the following colleagues and friends for their attention to and support of my work: Laura Landen, Vance Morgan, Tim Mahoney, Christopher Arroyo, Matthew Pugh, Joe Cammarano, Nick Longo, John Allard, OP, Laurie Grupp, Gabriel Pivarnik, OP, Sheila Adamus, and Hugh Lena. The students at Providence College, particularly those in my phenomenology courses, have been exceptional and have pushed me to do more with my own research. To the following students, I express my gratitude: Kelly Jones, Monica de Aguiar, Nick Horman, Dan Taylor, Dan Ginnetty, Nick Fleming, Stephen Mendelsohn, Chrissy Rojcewicz, Nate Pinches, Meag Doherty, Scottie Gratton, Courtney Fuller, Thomas Ongeri, Beth Leonardo, Cassandra Perl, and Kathryn McCann.

For reading and listening to earlier versions of this manuscript, I thank Vincent Colapietro, Richard Lee, and Daniel Conway, who were on my dissertation committee. I also thank the members of the Husserl Circle, who heard versions of a number of these chapters and who gave insightful feedback. James Marsh and Anthony Steinbock also read earlier versions of chapters in this book, and I am grateful to them for their help and feedback. In addition, I am indebted to the anonymous reviewers at the University of Toronto Press.

Throughout the many years I have spent writing this book, I have been involved with many fine philosophers. My conversations with them have been food and water for the journey. Thank you, David Ciavatta, Kym Maclaren, David Morris, Susan Bredlau, Greg Recco, Eric Sanday, Kirsten Jacobsen, Scott Maratto, Bruce Gilbert, Nathan Andersen, Jill Gilbert, Maria Talero, Jamie Crooks, Antonio Marcato, and Amilcare Boccuccia, FSC.

Finally, I am grateful to Providence College for financial support and for the course reduction through the Interdisciplinary Faculty Seminar, both of which helped greatly in the completion of this work.

LAYERS IN HUSSERL'S PHENOMENOLOGY

On Meaning and Intersubjectivity

Introduction

On a recent trip to a museum, I was struck by, and then became puzzled at, a still-life painting by Cezanne. What struck me about the painting was that the colours and the objects appeared as if in motion. It was as if the fruits were striving to push one another along their table, striving to be recognized by me as living on the canvas.[1] What puzzled me for a few moments was wondering how I could seem to see that. How could I recognize or construe as moving or striving what were clearly painted things?

As I drove home, I wondered about the proper description of my experience. Was I standing apart from the painting, inserting into it my own idiosyncratic vision of those blue-green-red-purple apples and milk-taupe tablecloth? Or was there some truth to my experience of these objects as animating themselves and me?

Later, remembering the museum from home, I asked myself whether I had to choose between myself as a separated viewer and the objects as moving towards me. What prevented me from acknowledging *both* accounts at the same time?

As I recount this experience now at the computer, I begin to think, within the memory of this experience, and while listening to a particularly interesting song on the stereo, of the call and response structure of jazz music. I think how jazz often requires that one or more members of the group move into the background for a certain time in order to provide space and time for a soloist.

The members of the group seem to me like different accounts of the same thing, accounts that depend on one another for both their unity and their distinctness. An individual musician's move into the background of the song does not have to mean breaking away or completely disengaging. Rather, the move to the background can mean, and often *does* mean, a kind of methodological openness to the continual reshaping of the music itself by means of the co-presence or intertwining of their accounts.

As an amateur listener, I cannot imagine how jazz could happen well if each musician were not always connected and 'in tune' with what the others were doing. Rather, in a piece of jazz that moves me to like it, the others' solos appear to me to be exactly what the pianist had called for in what she had just played. That is, the others' solos seem to be what the pianist would have 'said' herself if the piano had let her 'move' there in those registers.

However, the piano would *not* let the pianist move into those other registers. And it is the differences between the instruments, and the differences between the players and their ears and abilities, that motivate the pianist's move to the background. The pianist's attentive silence to the sax, bass, or drums, her movement to lay down a basic supportive chord structure – this move demonstrates how she feels compelled to let the others play their different solos in her place, with her, through her.

As I strive to listen to the music, I am struck by how difficult it is for me to articulate who is playing and to whom. The musicians, like the apples and tablecloth, seem to move and to strive towards one another and to me in some sort of pre-established system of meaning that I am catching up with as I hear it. The experience of the painting, the piece, the group, is so complex already, even on the first hearing, that I know the only way to get clearer about how the painting appears, how the group is playing, is to separate out the parts from the whole as far as possible. To clarify the way in which the art appears is to move back and forth from part to whole, from viewer to apple to painting, from listener to musicians to musical piece.

A need for clarification means that I need to listen again and again. And as I listen repeatedly, if I guide my reflection well, I do come to hear more about how the song works, about why it moves me. After an apprenticeship in listening, what I usually find is that each jazz piece reveals, in its own way, how the others are playing in and through the soloist and how the soloist is giving new shape to the piece. And I begin to hear, through these interactions, how the themes are playing themselves through the improvisation, how the improvisation allows the themes to resound more clearly and in ways that had not been previously anticipated.

In both these experiences – of the painting and of the jazz piece – I encounter objects and subjects as acting upon one another. As such, these experiences are not ones I arbitrarily choose to talk about. Rather, they are examples that show the truth of a certain account of human experience – an account that details the structure of perception and interaction as occurring by means of layers that require, support, challenge, and even conflict with one another. The point of this book is to examine this notion of layers and to argue that layers in the object call to and respond to layers in the subject. In its examination, the book's project is to further an account of how someone like Cezanne could paint objects as entering into dialogue with the act of perceiving them, of how something like a piece of jazz music can present the enactment of communication as its form and content.

The experiences of jazz and Cezanne, in other words, are ones I use as examples here because they are very condensed, very sophisticated arguments. They are philosophical and epistemological movements as well as aesthetic ones. And their very possibility (and, more important, their existence) lends credence to the descriptions of a method of philosophical description called phenomenology – more specifically, to the descriptions of the phenomenologist Edmund Husserl.

Throughout his published works, Husserl sought to show how a rigorous description of human experience necessarily uncovers the fact that the object and the subject are always already united. This was the insight that Husserl labelled 'intentionality.' But as he worked to describe this evident intertwining and interpenetration, Husserl discovered not only that objects and subjects were always together, but also that subjects were always already united with other subjects, that the self and the other were always together from the very start. Furthermore, he discovered that the structure of subjects always already being with other subjects – a structure he called 'intersubjectivity' – served as the basis for or foundation of the experience of objects as such.

Throughout his published works, Husserl would utilize the image of geological stratification, of layers or levels of sense, to describe these structures of intentionality and intersubjectivity. Indeed, this was such an important image to Husserl that in his introduction to *The Other Husserl*, Donn Welton insists that the approach to uncovering the sense and layers of Husserl's works should be patterned after Husserl's own approach to the intersection of subjects and objects. According to Welton, we must 'dismantle layer by layer the various levels of Husserl's account, using the one controlling image he was so fond of, that of stratification, as the working picture of how his own thought was put together.'[2]

In this book I trace the notion of layering, not, as others have done, to describe the *objects* of experience but rather to clarify the activities and the structure of the *subject*. I contend that the subject has layers and that she can experience them in herself and in objects, because the subject is both a *layer* and a *whole* within the experience of pairing and intersubjectivity. The subject perceives layers (and has them) because, at least in part, she *is* one.

On my choice to focus on the notion of layering, I will now comment briefly. I do so here, before outlining the chapters to come, because Husserl's own writing about the 'metaphor' of layering begins by doubting its efficacy. In section 124 of *Ideas I*,[3] which is one of his early and seminal works, Husserl, in the context of a discussion of the relationship between an expression and that which it expresses (or the expressed phenomenon), declares the following:

> For not too much should be expected of the metaphor [*Bild*] stratification [*Schichtung*]; expression is not something like a coat of varnish [*in übergelagerter Lack*], or like a piece of clothing covering it over [*ein darübergezogenes Kleid*]; it is a mental formation [*der intenionalen Unstersicht*] exercising new intentive functions on the intentive substratum and which, correlatively, is subjected to the intentive functions of the substratum. What this new metaphor [*neue Bild*] signifies for its part must be studied in the phenomena themselves and in all their essential modifications.

Indeed, it is precisely this kind of remark, which seems to encourage people not to take seriously the way in which this 'metaphor' reflects the phenomena of a linguistic, expressive subject, that prevents some readers of Husserl from thinking consistently about the occurrence of layers in Husserl's descriptions.

One such lack of consistency occurs in the translation and interpretation of a central set of terms in Husserl's description of the layers of a subject – namely, the German verb *decken* and its cognates. Most translators and commentators, such as Christopher Macann in *Presence and Coincidence*, do not recognize the philosophical connections among *Deckung* (overlaying), *Entdeckung* (discovery), and *Verdeckung* (concealing) in Husserl's work. And they accept as received wisdom that Heidegger first connected these within his description of the course of experience in the introduction to his *Being and Time*.[4]

In addition, and because of this oversight, most translators and commentators consistently translate *Deckung* as evoking the geometrical image of 'coincidence' (*Deckung*), as opposed to the more bodily and erotic 'overlaying' – a translation that the word definitely carries in German.[5] This lack of consistency and this tendency to mistranslate prevents many readers from noticing how far-sighted Husserl was with respect to accounting for how the subject recognizes absence, difference, and distance.

Nevertheless, to support the claims that one ought not to take too seriously the notion of layers in Husserl's descriptions, and that *Deckung* means 'coincidence,' I note that in his *Ideas* immediately prior to the remark cited above, Husserl uses the noun *Deckung* to indicate something like a coincidence between the expression and that which is expressed:

> As a consequence, the expressive stratum, with respect to the posited characteristic, is perfectly identical in essence with the stratum undergoing the expression, and in the coincidence [*in der Deckung*] takes up its essence into itself to such an extent that we call the expressive objectivating just objectivating itself ... The expressive stratum can have no other qualified posited or neutral position than the stratum subject to the expression, and in the coincidence [*in der Deckung*] we find not two positions which are to be separated [*zwei zu scheidende Thesen*] but only one position [*nur eine Thesis*]. (*Ideas I*, 297)

In response to this challenging textual evidence, which seems to prevent us from interpreting *Deckung* as overlaying, since in that case the expression would be like 'a coat of varnish,' what I will argue here and throughout the book, in order to defend my own claims regarding Husserl's continued development of the notion of layering and of the cognates related to *decken*, is simply that, in his work from the 1920s and 1930s, and perhaps even earlier, Husserl found 'in the phenomena themselves,' and, most important, in the phenomena of pairing with another's body and of the intuition of essences, evidence that layering was indeed more than a 'metaphor' and that layers produced something other than simple unanimity or coincidence. Rather, I will show that layering occurs for Husserl not despite but *because of* the gaps between layers that either were not fully coincident or were coincident only while preserving the distinction or conflict between them.

A preview of some of the work I pursue in the following chapters comes from a passage in one of Husserl's last published works, *The*

Crisis of the European Sciences. That book treats the problem of how the natural sciences no longer remain connected with the ground of their practice. And in his description of their groundlessness, Husserl singles out Galileo for specific attention. The problem with Galileo, Husserl argues, is twofold: first, Galileo is 'at once a discovering and concealing genius [*entdeckender und verdeckender Genius*]'; and second, Galileo the genius's work at mathematizing the world is itself 'discovery-conceal-ment [*Entdeckung-Verdeckung*] and to the present day we accept it as straightforward truth.'[6]

For Husserl, phenomenology must not follow Galileo in its blind adoption of a scientific method. Rather, phenomenology should dis-cover the structure and meaning of experience without concealing the ground of its very activity.[7] And thus phenomenology becomes, for him, the practice of becoming fully self-responsible by forging a new, rigorous science of description.[8]

In treating Husserl's rigorous description of the layers of the human subject, this book offers five chapters. Chapter 1 examines the notion of reflection deployed by Husserl, as well as the notion of the *epoché* and reduction that Husserl used to enter phenomenology. To that end, it analyses an example from *Experience and Judgment* of an experience of being puzzled in front of a store window by something inside that looks like both a mannequin and a human. And it explores how layers (or ac-counts) of such a puzzling object can work to provoke perceptual con-flict and the need for further reflection and description. Finally, chapter 1 shows, in light of the store window example, how Husserl's descrip-tion of one's own body in *Cartesian Meditations* provides evidence of layering, which can put one in conflict or in harmony with oneself, and which can open onto one's relationship with others.

Chapter 2 turns to Husserl's account of pairing with another's lived body in his *Cartesian Meditations*. Within the treatment of pairing, Hus-serl offers his clearest articulation of layering in terms of gaps, differ-ences, and alterities. This chapter also uses his noematic and noetic descriptions there to forge more than a terminological connection between the experience of other bodies and the intuition of essences, which he describes in a startlingly similar way. The chapter concludes that essences are intuitable by means of the Others with whom one is always already paired.

Chapter 3 moves from a description of pairing and intersubjectiv-ity, and the communal intuition of essences, back to a description of one's own lived body and ego. These self-experiences, according to the descriptions Husserl gives in *Ideas II*, are also structured according to layers. As such, the body and the ego, together, welcome the experience of layered objects. Finally, this chapter demonstrates how the transcendental ego for Husserl is embodied and how its body is the life-world, as discussed in his *Crisis of the European Sciences*.

Like chapter 2, chapter 4 moves from a consideration of concrete unities to the structural organization of experience, or to its conditions. It examines Husserl's descriptions of internal time-consciousness in his *On the Phenomenology of the Consciousness of Internal Time* and of the relations of wholes to parts in his *Logical Investigations*. Central to this chapter are the way in which the present relates to past and future and the way in which the subject is simultaneously a whole, a piece, and a moment – thereby serving as the initiator and receiver of layerings.

The concluding chapter examines how Husserl, in *Analyses Concerning Passive and Active Synthesis* and in his third volume of writings on intersubjectivity, used explicit mention of a kind of overlaying at a distance or through gaps. Then, by following the threads of this overlaying-at-a-distance, this chapter makes some overtures to later Continental philosophy, proposing in particular that Merleau-Ponty's discussion of the flesh arises out of Husserl's descriptions, as does Levinas's characterization of ethics as an optics.

Across these five chapters, my effort to defend Husserlian descriptions by examining his use of layers within subjectivity and intersubjectivity has relied on the help of a number of scholars. The sections of this book that treat intersubjectivity and intercorporeality owe a great deal to important previous discussions and defences of Husserl's account in his Fifth Cartesian Meditation – namely, those of Maxine Sheets-Johnstone, Marianne Sawicki, Natalie Depraz, Dan Zahavi, James Mensch, and Kathleen Haney. In addition, I am indebted to the work of James Marsh, Anthony Steinbock, and Donn Welton, whose insightful arguments for the consistency and legitimacy of Husserlian description have inspired and sustained my work.

Like many if not all of the scholars listed above, I am convinced that Husserl remains relevant to contemporary phenomenological discussions. In large part this is because I believe Husserl's description of layering to show, as Zahavi argues, that Husserl 'reveals himself as a thinker of alterity, facticity, and passivity, and by no means is he, as Derrida occasionally maintains, a thinker who remained stuck in the metaphysics of presence, stubbornly conceiving of absolute subjectivity in terms of a self-sufficient immanence purified from all types of exteriority and difference.'[9] Particularly by paying attention to how layers for Husserl imply distinction and difference as well as the gap between them, I intend to show how experience is always potentially shot through with the absences and alterities necessary to grasp itself.

1 What It Means to Experience an Alien Other

In this chapter, my argument proceeds across three sections. The first is largely a terminological introduction to Husserl, so Husserl scholars may want to turn directly to the second and third sections. As an introduction, the first section attempts to introduce the reader, by means of deploying them, to the specific terms that Husserl uses to describe the relationship between the subject and the object and between the subject and itself. A number of key resources on Husserl's phenomenology are included in the footnotes, and these serve as an important reading list for further exploration. This section also works towards the conclusion that Husserl's transcendental phenomenology attempts to unite the experiences of reflection and involvement. And it encourages the reader to think critically about the role of 'givenness' in experience as indicating the intertwining and agency of both subject and object.

In the second section, I move to explicate an important description in Husserl's *Experience and Judgment* of a perceptual conflict in front of a store window. In the window might be a mannequin or a human being. The experience of doubt and conflict that looking into the store window entails allows Husserl to show not only the pre-reflective origin of logical concepts and relations but also the way in which other persons are already necessarily implied in the pre-reflective experience of doubt itself.

The third section then combines the insights of the first two. Exploring the description of the other person's body within the sphere of ownness that Husserl makes in the *Cartesian Meditations,* I argue here that the world offers a gift to each subject by means of the manner of appearance of actual other persons. The way the other appears, as a doubling of one's body and subjectivity that even so retains its difference, ensures that the experiencing ego, one's own subjectivity, remains thoroughly embodied as a whole and thus is open to the layers of the meaning of the world.

On the whole, this chapter sketches out and presents, *in nuce*, the argument of the other four chapters. The Husserlian revision of reflection, its description of the origin of the experience of doubt, and its discovery of the openness of one's embodiment to the other person are what later chapters attend to and employ in order to clarify how the layers of self and of intersubjectivity propel us towards responsibility for the meanings we recognize.

I. The Natural Attitude and the Problem of Reflection

For Husserl, our everyday way of living in the world, our presuppositions and habits that usually go unnoticed, are what he calls the 'natural attitude.' And this natural attitude has one overarching presupposition: that the world and the things we experience within it *really are, really exist* outside of us and of our awareness of them. Closely related to this are, I would argue, two presuppositions about our own role in relation to the world: first, that the independent, all-permeating being of the world is what calls us to respond to it by *involving* ourselves with its objects in habitual action and knowledge; and second, that our habitual involvement with objects, if and when it is broken, can be restored by our efforts of stepping back from that involvement to look more carefully at the world and at our own understanding of it – that is, by *reflecting*.[1]

It is important to highlight this last fact: whenever conflicts arise, our 'natural attitude' motivates and employs our reflection to restore our involvement.[2] To do this, we must naturally assume that our involvement with the world is always partial, that it will encounter bumps. That is the price we pay for being separate from the world. But we also assume that our reflection is capable of attending to the world and to ourselves in their separation; and, we hope, that it is also capable of adjusting our involvement to meet the world more effectively.

Some examples: a physician struggles to find the right medicine to give a sick patient; a road crew discusses how to patch a recalcitrant pothole; a parent goes to great lengths to find a favourite food to soothe a child; a baseball team strategizes after a loss. In each of these cases in the natural attitude, the world makes such a claim on us that we are convinced that it is the world, not us, that is setting the terms for our experience, and our reflection has that superiority in view. Therefore our dominant assumption in response to problems is that we need simply to find other parts of the world – the right medicine, a better shortstop – in order to address this part here that appears broken and that can no longer sustain our involvement with it. If the problem lies not in the things but in ourselves, then we still look to the world for further education and assistance.

Reflection, within the natural attitude, might best be described then as a fault that shakes us further from the world in order to cement our relationship with it. If things are going well – if we, like things, appear to ourselves simply as moments of the world – then reflection does not appear to be necessary. And, again within the natural attitude, when reflection shakes us out of our dogmatic slumbers, we are eager to reclaim our lives of involvement after we use reflection to the best of our abilities.[3]

Of course, within the natural attitude, the relationship between oneself as reflective and oneself as involved participant does not come up as a problem. How reflection could operate in the first place, let alone be successful – such a question seems irrelevant or practically useless.

For a philosopher, however, these presuppositions, the isolation and delimitation of reflection, this unilateral dependence on the world, the relationship between oneself as reflective and involved, can present problems of clarification and evidence: How are we to understand the kind of involvement we have with the world? What evidence is there of the world's separate existence? How can we and the world ever establish (or re-establish) our togetherness if we are as separable as the natural attitude assumes? What kind of a being do I have to be such that I can reflect either on the world, on my experience of the world, or on myself as such?[4] What is the relationship between reflection and involvement such that we seem to 'turn off' reflection or transition from it back to our involvement with things?[5]

The answer is that, within the natural attitude at least, we do not know. We do not know how reflection and involvement are related or how reflection can indeed pass back into involvement, if the two are in fact different. What we do know is that reflection works. And it recedes. So, because it works and recedes, we accept the limits to reflection that the natural attitude sets. We do not reflect on the relation between reflection and involvement, between consciousness and world. We simply enact it. We enact the relation, finally, in order to submerge the sense of our own being in the being of the world. And we tacitly agree to reflect, to come home to ourselves, only to better understand the world and the way the world can envelop us.[6]

This rather blind enactment of the stance that posits the separation, superiority, and self-evidence of the being of the world, this acceptance of the limits to reflection, in fact applies even to the way in which abstract scientific concepts or measurements effect real change in the world around us. From within the natural attitude, we simply take for granted that architects use geometrical concepts and drawings in order to build structures that withstand wind, snow, weight, and time. Exactly how do these geometrical concepts work on rough or bumpy material in a three-dimensional world? We do not know.[7] We simply take for granted that the world is measurable according to the rules that reflection tells us are necessary to comprehend space and buildings in this objective sense.

Perhaps one or two buildings fall down, though – very large buildings. And perhaps, in a series of events connected to those buildings' demise, a country loses a sense of its constitution and its purpose. In other words, perhaps some very large problem occurs such that reflection recognizes it as a crisis, in contrast to just an ordinary problem of the sort that 'working on it' in the natural way will alleviate.[8] Perhaps then the limits set to reflection in the natural attitude by means of an uncritical acceptance of the world's separate existence is not so comfortable – perhaps the natural attitude passes into anxiety that there is no corner of the world where we can look for ways or medicines to redress the problem.[9] Perhaps because we have lived for so long in the natural attitude, we, like characters in the Chinua Achebe novel, simply fall apart. When that happens, we feel the need for something other than the presuppositions of the natural attitude.[10]

Within the natural attitude, there are two main attempts to address this apparent problem of the dissonance or distinction between the experiences of reflection and those of involvement – before such a crisis occurs. One of the responses to the apparent dissonance between reflection and involvement is realism. Realism claims the following: If my natural attitude dictates that I am separate from objects and others, then I ought to stick by that. Objects and others *really are* separate from me, and any relation I have with them is itself a real thing, able to be broken down and explained by means of things and events within the world – things like family narratives, chemical imbalances, or genetic codes.

But coming to self-awareness or reflection within the realist position would be helpful only insofar as it tells more about what the universe *is*. Reflection, for a realist, is to be employed in order to develop a greater appreciation of real things. And realists, to be consistent, would have to be materialists. That is, they would have to argue that reflective procedures will eventually decode the relationship of reflection itself – perhaps by identifying its genetic structure, the chemicals that sustain it, the measure of the neurons that constitute it.

The other response to the apparent dissonance between reflection and involvement is idealism.[11] From the position of idealism, one sees the experience of the separation of the world from oneself, of the being of the world, as a necessary illusion. Indeed, I must take the world to be separate in order to shake myself towards the greater significance of what I am as mind or subjectivity. To know a piece of wax through changes, as Descartes said, is really to know more about the power of my own mind and its powers of synthesis.

When pressed further with the problem of the *experience* of separation itself, with the problem of the world or of other minds, the idealist might well take refuge in the argument that mind as such, which for idealism is an essential truth, needs to differentiate itself into what appeared as a world, as separate things and other minds, in order to continue to demonstrate to itself its overarching enclosure of all meaning. In idealism, the mind returns to itself by addressing its inner divisions, by *arguing* how what appears to be external and conflicting is really internal and harmonious. In other words, for the idealist, things are simply concepts that the mind gives itself to think in order to move itself (mind) through apparent contradictions or problems towards greater self-awareness. Things are shorthand expressions for what the mind *is*.

In taking the path towards phenomenology, Husserl does not choose between the two possible options of realism and idealism,[12] since he sees no compelling reason to attempt to reduce reflection to involvement, or vice versa. Rather, dissatisfied with both philosophical arguments and with the oppositions between them, he returns to the first position or assumption one makes in the natural attitude – namely, that things and the subject (or mind) *are*, and he asks whether that is the only way to relate to the question of being.[13]

In asking this question and answering it in the negative, Husserl enacts a third, more authentically philosophical position than either realism or idealism by discovering an attitude that is more radical than the natural attitude, an attitude he calls 'transcendental,' which attempts to do justice to the original and final unity[14] of reflection *and* involvement even as reflection takes its distance.[15] If an 'attitude' suggests something akin to mood – to a passive deployment of an overarching 'take' on the world – then perhaps this transcendental move is not quite an attitude. For this transcendental attitude is something one enacts by means of an explicit, voluntary, self-aware act of bracketing or *epoché*, which suspends our everyday uncritical acceptance of the being of the world.[16]

For Husserl, the *epoché* is the means by which one inoculates oneself against making uncritical pronouncements as to what *is*. What it then promotes is the description of experiences on the experiences' own terms, without uncritical metaphysical presuppositions.[17] Without presuppositions, we are free to become a witness to our being fascinated by an unclear view of the world and thereby to witness both reflection and involvement as needing further attention.[18]

The further attention, made possible by the performance of the *epoché*, is something we extend into productive phenomenological descriptions by what Husserl calls a 'transcendental reduction.'[19] The reduction is more than the *epoché*, more than the cessation of the uncritical acceptance of the being of the world. It is an active restriction of the presupposition of the being of the world, the fact that was central to the natural attitude, to our awareness or consciousness of that being.

When we have thereby become aware of, or reduced, the claim of the world's being to a claim of understandability, we find a surprising correlation. We find a correlation between the *meaning* or sense of the world as existing, on the one hand, and the meaning or sense of our own structures and responses, on the other.[20]

Unlike simple idealism or realism, the position that notices this correlation does not argue that the being of the world is just our own mind or vice versa. Rather, this position, which Husserl calls transcendental idealism or transcendental phenomenology, focuses on the correlation itself without reducing the members to one another. Indeed, in order to differentiate his transcendental idealism from both realism and idealism, Husserl immediately and consistently focuses on the description of the correlation itself, which he calls intentionality.[21]

Intentionality for Husserl can be cashed out by showing how, for each act of intertwining or attention or recognition of the subject, a corresponding revelation of the object, of the world, is attached. Each act, each ray of one's attentive regard – each *noesis*, to use Husserl's language – is attached to a layer, a stratum, an appearance of an aspect of the object, which within the reduction is now something Husserl calls a *noema*. The process of becoming clear about the meanings entailed by the *noema*, within the noetic acts that attune to its sense, is something Husserl calls a 'synthesis of identification.'[22]

In such a noetic–noematic correlation, there is no consciousness that is not involved with the object; there is no consciousness that is not 'consciousness of.' Conversely, there is no world that demands the total subordination of subjectivity. Husserl claims that within the reduction that attunes us to the noetic–noematic correlation, the being of the world depends on the being of consciousness for its very efficacy. But 'consciousness' within the reduction needs to be understood *not* in the way the natural attitude did – as simply a thing among other things that confronts the world – but rather in the sense of the all-embracing correlation of world and subjectivity, a correlation that persistently refuses to allow the subject to be fully and simply present to itself by itself.

If consciousness is, in transcendental phenomenology, that which is thoroughly open to objects, then the self-presence of consciousness becomes a problem to investigate. That is, if consciousness is now not simply the person who uneasily confronts the world in the natural attitude and who wishes to dissolve back into it, then a question arises as to what consciousness is within this transcendental reduction. For Husserl, the consciousness revealed to the one who performs the transcendental *epoché* and reduction is a new layer of subjectivity, one that both claims identification with the self of the natural attitude and enacts a novel distance or difference from it. Husserl's term for this new layer of subjectivity is the transcendental ego.[23]

These terms, *noesis*, *noema*, and transcendental ego, are Husserl's attempts to describe how intricately the subject and object map onto one another. These terms keep the very issue of being, of existence alive. Their very novelty helps to thematize, sustain, and describe the sense of the world's existence, the object's existence, the other person's existence as these intertwine with one's own.[24]

If we look briefly at what all of this means for the description of a perception of an object, we see the following: for the transcendental ego who is attending to the experience of an object, any visually perceived *noema* (say a *noema* of a table) is tied to a particular set of visual and kinesthetic acts, which help comprise the noetic acts of perceiving that I perform, that reveal more of what the table means.[25] If I separate each noetic act from the others temporally, I see just how impossible it is within transcendental phenomenology to reduce, once and for all, the object to my own life.

For in each moment of noetic life, although my current noetic act or ray of regard only has within its explicit grasp the sense of a profile of the table, the table from here where I am standing, nevertheless in each profile, in each separate noetic act, there dwells the noematic sense of the *whole* table. I see from here 'the' table and not simply a perspective or a slice of it. The underside of the table, the way it relates spatially and aesthetically with the rest of the room, the way in which the other person at the end of the table sees it – these are all to varying degrees noematic senses that are unverifiable from within the present moment of experience. But in each case these unverifiable profiles or meanings are *given* or pre-delineated with the current profile. They accompany and permeate its sense. Thus, the whole *noema*, the whole table, is sketched out within the current profile, and to that extent, as a sketch, it is within my current grasp.

As giving its sketch, however, the *noema* indicates its power to implicate consciousness in a process of explication that consciousness merely unfolds without dominating. The whole, the further profiles, are *co-given* with the profile that is currently accessible, and the very *givenness*[26] of the yet-to-be-verified ones immediately indicates how much more noetic work one has to do in order to describe or to know them exhaustively and explicitly. It is as if the *noema* of the table were already in motion, already exhorting me to walk around it and to see for myself whether what was given with itself, in a rather empty or anticipatory way, can indeed be verified as the unitary colour, symmetrical shape, and so on, that has been both promised and referred.[27] It is as if the *noema* as a whole were engaged in playing with me, with my future acts, giving me a future, a responsibility, by means of a gift of itself.[28]

Perhaps the anthropomorphizing of the table is attributing too much agency to it. Even so, it is certainly true that at any moment, the table means more than I can explicitly verify within that specific noetic act. The *noema* of the table is certainly tied through its references to its other sides to my future noetic acts.[29] It indexes them, as Husserl says. But it is precisely that fact – the fact of the *noema*'s function as the index of my future acts of explicating it, or of the *noema*'s excess – it is that fact by which being manifests itself within the transcendental ego.[30]

The experience of the being of the world and of things and others within it – this experience transcendentally reduced means that we come alive to the realm of *meaning* and how it is within the given system of meanings enjoined upon us by our irreducible correlation with objects that we perceive and move and have our being. It is the given meanings of these things that serve – more than any certainty of the world's being in the natural attitude – as propulsions to self-examination and self-development with and across them.[31]

On the whole, then, the transcendental reduction of uncritical being to givenness is a change in register, like the way the other members in a jazz group allow a soloist to come to the foreground. Only within this new register can one recognize the particular ways in which objects and subjects map onto one another, can one describe, as Husserl insists we do, the *manners* of givenness of the phenomena and the way that those manners of givenness call for our own acts of making sense of them. Within this transcendental register, we see that neither the world nor consciousness could be without the other, and we see, as Zahavi points out, that Husserl's transcendental phenomenology 'supersedes the objectivistic distinction between meaning and being.'[32]

When we stop participating in the naive, natural attitude belief that the world sets the terms for experience, that the world requires us to lose ourselves in it except in moments of breakdown, we begin to see the world in a new way. The world appears as *horizon*,[33] to use Husserl's term, as co-given with the things in the foreground. And both the world and the things appear as co-given with and to subjectivity. In other words, because, through the transcendental reduction, we see that the being of things and the world is co-given as (and mapped onto) the indexical being of our own synthetic acts, we also see that we perceive the things – the soloist, for example – directly, and thus potentially on her own terms, without the presuppositions usually afforded through the natural attitude.

Let us return briefly to the notion of givenness emphasized above. There is an irreducible passivity implied in being 'given.' And while we are reflecting, it is that passivity that motivates and sustains our involvement with the things as things, and not as our simple products. To be given something suggests that that thing appears (as gift) only as carrying the reference to its own pre-existence. At birthday parties, when we open the gifts, we may not know whether a particular gift was brand new or used. We may not know the giver, especially if there is no card attached. But that is precisely the cause of a gift's powerful attraction. It comes from we know not where, and we must now come to know it by paying attention to it *as* given and not simply as a product of our own volition.[34]

That which is given *is* in the mode of its givenness. It *is*, not because we take its being to be unproblematic, but precisely because its givenness allows us to realize that its being, its pedigree, its existence *is a problem*. In its givenness, the world *is*, not perhaps in its continuous maintenance of a reference to a divine giver who is not us, but in its structure as 'horizon.'

As horizon, the world is like the painting or the music that one's eyes move across or one's ears resound with. One has not simply left the canvas or the frame behind to see the apple or tablecloth. One must still hear the rest of the music and silence while listening to the soloist – in fact, one would not hear the soloist as playing a solo without hearing the rest, too. In short, the reduced experience of the world is an experience of the world as pregnant with objects, which are also pregnant with the world. It is this double set of references – the world as horizon and as objects within the horizon – that Husserl's reduction notices, along with the world's double references to consciousness, which itself appears *within* the world and yet carries the world *within* itself.

With the *epoché* and reduction together, then, we perform a reflection that notices the world as a structure of meaning that is *within* our consciousness. This appearance within consciousness occurs, however, *while* the world claims its being as outside of consciousness. The world *is* by virtue of and within its givenness, and thereby it appears as sustaining a reflection that is simultaneously a more sophisticated involvement. For the world now appears as getting its teeth from its involvement with us. And we appear as owing our power of reflection from our *a priori* interconnection with that which transcends us. As Zahavi puts it, 'reflection is not an act sui generis, it does not appear out of nowhere, but presupposes, like all intentional activity, a motivation. According to Husserl, to be motivated is to be affected by something, and then to respond to it.'[35]

What now no longer compels us is the presupposition of the meaning, separation, and superiority of the world's being. We are no longer convinced that things only appear by virtue of receiving their power from the world. Rather, we notice that figure and ground, object and world, are given together with us, that in some sense the being of subjectivity and the being of world are always already together and that we are the 'third term' by which object and world dance together with us.[36]

By means of the *epoché* and phenomenological reduction, and by focusing our attention on the field of givenness, Husserl attempts to show how we build up the ability to say, with evidence, what the world and what consciousness are. We build up our ability to describe our relatedness, our involvement that is at the same time the sustenance and the motor of our reflection, through what Husserl calls 'constitution.' We constitute, we recognize, we lay out, the structure of the given and then make it explicit. Not as a kind of creation and not simply as a kind of explication of what was always already available. Rather, unlike the process of reconstituting powdered milk, we constitute in the sense that we participate with the world and with other people in giving shape and meaning to what surges forth towards us. We do not reconstitute but we co-constitute, and we can do so anew and for the first time.

As Zahavi notes, Husserl 'occasionally speaks about the reciprocal co-dependency existing between the constitution of space and spatial objects on one hand and the self-constitution of the ego and the body on the other.'[37] To constitute or recognize spatial things is to be constituted or concretized by their givenness. The being-given of the object, and world, in other words, calls out for the spatial and bodily being of the subject. The co-givenness of ego and body require that we recognize their intertwining structures such that both appear as layers of each other. With Husserlian phenomenology, then, we can recognize how we are intertwined with the world in ways much deeper than is visible in the natural attitude, and how this intertwining supports and calls for the development and extension of a new relationship between reflection and involvement.

In sum, what Husserl saw, like Hegel, was that being is itself constantly showing itself to be relational; it reveals itself within an intentional, subjective nexus of relations. As Husserl explores this nexus, he comes to see that the transcendental ego, the process of constitution of the intentional correlation, is not simply one's own. Rather, the transcendental ego gathers meaning from and inserts meaning into the world by means of the ego's already bearing within itself other egos, other persons. The transcendental ego, for Husserl, has always already been a transcendental intersubjectivity.

Through his *epoché* and transcendental reduction, and within the recognition of the transcendental ego as transcendental intersubjectivity, Husserl discovered two complementary positions that address the apparent tension between object and subject: first, that persons are to themselves and to one another the indices or clues of what objects are (and thus we use our bodies and one another to discover the being and significance of objects); and second, at the same time, that objects are the indices or the traces of these selves and other persons, all of whom discover objects to be given within experience as opportunities and obstacles (and thus we use objects to discover the being and significance of ourselves and of one another).

This whole initial discussion, then, of Husserl's re-vision of reflection, the introduction and deployment of his novel terms, is a necessary step in coming to terms with his project of describing the subject in terms of layers. Reflection cannot be for Husserl a completely separate, divorced act. Rather, phenomenological reflection, as the enactment of a transcendental layer of subjectivity simultaneously united with and distant from itself, allows for consciousness to be more involved (and to notice more) within straightforward experience.

II. The Possibility That Alien Other Persons Are among Us

In order to clarify the method of Husserl's phenomenology, which we have defined as a break from the presuppositions of the natural attitude and the enactment of an attentive openness to the givenness of objects and subjects within consciousness, I start with an example from Husserl's *Experience and Judgment* (hereafter *EJ*) and with the description there of a very concrete experience – *not* of an actual encounter with an alien other person but with a *possible* encounter with such. The experience is an apparently simple one, one that could happen on any particular day while within the natural attitude. It usually lasts only several moments, perhaps the duration of a few glances. But the example is quite important, since it establishes not only the way in which consciousness makes sense of conflicting appearances but also the way in which consciousness itself is mobilized by the very possibility that another person perceives it.

In Husserl's example, one is walking by a store window, sees something within it, and 'hesitates' – is that a person or a mannequin inside? This hesitation or doubt is the very experience of a possibility of an alien other person (someone who is not me, who might challenge, who might entertain me). It is not an actual encounter, since after all it might be a hard, plastic figure there in the window. I here cite the relevant text at length, noting the explicit use of the German verb *überschieben*, 'to overlap,' which is often paired with *decken*, 'to overlay,' in other texts of Husserl's:

> Perhaps we see a figure standing in a store window, something which at first we take to be a real man, perhaps an employee working there. Then, however, we become hesitant and ask ourselves whether it is not just a

mere mannequin. With closer observation the doubt can be resolved in favor of one side or the other, but there can also be a period of hesitation during which there is doubt whether it is a man or a mannequin. In this way, two perceptual apprehensions overlap [*überschieben sich*] ... The full concrete content in the actual appearance now obtains all at once a second content, which slips over [*darüber schiebenden*] it ... One and the same complex of sense data is the common foundation of two apprehensions superimposed on each other [*übereinander gelagerten Auffassungen*]. Neither of the two is canceled out during the period of doubt. They stand in mutual conflict [*wechselseitigem Streit*]; each one has in a certain way its own force, each is motivated, almost summoned, by the preceding perceptual situation and its intentional content. But demand is opposed to demand; one challenges the other, and vice versa. In doubt, there remains an undecided conflict [*unentschiedener Streit*].[38]

The ego vacillates [*schwankt*] between the apprehensions: man or mannequin. The expectant anticipatory intentions belonging to the perception do not give a univocal prescription but only an ambiguous one. This leads to a conflict [*Widerstreit*] of consciousness, with inclinations to believe either of the two sides ... It is in this conflict of inclinations of belief [*Streit von Glaubensneigungen*], correlatively of presumptions of being, that a concept of possibility [*Begriff von Mögllichkeit*] has its origin. Being-possible, possibility, is thus a phenomenon which, like negation, already appears in the prepredicative sphere and is most originally at home there.[39]

Now, after reading this passage, it might seem that Husserl is concerned here more with the experience of doubt and with the origin of the concepts of possibility and negation in general[40] than with the particular experience of doubting the existence of an alien other person as such. The point seems merely to be about how logical concepts have their 'origin' in pre-predicative, pre-reflective experience.[41]

If that were the case, if Husserl's point were merely to show the origin of logical concepts, then the relevant example could have been the experience of doubt in the face of *any* 'ambiguous' object. However, I argue that Husserl needed to choose this possible encounter with an alien in order to bolster his conclusion that possibility 'like negation, already appears in the pre-predicative sphere and is most originally at home there.' It is the possibility of a body being perceived as a logic-deploying subjectivity like oneself that guarantees the very concept of possibility in experience.[42]

First, let us use the example to describe doubt more carefully. To doubt is to experience an 'uneasiness' even before one can think to formulate that word. I can doubt and then reflect on that doubt and say, 'I was really already in doubt as to whether that shirt was blue before I put it on.' Doubt is pre-predicatively begun (before I can assign it values and a sentence structure) and then predicatively and reflectively stated and resolved.

As Husserl intimates, however, to doubt is already to engage in a kind of logical operation. Doubt is the ability to link the concept of possibility, 'this might be that,' to the concept of negation, 'this is not that.' Doubt is the ability to experience 'this might *not* be that.' Doubt, in a very bodily feeling of irritation or uneasiness, doubt in the face of competing sights and sounds, is thus already the place of conceptual relations even in the pre-predicative sphere, and doubt shows that at least some logical concepts are most 'at home' in a realm of pre-reflective involvement with objects.

Doubt is something that the subject enacts as a response to the object. For Husserl, the ego 'vacillates' in the doubting experience – that is, the subject *moves* back and forth between the multiple senses that the object could be. The subject thus does not draw its concepts of possibility and negation (which are united in doubt in particular ways) from outside the situation of its involvement with objects. Rather, the concepts appear within the very movement between objects and their 'summons,' which the subject responds to in a 'conflicting' way.

Now it is true that *structurally* the description of the experience of the mannequin/human could have been a description of myriad other things. I can experience doubt as to whether the colour of a piece of clothing is blue or black, as to whether the theme the jazz piece revolves around is Strayhorn's 'Take the A Train' or another Ellington song I have forgotten the name of. In both cases, of colour and sound, the same structure of doubt and overlapping contents, and the same *kind* of experience of conflict, occur – Husserl would not deny this. In all cases of doubting, my own vacillation is the response to the overlapping contents, and a conflict is created insofar as I compelled to move in multiple directions while I intend to move in only one – towards 'the' answer. What, then, is so special about the fact that Husserl here talks about the experience of doubt in front of a figure that could be mannequin or human?

In this case the *content* sets this experience apart. In this particular experience, *all* logical concepts and tools that one has and is, the very functioning of the totality of one's logical system, are being called upon. For what is being doubted is not just a quality or existence of some object, which requires some part or facet of one's subjectivity to know it. What is being doubted is the very possibility of subjectivity itself (that which *is* logical) as embodied, the possibility of all of one's own concepts, all of one's own objects and relations, all of one's logical operations, becoming visibly deployed in and by an object there, an object as subject.

This experience, then, is not the experience of either embodied subjectivity or moulded plastic but of the question of the possibility of the perception of another, alien subjectivity as such.[43] In this case, unlike other cases of doubt as to the quality or existence of 'lesser' things, it is the mannequin/human itself that must do or not do something in order to prove what it is. In the case of colours, I can modify the light, do tests against other colours. In the case of sounds, I can go listen to the other two songs and decide. But in the case of the mannequin, it is the thing itself, the alien or possible alien, that has the evidence within it and that must enact (or fail to enact) that evidence, which is the evidence of all one's own logical operations. Only then can logic be useful, only then can a judgment emerge.

Because the experience itself reveals that *in principle* this doubt of a mannequin/human can only be resolved by the behaviour (or lack thereof) of the object of one's perception, it is possible that this doubt might *not* be resolved, that the conflict might continue indefinitely. Now it is not likely that such an experience will continue indefinitely, for a person can hold still only for so long and will eventually notice the mannequin's plastic construction at some specific distance. But this empirical contingency (that such an experience usually does not last very long) does not change the fact that the experience is one that in principle requires the object to reveal its capacity or lack of capacity for organized action and logical self-direction. And this means that the mannequin/human doubt-experience is more central, more fundamental than other doubt experiences, since it presents one with the necessity to examine on some level (even if only fleetingly) the conditions of the appearance of subjectivity as such.

To reiterate: it is not simply that one experiences a doubling and overlapping of the layers of one's specific and momentary intentions or their correlated *noemata* here. One experiences the *particular and explicit* possibility (because one is aware that the object may turn out to be another human) of an overlapping of an entire subjectivity similar to one's own with a non-subjective object. One experiences two layers conflicting with each other that one's own logical operations cannot in principle work out.[44]

As I will show throughout this book, beginning here and especially in the discussion of essential intuition in chapter 2, it is not just a store window, not just a full-fledged object that has similarities to the human body, that brings forth the relation of subjectivity to objectivity. Rather, the alien other person, and the other's relation of what is subject to what is object, is at least potentially at play in any experience of *any* object as such. How is this possible?

It is possible insofar as the experience of the mannequin/human was really two competing experiences. On the one hand, the experience is that of an alien, another human. The body presented itself as at least in some way *really* similar to the body of another. On the other hand, the experience is that of a mannequin. The body presented itself as a simple body like rocks and baseballs, a body somewhat similar to the body of another but only insofar as it was created to *seem* that way. These two competing experiences involved different senses – one of reality, the other of seeming; one of a subjectivity living its body, the other of a body that had the veneer of a subject.

Let us take closer notice of this experience of *seeming* to be another. To do that, let us assume that the experience ended with the perception of the being in the window as, definitely, a mannequin. To appear as a mannequin is to appear as created, moulded, and displayed by another who understands what it is to appear as a human, what it is to be another human walking by and looking at a store window. To experience a mannequin is to experience – at least indirectly, and in a rather distant or alienated way – the others who made and dressed the mannequin. The mannequin works on me, at least in part, then, because it carries within it the very purpose of the creators, this in addition to the very basic veneer of physical similarities to my own body. To experience a mannequin is to experience a host of social, cultural, and economic concepts and perspectives: the perspective of the store, of the plastic company, of the 'market' that would require a mannequin of this type, and so on.

These accompanying concepts are not irrelevant to the perception of the mannequin as seeming human. And they are certainly implicit, pre-predicatively, in the experience of doubt before it. The pre-predicative experience has implicit within it a host of items that are calling for one's attention. Yet they are not explicit. However, the lack of their explication does not mean that they work on one's perceptual involvement with the street and store window any less than the basic physical form does. In fact, the notice of the store window as a *store* window is precisely what keeps in play these various threads of meaning, and the 'hesitation' and 'vacillation.' After all, there are 'reasons' why this could be a mannequin.

All right, one might say, I see how references to other persons, alien to me, are contained in the form and substance of the mannequin. But how do *all* objects, and not just ones made by humans, carry these implicit references to others? For after all, not all objects are mannequins, not all are designed to have human form, not all are designed as such by humans, and so on.

The further piece of the argument is just this: to doubt a sound, a colour, or anything else, to doubt whether a rock is quartz or marble, is implicitly to acknowledge that there is a perspective other than one's current perspective that could rectify one's experience. To doubt is to acknowledge the possibility of doubling one's subjectivity, of creating another place from which to experience the same. To doubt is to treat the current object, the occasion of the doubting, as that which bears within it other sides, as an index of possible movements and responses on one's own part.

To doubt is to see the object from more than one perspective at a time, even if, in reflection, one can only see *one* at a time. Is it this song or that one? It seems that a good case can be made for both. In a sense I hear *both* insofar as they remain together as competing answers. But when I reflect on which one it is, I can only hear now Strayhorn and now Ellington. Thus, to doubt, to hesitate, to vacillate, is to acknowledge that one cannot actually account for how these competing, conflicting views are already united into one problem or experience. To doubt is thus to claim that, if one were someone else (someone with a clearer vision or memory), or if another with clearer senses were present, or if one could see or hear both at once, then the conflict would be cancelled, and the uneasy unity of 'mutually conflicting' possibilities would be ended in favour of the evidence of the truth.

Since one can only ever take up one layer, position, or moment at a time, the very notion of possibility implies the other persons who would both offer and guarantee the other layers, positions, and moments that are necessary for clarity right here and now. Doubt is experienced now. The possibility of doubling oneself is experienced now. If one were limited strictly to one's own resources, to one's own evidence, then doubt, possibility, and conflict could never arise as concepts.

Let us return to Husserl's description above. What is most intriguing about that description is that he discovers that these competing visions, mannequin/human, actually *'overlap'* or are *'superimposed.'*[45] The doubt is in effect a *single experience of competing layers*. The strands or layers themselves are *already* one. They play at the same time, as it were. This is why I am bothered, why I hesitate. Both are going on in my experience, and I recognize not simply disparate contents but *a single* conflict, yet I am not equal to the very unity that is a part of my experience. I can only experience 'vacillation' or one view at a time in explicit recognition, although they have made themselves a single unity, a conflict, in my attention.[46]

One is always confined to one explicit perspective at a time. How, then, can the unity 'conflict' or 'doubt' appear at all? The only way that multiple, simultaneous perspectives can present themselves, the only way that doubt can present itself not as *total confusion* or *total impossibility* but as *possibility for resolution* is if the object presents itself, within the *doubling of its senses*, as the bearer of multiple (at least double) views. The dubitable object, *any* object, thus presents itself as shot through with the possibility of an alien, of another who invests that object from other perspectives with whom one works to gain clarity and explicit awareness.

Now in the natural attitude, when we doubt, we do not recognize an alien person either potentially or actually as the condition of our resolving the conflict. We simply change perspectives. We move from this distance away to another one in order to grasp the object more precisely. In this case, the other perspectives that were presented as possible, as implicit in the experience of doubt, do in fact become explicit. We take them up. Moreover, these other perspectives are ones that we *are*, not alien ones, since we each become the bearer of the clearer view after a time. If the perspectives that we are yet to take are alien at all, they are alien only to the extent that they are perspectives we have not yet taken, just as Will Rogers once said that strangers were simply friends he had not yet met.

Yet something is still not quite right. It may be that in the natural attitude, doubts get resolved as if aliens, other people, had very little (or nothing) to do with our process of resolution. But is that really true? These other perspectives that we come to take in order to resolve our doubts about these non-human things, are they not presented contemporaneously? Are they not possible at the same moment in order to motivate our sequential shift from one to the other? They are. But that means that we only get to take that other view because we have grasped the fact that more than one view is possible at the same time. And this grasp of simultaneity comes from, originates in, an understanding of what is alien as co-given with oneself.

For it is only if the alien other person were necessary for the logical conception of possibility, of the full view of any object given in a profile, that the alien other could appear by means of an object. If the alien other were not implicated within our logical structure, if the stranger were not a full and complete doubling of our own powers that nevertheless *completed* them, then they would never be given *as* alien. They would only ever be bodies, like all other accoutrements in shop windows. Only as both the doubling and the completion or guarantee of our own pre-predicative judgments can we mistake a mannequin for a human or feel delighted or bothered, as in Sartre's account of the Look, by a stair creaking behind us.[47]

III. An Actual Alien Other – There in the Flesh!

If the previous argument about the other person guaranteeing the logical concept of possibility seemed to require further evidence, perhaps that is because the example was one of simple possibility instead of a direct description of an encounter with an actual other person. Let us attempt to offer more evidence for the implications and layering of other subjects within one's own subjectivity by following Husserl when he moves from the description of a possible alien to the description of an actual one. In that move, Husserl shows even more clearly how the experience of an actual alien other person confirms that my transcendental ego, my consciousness as such, is what it is only through its being embodied; and that, through my embodiment, I am fully linked with all other actual (and possible) egos who stand as guarantors of the entirety of my own powers of reflection and involvement.

For this section, I follow Husserl's description of the experience of the alien other person (*Fremderfahrung*) at the beginning of the fifth of his *Cartesian Meditations*. There Husserl assumes the performance of the *epoché* and the reduction, and his description involves the transcendental ego's grasp of its own body and the extension of that sense of body to the other person who enters the field of perception.

A. *My Transcendental Ego Has Its Own Body*

What I will do in this section is show how, for Husserl, even the essential structures of subjectivity – which we, following Descartes, usually take to be an abstract unity of the faculties of thinking, doubting, affirming, perceiving, and willing – are given together, *contra* Descartes, with one's embodiment. For Husserl, the philosophical experiment of reducing myself to what I am alone as a subject – the attempt to experience myself purely on my own terms – cannot rid me of my specificity and particularity. Rather, what I discover is that it is by way of my bodily experience of my own subjectivity that I am given to myself at all.

What might be helpful to keep in mind here is the genetic development of a human infant. For while this kind of description falls largely outside the eidetic description that Husserl engages in in the first four *Cartesian Meditations*, genetic accounts of experience are ones he acknowledges as relevant, particularly in section 50 of the *Fifth Meditation*, where he discusses the way a child first comes to an experience of scissors.

To take up the genetic example, then, we can watch an infant. We can see how she slowly gathers her powers of recognition in tandem with the development of her powers to move. At one month old, her feet are still 'out of sight' for her and she does not play with them. But soon after that, her feet become 'owned' by her eyes and hands and, most important, her mouth. Based on what can only appear as a gradual familiarization, reflexive movements (the feet in the mouth) suddenly emerge and she gathers a clearer sense of her whole body. For her, to recognize or own her foot is to come to be able to put it in her mouth. Months later, the recognition of the permanence of objects within her experiential field develops only with the ability to crane her neck or move from a sitting to a crawling position, or vice versa. In other words, it would seem from the way she is growing that consciousness and its conceptual power develop only insofar as her body does.[48]

Now let us turn to Husserl's own account. In the first four of his *Cartesian Meditations*, as in his first volume of the *Ideas*, he is primarily engaged with separating himself from the natural attitude and inaugurating the practices of transcendental phenomenology. In both works, he describes the transcendental reduction as the way in which the ego reduces the experiences it has of objects to the *sense* of those objects for consciousness. To review, that means, for him, that one brackets the naive acceptance of the being of the world and its objects and instead pursues the way that those make demands on and respond to consciousness's own acts.

The focus of the first four meditations quickly becomes the way in which the structures of one's subjectivity, of one's 'pure' ego, trace the outline for any objective sense that one may encounter.[49] The object, in other words, is within transcendental phenomenology an index of what subjectivity can do to reveal it, of how the subject responds in order to experience and to judge the givenness of the object in its relations to other objects and to the subject. Indeed, Husserl moves away almost completely in CM from any analysis of particular experiences of this or that thing here. Rather, he employs a number of 'reductions' that engage the eidos[50] or essence of a region or field of particular experiences.[51] It is no longer the actual experience that Husserl is interested in accounting for, but the possible ones: 'since every fact can be thought of merely as exemplifying a pure possibility' (CM, 71). And, correlatively, it is not the actual subjectivity that I am here in the flesh that interests him (at least not primarily) but the essential or possible subjectivity that I am, the 'eidos transcendental ego'[52] that he deals with: 'with each eidetically pure type we find ourselves not indeed within the de facto ego but inside an eidos ego; and constitution of one actually pure possibility among others carries with it implicitly…a purely possible ego, a pure possibility variant of my de facto ego' (CM, 72). All of this work seems guaranteed not to acknowledge bodies as such and certainly not the actual alien other person at all.

However, in the Fifth Cartesian Meditation, Husserl works to overcome a possible objection to all this eidetic work – the objection that all of these insights are true only for the solipsistic subject – by performing an additional reduction or restriction. He requires, in short, that 'we disregard all constitutional effects of intentionality relating immediately or mediately to other subjectivity and delimit first of all the total nexus of that actual and potential intentionality in which the ego constitutes within himself a peculiar ownness' (CM, 93; my emphasis). Husserl wants to get at the eidos ego, and he wants to do so in the manner in which the eidos is lived as in each case one's own. Yet it is in retreating from the possibility of the other person there in the flesh, it is in restricting the experience of the essence of consciousness, that Husserl notes that one's own body is part of one's subjectivity through and through and that the eidos 'transcendental ego' is lived only by being referred internally to a richer notion of the whole of oneself with others.

Let us see how Husserl shows the transcendental ego to be immediately bodily and to be intercorporeal. First, he notes that the transcendental ego, insofar as it is an *experiencing* ego, when it reduces its experience to what is its *own*, discovers that its body gains central stage: 'among the bodies belonging to this "Nature" and included in my peculiar ownness, I then find my animate organism [*Leib*] as uniquely singled out – namely as the only one of them that is not just a body [*Körper*]' (*CM*, 97). Experience then is bodily, and marks itself out as such, even when one is reducing experience to its essential structures, to what is one's own.[53] Indeed, the very meaning of the concept 'ownness' lies in the essential uniqueness of the appearance of one's lived body.

Moreover, this bodily essence that defines what it means to 'own' experience is reflexive insofar as the body that I *am* can experience objects and itself by means of its organs taking on the role of objects, at least for a time: 'As perceptively active, I experience (or can experience) all of nature, including my own animate organism ... That becomes possible because I can perceive one hand by means of the other ... a procedure in which the functioning organ must become an Object and the Object a functioning organ' (*CM*, 97). It is the possibility of my actual organs taking on the role of object, of taking on another perspective, and then moving back again into their role as organ – it is this possibility that sustains my possible experience of my body as a *whole*. As my hand turns from touching to touched and then back to touching, I enact the body as the background that supports the hand's alternation. Without being able to grasp it explicitly, the hand's very turning to object and back to organ has made reference to the actual, whole body that I am so that it can also become more explicitly 'reflexively related to itself in practice' (*CM*, 97).

But the fact that my lived body has organs that turn into objects does more than enable the enactment of reflexive self-experience of my whole body. The organ-into-object-into-organ movement also opens my perception onto objects. It is not just 'my own animate organism' but also 'all of nature' that responds to my organs. And this happens – this nature responds and offers more to me in my perception than I have explicitly – because I share, in the turning movement of my organs, in the structure of objects as *Körper*.

To feel or to see the world is to feel or to see things as corresponding with my own structure, as meant for my organs, as things that can sit in the hollows of my hands or in the pupils and retinas of my eyes as objects of use or of enjoyment. To feel an object is to experience my own capacity to exist as *Körper*, to feel myself as resonating with the object as *Körper*. But to feel an object is also to see things, like me, as *Leib*; and indeed, Husserl often describes the experience of objects, when we describe them in their givenness, as *leibhaftig*, as there in person, in the flesh, as active, as always resonating more than their adequacy for my organic movement. To perceive objects, therefore, is to perceive them as things that can, in their brightness or heat, resonate with my body as an entire *Leibkörper*. In so doing, I perceive things both as both appealing to my organs to pick them up and as enforcing the experience of my organs as objects, as susceptible to disease or disorder within the world.

In fact, things would not be grasped by me unless they carried with them this dual power, the possibility of attracting me to them and the possibility of directing me from my experience of them to my experience of my body and its organs. Let us stay for a moment with this directive power of objects. The active, directive, *leibhaftig* power of the object to engage my hand or my eye as object is also for the object to sketch out what I can do with these organs in the future. The object from here fits in with my power to verify the other sides of it, which are given emptily in my present view or grasp. The things appear as engaging the whole (and the future) that I already *am*, then, because their ability to object-ify me matches (or can turn into) my ability to organ-ize myself. That is, things re-mind me that my body is both my way of gearing into the world and my way of returning from the world to engage and redirect my body as a whole.

In looking intently at this computer screen for a length of time, for example, my eyes begin to hurt. I have to stop looking. Then, if I rub my hand across my eyes when they itch, the break in my direct experience of the screen and of what I am writing allows me to verify that these two sight organs are grounded in my touch field, that they are organs of my body that work on behalf of the whole and that the whole can work to reintegrate and support. My rubbing indicates again to myself that my eyes are not only organs of seeing but also objects that I can put glasses in front of, organs that can tire through their functioning, and so on.

If I follow through with this recognition, I see that the organ–object–organ structure of the eyes is something I can also verify for (or impart to) the whole of my body (or a large portion of it, anyway) through their very activity. The eyes work to give me this sense of my whole body by, as it were, projecting their own ability to be taken as objects, as they bring the other parts of my body into view. The eyes can see my fingers typing and the computer screen, and with my eyes I can, at the notice of an inadvertent misspelling, turn my fingers from immediately functioning organs of my thought back into objects that have to hit the delete button, retype, and so on. In the act of revising what I had typed, I glance down at the keyboard, glance up at the screen, negotiate the relation of my fingers to my eyes, and restore the position of the fingers where they ought to be – on the mouse, at the keyboard – in order to return to an immediate use of the fingers by my thought, and so on.

In general, then, the organ–object–organ structure pervades my experience. And it is because of this pervasiveness, because the organ–object–organ structure is initiated from (and supportive of) the level of my whole body as *Leibkörper*, that I can be inserted *into the world*. It is because all my organs can become objects on behalf of a whole that I can be *like* an object sufficiently.

However, even though the experience of this *Leibkörper* structure and its compatibility with the *leibhaftig* appearance of things has been sufficiently demonstrated, there is still a problem for Husserl to address. While we remain within the restriction to ownness, we experience, but we *cannot account for*, the character of the whole body that the organ–object–organ movement requires as its background. When the right hand moves from a touching action to a being-touched, from an organ to an object, it undergoes a qualitative shift of such magnitude that by all rights it would seem that it was no longer 'mine' in the same sense. The right hand can only live one perspective, one view, either organ or object, at a time. Yet the body unites these senses, preserves the touched hand's possibility of returning to function as an organ. How is this possible?

To frame this question slightly differently: one's lived body unites the hand as object with the hand as organ. One's lived body thus treats as two layers of its own sense the two roles of the hand. That must be the case if the body as a whole lives in and through the transition the hand makes between the two positions. But taking the hand's dual role as layers of its own life means that the body is both synthesizing the competing moments together (touched and touching) and preserving their distinctions. How can one's own lived body enact such a synthesis without a full, adequate grasp of *how* it does so? The short answer is that, within the restriction to ownness, and focusing solely on ourselves, we do not know.

None of our organs are sufficient to give a full view, a full hearing, or a full touching of our body's inside and outside. No organ can objectify the whole body – including itself – while simultaneously maintaining itself as a perceiving organ. But in the face of this inadequacy, how does the whole body as a *Leibkörper* come to our attention at all within own-ness? How can our claims to ownership extend beyond what we have explicitly in view?

What we find, following Husserl, is that the transcendental ego cannot discern how its ownership of its lived body as a whole is possible if we remain within the initial, rather radical restriction to one's own body within the sphere of ownness. Left squarely on my own, gazing simply at myself, I cannot verify my own appearance as a totality; I cannot 'own up' to my own power and expanse.

If we return to the example of the infant's development with which we began this section, we can see how the actual, genetic account of human development attests to the experimental character (and limited outcome) of this whole effort to restrict our grasp of our bodily experience to the resources that appear within our 'ownness.' For, like the transcendental ego in its ownness, the baby too is originally given a whole sense of herself, of her body, only in a purely passive way. In this passivity, her wholeness is at one level always already available, without the assistance of other persons, insofar as she can feel pleasure or pain anywhere on (or in) her body. But she also becomes actively alive to her whole body as it grows. She reaches out, grasps, and in doing so claims the project of making explicit to herself what she lives only passively, only as a support. And she does so only by engaging the touch and care of the parent or caregiver.

It is only as the baby is carried around the house, from the height of a chest or shoulder, that she as such begins to reckon more completely with, to expect more from, her own body and her world. Or it is as she discovers her older sister that she discovers (or at the very least enacts) her own power to laugh at, to imitate, and, apparently, to favour in a singular way the appearance of that sibling as the clearest echo of her own bodily life.

Husserl's initial focus within the restriction to ownness does not immediately produce the resources to show *how* we experience our bodies as wholes; this indicates that his focus must be enlarged or amended. In his focusing on strictly *self*-experience within ownness, the phenomenologist did discover something quite important – namely, the fact that subjectivity is, at its core, bodily. However, the phenomenologist also saw – almost immediately, in fact – that in the very act of living it out, our bodily self-experience appears to us as more than we can account for on our own. As we will now go on to read in the next section, for Husserl it is clear that I can grasp more explicitly the wholeness of my own body, the very meaning of ownness, only if I broaden my focus within ownness to include my experience of the other person, whose *Leibkörper* appears, unlike my own, as one I can in fact directly witness as a whole.

B. *The Body (That One) of the Alien Person Exists*

As I have intimated in the earlier description of the baby, I argue, following Husserl, that the explicit and full description of one's own lived body, the description of its whole–part logic and of its function as the term that grounds the organ–object–organ movement – all this only becomes possible within the description of the experience of the alien body. It is the other person, through and as her own body, who in her actual intertwining with my own body can view, make explicit, and thus guarantee the whole of my own. A jazz musician can only solo if the other players in the group make room for her, and she can only rejoin them if they welcome her back into the fold. In much the same way, it is the alien person's body that gives me explicative access to the power of my own body to be a perpetual horizon and support for my own increasingly sophisticated, increasingly organ-ized acts.[54]

But in order to substantiate this claim that the alien body is what allows me to live (and account for) my own body as a whole, we must first show how the alien person appears and what her body announces.[55] In the Fifth Cartesian Meditation, Husserl allows the experience of another person to occur in the sphere of ownness. He does so by allowing any kind of other person, any gender, any race, any kind of appearance of another person at all, to appear perceptually to me. In making this allowance, Husserl describes the other as if he or she were finally allowed to enter my perceptual field for the first time.

By allowing the previously forbidden other to appear within the ownness restriction, Husserl shows that, despite the non-specific nature of the other person that we allow ourselves to perceive, that experience nevertheless works to shock, decentre, double, and totally re-organize ownness.

Previously, when I had reduced my experience to what was included in my sphere of ownness, I had experienced my own *Leibkörper* as uniquely singled out. But when I allow myself to see or hear or touch the other person, when I allow myself to experience him or her from within my own resources, I see the other's lived body as *also* uniquely singled out. I see two unique and equiprimordial lived bodies, both of which are experienced by me as correlates of my own noetic acts.

To put all this firmly in Husserlian language: in the appearance of the body of the alien person within one's own sphere, one perceives a clearly, primordially, self-existing *noema*. As a *noema* as such, the alien other person still appears as a correlate of my own consciousness. However, insofar as this *noema* bears the sense of *alien*, it appears as the only other correlate of consciousness, which, besides oneself as transcendental ego, one cannot doubt in its connection to *existence*. This *noema*, alien other person, is thus uniquely given as both a correlate of mine and as a self-existing, non-correlative experience. To capture this tension, Husserl describes this *noema* as *apodictically* but *not adequately* given. And this means that the alien other person signals to us that we cannot plumb his or her full significance without further *shared* work.

The reason we have to do more work, the reason that the perception of the alien other person cannot bear witness immediately to what remains problematic in 'ownness,' is that the alien other person only appears bodily through being fundamentally out of reach:

> Experience is original consciousness ... The other is himself there before us *'in person'* ['*leibhaftig*']. On the other hand, this being there in person does not keep is from admitting forthwith that, properly speaking, neither the other ego [*Ich*] himself, nor his subjective processes [*Erlebnissen*] ... becomes given in our experience originally. (*CM*, 109; my emphasis)

As being given bodily (*leibhaftig*) without ever being originally given, the appearance of the alien person, even though it is my *noema*, maintains its own self-governance. It interrupts the normal flow between me as a subject and the manner of givenness of an object. The other person is not given simply as an index of my own future movements.

If the other person's 'I' (*Ich*) and her lived experiences (*Erlebnissen*) were given originally, as such an index, they would be, in principle, mine. Like a table, which is originally given as a whole within my grasp of its profile, the other person would appear as something I could simply walk around or turn over in order to see and verify all of her. If the other person were given originally, then the appearance of her as a whole would not bother me since the very upsurge, the origin, of her appearance would show itself as having come from me.

But the other person appears non-originarily within my ownness, as showing sides that will never fully reveal themselves to me. This fact makes me, as St Augustine claims, 'restless' to pursue her for further explanation, as the 'origin,' as the one who is responsible for her own simultaneous givenness to and removal from my view.

In terms of its essential content, its basic givenness, then, the sense of the alien body is that of my own. For the other person presents herself to me as a copy of ownness, as another lived body, as another subjectivity, as another process of giving meaning to what appears within a correlative process of subject and object. In that sense, in giving herself as a double, her arrival therefore does not shatter ownness, and my change in focus has been from ownness here to ownness over there.

However, the change in focus is not unproblematic, even if it does not shatter ownness. In terms of the *manner* of givenness of the other person – that is, in terms of the *how* of this appearing alien body – the sense of *not mine* and thus as *mediate* also arises as given: 'A certain mediacy of intentionality must be present here, going out from the substratum "primordial world," (which in any case is the incessantly underlying basis) and making present to consciousness a "there too"' (*CM*, 109). In my own experience of the other person, I sense that there 'must be' a source, an intentionality, a noetic activity, that gives the other's appearance, a source that is traceable to the 'primordial world' in my ownness. What makes the appearance of the other person problematic, in other words, is that it causes my own world to appear as strange to me.

Though the world remains mine, I cannot force the world to show me an adequate picture of what the other's intentionality is. For the world indicates that it, the world, is the 'site' from which the mediate intentionality 'goes out.' The world, my world, thereby shows itself as a participant in the simultaneous appearance and withdrawal of the other. The world sustains our sharing of it. In its 'betrayal,' the world thereby also offers 'reconciliation' – that is, it offers the possibility of further concrete work, with the other person, on what it means for the other person to be 'there too.'

The mixture of immediacy and mediacy that the world sustains, this strange system of doubled ownness-spheres presenting themselves as lived bodies, provokes Husserl to name this kind of appearance of the other person an 'appresentation' or 'a kind of making co-present' (*CM*, 109). Insofar as the appresentation of the other person occurs in my world, then, it occurs as if she or he appeared because of a simultaneous exertion on both of our parts. In its involvement with the appearance of the other person, the world appears simply as the trace of a shared effort that cannot come immediately to view. Further explication, further evidence for the alienness of the alien, evidence that would help me make sense of what is not mine about the alien other person, thus ultimately rests with (a) my willingness to pursue contact with the alien person, (b) her willingness to pursue contact with me, and (c) our mutual willingness to pursue, in the world, the trace of our 'forgotten' cooperation.

As an alien, the interruption that she embodies to me, her self-originating presentation of ownness as another bodily life, is something I can negotiate only with the other person. Only by concretizing the initial appearance as a co-presentation through further mutual work – that is, through speaking, interacting, listening, touching with her – can we clarify the relationship between the world, myself, and the other person. My continuous perception of her thus depends on our coming together within a 'functional community of one perception' (CM, 122) in which I allow her, her body, her activities of experiential syntheses to have their say in our shared projects.

C. From the Alien to the Familiar

Let us review: In the second section of this chapter we discussed the experience of the 'possible' alien other person in Experience and Judgment, and the possibility of logical concepts and structures being embodied there in the store window. In this third section, we have just finished discussing the actual encounter with a logic of ownness, a logic of essence as existence, which doubles our own actual logical structure as rooted in embodied life. In the actuality of the encounter with the alien, we discover that whole subjectivities are given together both as compatible and as at a primordial distance from one another. Further clarification of how this experience of the other person could now propel us towards further explication, towards the unfolding of the meaning and being of objects within the world and of our own bodies as geared into that world and into one another – this remains for us to do.

Here I further explore two key ideas or terms in Husserl's account of Fremderfahrung in Cartesian Meditations – appresentation and apperception. In each case, the excessive character of experience will become manifest. Appresentation, as we have just noted, will involve the noematic co-givenness of meanings beyond what is immediately in grasp, as in the backside of the table being given in the view of the front. Apperception will put forward the noetic excess of the multiplicity of acts of co-perceiving that occur within, say, the experience of listening to music, speaking to a philosophy class, or attending a baseball game.

Appresentation and apperception, working together as noematic meanings and noetic acts, will help articulate the way in which one's own body is always already intercorporeal. In addition, these two terms and the sense they bring to light will help make comprehensible how the turning of my hand into an object and back into a hand is possible. As we will see, the conversion of the hand is possible only on the basis of the way in which my whole body is given within a network of bodies, of bodily meanings and acts of perceiving.

Let us now turn to the description of appresentation. For Husserl, one of the ways in which the experience of the other person helps propel us towards our own experience is in the other's appearance as 'appresented.' Appresentation, Husserl says, is a synthesis that makes possible the experience of objects as ongoing locales of discovery: 'An appresentation occurs even in external experience, since the strictly seen front of a physical thing always and necessarily appresents a rear aspect and prescribes for it a more or less determinate content' (*CM*, 109). Appresentation is the way that immediacy, the experience of this table, for example, is given by means of an excess, a mediacy that leads one to see further more than is in view at the moment.

However, as was pointed out in the previous section, such appresentation does not provide the possibility for the appresentation of the other person: 'on the other hand, experiencing someone else cannot be a matter of just this kind of appresentation' (*CM*, 109). In the experience of the other person, the 'other sides' of her subjectivity are never fully in view, not even ideally, and they are not preserved as noematic references to my future and past acts.

Even if I can ask the other person what makes him to be him and not me, I cannot thereby receive a full answer, even if he wants to give one. The other person, for example, does not just *think* his likes and dislikes. He *lives* them. And this means that, especially *as* I take them up, his lived relation to what he likes can change, does change in my bringing those things he likes into view for him.

The same is true with his political affiliations. As I repeat back to him what he has said politically, in being confronted with the appresentation of his commitments, he may very easily refuse to acknowledge that which I have in view as permitting a sufficient grasp of his political life. This is because the act of living through what he believes, has preexisted and motivated any appearance (or reappearance) of his political expression.

Little by little, in the very appearing of his desiring or political life, he escapes me into other positions. His act of living every determination of his essence, in other words, makes a clear and sufficient grasp of them, and of him, impossible for me.

So in what sense, then, does the same word 'appresentation' apply both to the experience of the table's other sides and to the experience of the other person's inaccessibility? For Husserl, the same word applies to the manner of appearance of both kinds of objects, a table and another person, insofar as the latter founds or supports the former.

The appresentation of the other person founds or makes possible the appresentation of the table insofar as I perceive her as both similar to and removed from me. To the degree that I experience the other person as similar to me, she appresents her whole body as her consciousness. This appearance engages my *whole body*, as the similarity is not just of a foot or of a hand but of ownness as such, embodiment as such.

To the degree that she appears as removed, she takes up a position, she enacts a stance that I am not enacting. In this way, the other gives me to myself, then, but at a distance. She sketches out what I might yet do, and thus she provides the distance, the vantage point I needed in order to 'come home' to my own wholeness, my own self. I could not get all of my own body in view with one of my own organs. But in her distance from me, she functions as that organ that can 'see' all of me. She re-minds me of my own activity of being a whole – a whole that, if I remain within the strict restriction to ownness with which Husserl begins, I cannot describe or deploy adequately.

Not despite but *because of* her givenness as removed, then, the other person thereby makes possible, in her connection with me, my grasp of 'the' table within a profile of it. She makes possible the union of myself here with myself who is not yet, who is in the future; she shows how my current viewpoint can also engage my future ones. She does this because, by virtue of her presence and absence within my own sphere, she connects her noetic acts of perceiving with my own. By virtue of our appresentation, then, as similar wholes, as wholes within the sphere of ownness, we always also *apperceive* one another as actively gearing into our shared 'primordial world.'

In grasping the appresentation of the other person, then, I also immediately intuit, I *apperceive*, her own acts of perceiving as interwined with mine. I experience that she sees all of me, or can do so; that she judges, or could, all of me as attractive or giddy or unstable or dangerous. I also experience that she sees, or can see, what I see from other perspectives, which are not mine.[56]

Perhaps I become interested in her reading of a text, her view of a picture, her emotional and intellectual experience of a piece of music. And I listen or read or view again, as if from other sides, as if from hers, trying to see or hear or read as she would. In doing so, I may or may not 'get' what she does. If I am far behind her in terms of practising how to listen to free improvisation, it is almost guaranteed that a single act of listening will still not help me hear anything but 'noise.' But in my attempt to be like her, I will begin to perceive my own hearing of 'noise' differently. And I will discern the possibility of being different, of maintaining a different relation to free improvisation by means of her acuity, which I perceive in her face, in her speech, in her attitude.

The appresentation of the other person, in other words, is also the means by which we apperceive with (and as) each other. This intertwining of appresentation and apperception allows me to grasp that my whole body can be called into play by a *noema*. It first occurs with the other person. It occurs, by way of the other person, with all other noematic correlates. Within our mutual apperception, we function as particular organs that, together, uncover greater significance within an ongoing, paired relationship.

Indeed, Husserl makes this last argument – that the other person assists me in my gearing into the world – explicitly in the *Cartesian Meditations*. To experience the other person as non-originally given is possible, he says, only if 'our perception of the primordially reduced world, with its previously described articulation' *calls for* or 'motivates' the perception of the other as an unverifiable certainty (*CM*, 110). He asks 'How does the motivation run? What becomes uncovered as involved in the very complicated intentional performance of the appresentation' (*CM*, 110)? Within ownness, then, the world that we experience, the total world, has always already 'leaked' evidence of the other. Something in the world colludes with the other person's coming to appearance; something betrays our attempt to restrict our focus within ownness. As Husserl implies, something in the noematic sense of the world *acts*, it calls forth, it requires, it acknowledges the role of the other person. Within one's own very *having* of this owned world, in the very process of an organ–object–organ movement, then, we are always already on the way to a 'perception of the other.'

To further emphasize the way in which the other and myself are co-given originally, Husserl notes that the appresentation of the other person immediately demands something of my own body, something I was not aware of until I examined how the appresentation of the alien body was possible: 'the body over there, which is nevertheless apprehended as an animate organism, must have *derived* this sense by an *apperceptive transfer* from my animate organism, and done so in a manner that excludes an actually direct, and hence primordial, showing of the predicates belonging to an animate organism' (*CM*, 110–11; my emphasis). My own 'perception of the primordially reduced world,' the sense, the experience of the world itself rose up to meet the other and did so by transferring the sense I have of myself, of my own body as organ–object, without really *showing me* what it transferred *directly*.

My objects, my world, my sense of my body have all doubled themselves. They remain as senses, but they also leave me and move to the alien person there. They 'exclude' me by not leaving in their wake the 'predicates' that would have paved the way for me to understand how they can be mine but also be shared.

The world left me and went to her, Sartre would say. But that is not true for Husserl. According to Husserl's description, the world both stayed with *me* and went to *her*. The fact of our sharing the world does not immediately or necessarily descend into a competition for mastery of the sense of one's experience. If we follow Husserl's account, meaning is an issue for me, the world is *for me* to know because I appear *within the world* and allow the world and others to do their work on me.

This mutual appearance to one another is something that Husserl describes as occurring due to an appresentative *similarity* that supports our mutual apperceptive transfer: 'It is clear from the very beginning that only a *similarity* connecting, within my primordial sphere, that body over there with my body can serve as the motivational basis for the analogizing apprehension of that body as another animate organism' (*CM*, 111). The world of correlates, the world that I claimed as simply what I constitute as transcendental ego, then, is a world that I do not simply (idealistically) control as if its status as correlate meant that it was my creation. Instead, as we claimed previously, the world *itself* appears as having an agency that we must have always already permitted and authorized, an agency that shows pre-predicatively to me and to alien others that we are not only mutually appresented objects but also subjects who co-perceive the world (and one another) together.

By motivating our apperception, by 'leaking' my transfer to the other, the world enabled its own verification by making possible a link between what could not be verified, between oneself and the alien. Ours is the appresented similarity that occurs, therefore, as if behind our backs, as if by the world's separable agency – and this apperception of one another, and of the trace of a worldly agency, is the indication that bodily subjectivity as such is both multiple *and necessary*.

There must be a reason, given within our givenness to one another, for our being together. There must be a *telos* to our taking up the world as the site and source of our intertwining. And there is. This reason, this *telos* is the opportunity to attend to the excessive character of the world's meaning, to perceive with one another our shared eruption together across our 'primordial world.'

In other words, if I sense that the world is in some way responsible for our mutual apperceptive transfer, then that is because the world, which remains mine, which remains in some sense my noematic correlate, offers our transfer to us as an excess, as a gift of our co-perceiving. Our world, which is still in each case experienced as one's own, then functions as if an anonymous gift from the future, as if from our future selves, towards each of us in the present. And the *gift* the world made by helping transfer the sense of one's own animate organism to the alien (and vice versa) is the gift of meaning, of possibility, and of fields of further exploration.

After all, the 'exclusion' of direct verification of exactly what constitutes this 'similarity' between oneself and the other person does not mean that we must not seek *further* or *concrete* verification. On the contrary, the exclusion of direct verification bothers us. And we seek the reason for it together in the world. The inability we have to dominate one another's perceptual acts, the possibility of shared perceptions – these are problems and possibilities for us that motivate us to take up what we share as the worldly beings we are.

As I have intimated to this point in the book, one possibility marked out by the lack of direct verification of our interrelationship is further phenomenological description. To pursue our givenness to one another as indefinitely but never adequately verifiable, we could engage in the shared, methodical work of presuppositionless description in order to find out why there is no full disclosure. In this pursuit, our lack of direct verification might translate into authentic, ethical stances. That is, if we took this phenomenological possibility seriously, we could pursue the way in which the impossibility of finding out the source of our relationship might open up new, worldly ways of seeing what we *can* open up together – interpretations of texts, of beauty and justice, of music, art, and politics.

In this sense of taking up a shared responsibility for the lack of verification of our mutual transfer and our fundamental similarity, we turn now to Husserl's further account of how our mutual transfer structures our ongoing perceptual experience of the world as such. Like the transfer involved in the experience of another person, Husserl says, so too 'each everyday experience involves an analogizing transfer of an originally instituted objective sense to a new case, with its anticipative apprehension of the object as having a similar sense' (*CM*, 111). Objects can sustain histories and sciences of experience because first *we* do. We sense 'scissors' for the first time, or what a party is for the first time, because we use or deploy in a directed, partial way the transfer that we already are *as whole bodies and subjectivities*. We transfer partial senses onto others within experience because we, as sense-transferring whole beings, are ourselves always already transferred to one another.

The world's gift, then, is that the division between myself and the alien has already been fundamentally appreciated, negotiated, and *directed* by a source that operates at a higher level than the difference itself: 'Ultimately we always get back to the radical differentiation of apperceptions into those that, according to their genesis, belong purely to the primordial sphere and those that present themselves with the sense "alter ego" and, upon this sense, have built a new one – thanks to a genesis at a higher level' (*CM*, 111). Our division, the alien and the primordial, the other and the self, is a division that is 'radical.' What I perceive as truly 'my own' marks itself out as different from what I perceive together with the 'alter ego' or on her behalf. Yet, Husserl suggests here, the radical differentiation we experience is not the experience of a complete splitting. Neither set of apperceptions, one's own or the other's, dominates the other within the structure of the transfer as such; therefore, when we take up a transcendental description of our life together, what we are as perceptual beings is a co-functioning system of 'apperceptions.'

The 'radical differentiation' therefore maintains itself as a unity, as something to be experienced, only within the 'settled' unity of the entire perceptual system. This difference, by virtue of its answerability to that shared source, that 'higher genesis' of the system itself, therefore does not preclude the possibility of connections among multiple, concrete apperceptions, differences, and variations, which all coalesce or sediment themselves in more or less stable, particular patterns or familiarities.

We are engendered at a higher level, Husserl argues, and that higher level is the shared world and the perceptual system themselves. Each of us is unified by means of radical differences, with the alien other persons by being made *for* a fully and mutually determined world, the promise of which always leads us on together. Yes, it is true, the higher genesis of our relationship will never exhaustively appear or fully account for itself; we will never 'rest' together, as Augustine thought we might, within the full description of the world, within a single, united vision of the concretely determinable 'purpose' of the universe and human community. However, this fact need not shut down our time together; it can on the contrary continue to motivate us to press together towards this 'higher genesis,' this full world of transcendental intersubjectivity, which calls us into our perceptual lives.

As we move on from this chapter into the next one, we will take up more particularly the way in which our togetherness, given within our mutual appresentation and apperceptive transfer, makes possible the adequate description of our own experience *as* our own. We will see how our fundamental perceptual similarities, and their distances from one another, are implicated within our own power to anticipate, within the grasp of this side, what we might *possibly* discover in the other sides of a perceptual object. And we will also see how we can provide evidence for the argument that, because I am not the alien other person, but because I am given with her, I can take her anonymous but *actual* position on a table, a piece of music, or a blossoming tree and come to reckon with and thus to know those objects better.

In light of our discussion of ownness, it might be helpful here, at the conclusion of this chapter, to note that ownness, my own sense of experience, is a problematic notion that needs to be further explored. For Husserl, ownness is not simply preserved, but neither is it erased. The togetherness of self and other is what fosters this uneasy maintenance of the 'radical differentiation.'

If we take jazz as an example for this, we might easily agree that the differences between persons and instruments are preserved in a group. Yet we could also see that solo performances, the chance to 'say' something of one's own within a jazz group, are earned only through hard, specific work with one another. For the most part, a chance to solo is earned when the soloist learns how to move into and out of the group, when she learns to trace and listen to the others, to the group, who is with her at the base of her musical or philosophical experience. When she learns how her body is implied in the instrument, in the logic of music, in the history of jazz, in this group, with this sax player and drummer and bassist, she is able to play, as if for the first time, explicitly, the piano solo as if it were what was always being called for – a solo of free improvisation that is different from even while nevertheless still building upon the others' efforts.

2 Intersubjectivity – Syntheses and Product of Encounters with Alien Others

Introduction

Doubt, one's own lived body, other people – these are all unities that are clearly original experiences. We are at one with our doubt and with the difference that we experience between doubt and certainty. We experience immediately the power to live as and govern through our bodies. We encounter alien bodies from the beginning as other persons, other egos. Yet, although we know *that* we experience them, although we know something about the *manners* of givenness of these unities, still we lack a great deal of clarity as to how they arise within experience.

If the power of phenomenological reflection that Husserl inaugurates as maintaining a link to our involvement with the unities of experience is to help us in a significant way, it needs to assist us in clarifying the appearance of these unities as the kind of unities they are. In particular, as we mentioned in the preceding chapter, Husserlian phenomenology needs to clarify how the alien person's body presents itself without directly demonstrating which predicates of an animate organism have been transferred from oneself to make the encounter possible.

This second chapter has two sections. In the first, I explicate the particular syntheses that Husserl identifies as at work in the pairing with another's lived body in the *Cartesian Meditations* (*Husserliana I*, hereafter *CM*). And it is here that the relationship of overlaying (*Deckung*) achieves prominence in a way that will be relevant to the rest of this book. What the deployment of this term by Husserl signifies in the pairing with other bodies, I argue, is that distance and alterity are recognized without being totalized or reduced.

In the second section, I explore within the account given in *Expe-

rience and Judgment (hereafter *EJ*) how the overlaying with the other person is fundamentally employed in order to recognize essences. This argument, in its explication of the *reason* for isomorphic descriptions of pairing and essential intuition, is new, but it derives, I claim, from the earlier consideration of doubt as a pre-reflective gift of the possibility of other persons.[1]

What this chapter does not consider yet are two important conditions for intercorporeality and essential intuition – namely, time-consciousness and the logic of part–whole relations. These I save to discuss in chapter 4, in which they will be seen both as gifts of intercorporeality and as conditions for it.

Initial Definition

The remainder of Husserl's Fifth Cartesian Meditation, much of his *Crisis of the European Sciences* (*Husserliana VI*), and numerous volumes of his lecture and working notes are attempts to explicate the experience of our encounters with alien other persons. The experience of others has numerous conditions, numerous structures, that make possible our actual perceptions of them. But the general name for these conditions or structures is intersubjectivity, by which Husserl means the linking or intertwining of the powers of the transcendental ego that is in each case one's own.

For Husserl, intersubjectivity is not an abstract set of categories that are visible only when we consider other persons. It is not a thing or a concept. Rather, it is the origin, process, and goal – the prepared, unfolding organization of the syntheses that are already at play – of every experience that a subject has. Intersubjectivity is the 'higher level genesis,' the pattern that our intercorporeal, bodily experience is imitating and echoing. And it is the call of these bodies to mutual recognition.

In the act of listening to the jazz piece played by a group, one hears a whole that the parts could not have produced on their own, a whole that organizes the players and the notes. However, that same song is nothing else than the players and their breath and hand motions in their responses and calls to flesh out the theme. This sense of the whole piece of music as both independent of its parts and dependent on those same parts (which are themselves wholes) is the sense of reciprocity given musically.

The intertwining of the players' bodies, the way each player makes room for the others, only happens given a whole that is their explicit organizational principle. Their bodies respond, encounter one another, within an overarching structure. Yet that structure is nothing – marks on a page, perhaps – without those bodies to take it up and carry it out. Particularly in jazz, it matters essentially who the players are, whether and how they anticipate one another, and how they take up the same theme and what they do with, through, and to it. In short, in jazz one sees, hears, and feels the bodies and the piece call to one another, just as the bodies and intersubjectivity do in Husserl's descriptions below.

I. The Syntheses at Work in Encounters with Alien Others

As we discussed at the end of chapter 1, the experience of the alien person's body occurs without our immediately knowing exactly and exhaustively *how* it *could* occur. The experience happens as if behind our backs, as if some higher function of our powers – powers we did not know we had – were already engaged in recognizing the alien. The experience of the alien thus appears as if the truth of the experience were a higher unity that we had already formed with the other.

It is precisely this character of appearing *without* a clear pedigree that Husserl examines. When Husserl looks more closely at the 'intentional situation' of the appresentation of (and of the bodily, apperceptive transfer of sense to) the alien, he finds several powers, several 'syntheses' at play – namely, similarity, overreaching, awakening, and overlaying. These syntheses are the conditions for the appearance of the alien in a perceptual encounter. They are the predicates that are at least initially excluded from a direct showing.

It must be the case, in other words, that the appresentation and apperceptive transfer that occurs in an alien encounter does so because one is 'awakened' by the other – that the noematic contents of oneself and the other have appeared as 'similar,' as finally 'overlaying' their sense with one's own. Husserl's discussion of intersubjectivity, at least in the fifth of the *Cartesian Meditations*, thus is the recovery of a necessary 'history' of the acts of recognition that are brought together in the single and immediate experience of *Fremderfahrung*. It is these acts of recognition lived as a unified whole that form intersubjectivity, which is more precisely a way of seeing and a way of *being* the intertwining that one has with others.

The experience of the alien other's body *calls for* the recognition and reflection that oneself and the alien other were already *joined together* in mutual, passive and active syntheses of meaning. The appresentation and transfer of that body requires that we acknowledge that we already are subjects that are intertwined with one another such that other things could be experienced together as paired, as calling forth a response that has implicated our own bodies.[2]

A. Similarity

Although we have already spoken at some length about the way in which Husserl describes the appresentation of the other person as a relationship of similarity, I would like to return briefly to it here. What I want to emphasize is the way in which a noematic similarity motivates or founds the more noetic act of overlaying.

In her experience, the phenomenologist searches for the layers of sense that go into the encounter with the alien body. She discovers in her search that she can recognize a passive source of her intentionality of the other person, a similarity or *Ähnlichkeit*, within ownness: 'It is clear from the very beginning that *only a similarity* [*Ähnlichkeit*] connecting, within my primordial sphere, that body over there with my body can serve as the *motivational basis* for the "analogizing" apprehension of that body as another animate organism' (*CM*, 111; my emphasis). One can recognize another person as another lived body like one's own only if the experience of another person is prepared passively, only if, 'from the beginning,' one already sustains a 'motivation' to recognize a relationship as such that can be further specified as an 'analogizing apprehension.' Similarity does not privilege either oneself or the other. It is an impartial, non-self-conscious insight that 'takes in' at one blow the entirety and the certainty of the encounter.

Such a passive preparation of a relationship is something we often experience even when not doing phenomenology. If we stop after some years to take account of how we became friends with someone, often the exhaustive account of the beginning of the relationship is hidden. We are left with an intuition of a compatibility that we must have recognized straight away, without being quite aware of our perception. Why else but for a passively recognized similarity or compatibility would we have pursued this person at all and not these others who were there at the same time? This kind of compatibility or similarity that we discover at the bottom of our explicit awareness of a friendship is rooted, Husserl is arguing, in an unexplicated experience of similarity at an even more passive level of bodily involvement with others. It is this sort of a structure of similarity, which nevertheless can itself be experienced by means of phenomenological reflection, that makes possible any and all involvement in language and action.

In other words, the experience of similarity is a passively intended, concrete presentation of others within one's 'primordial sphere.' Now it is in its concreteness that the similarity itself matters and calls on us to act on it.[3] She calls to me with a voice like mine, and our similarity hits me in the midst of what I am doing. Hers is not any cry or sound; it is one I share, a voice that always already has a grip on me. I walk like my father, and you can see that when we walk together, his gait is just the way I also walk. And even if I try to undo the similarity, I cannot. However, in these two examples, despite the initial concreteness of moments or organs of the experience of similarity, the totality and range of the similarity – of the 'predicates' proper to *Leib* and productive of the similarity – are, for essential reasons pertaining to the very meaning of 'alien,' not able to be adequately (thus explicitly) intuited by me. How does her voice immediately claim mine? What is it about a human voice, or, for that matter, the call of a loon on the water, that inaugurates the similarity? How do I walk like my father? How is walking built as a stylistic and not just a functional similarity? These questions move towards the recognition that the similarity announced in these examples, this inherently experienceable relation or structure, is something that is, as a whole, passively and pre-predicatively established.

Though it be established pre-predicatively, however, the similarity between oneself and the other person does point back, from within its concrete development, as precluding at least one description of it. That is, the similarity between one's own lived body and that of the other person is *not* capable of being described as a relation of original and copy. This is because, as we live our similarity with others in concrete ways, we find ourselves unable to control the relation.

In the friendship example, neither friend can say that she is the unique and sole original lived body to which all others appear as subordinate, as merely similar copies. Our similarity and compatibility with each other as friends announces a sharing that cannot divide into master and mastered. This is also the case with a less sophisticated example.

While I am walking down a street, I have an experience of a woman who waves at me. In seeing her hand waving urgently, I find myself almost immediately waving back in a similar way, without thinking, even though I realize, from the beginning, that I do not know her. That is, I find myself beginning to raise my hand and to wave it back to her,

as if completing a circuit, without explicit awareness of what I am doing. My similarity with her, that of my body with hers, that of her wave
with mine, seems to announce itself to me as that of an original (the
woman waving) and a copy (my, subsequent and rather non-reflective
act).

But this is not so. The woman waved because she had already passively grasped that we were similar as total bodies. She waved as a
recognition of the fact that we were given together as similar bodily
wholes, and that I could be compelled by our separate hands *as if* they
were organs of our pre-established overarching, communicative relationship. She may have originated our explicit communication, but she
depended on a prior similarity that (passively) appeared to her – that
is, of me as someone who, like her, experienced waving as a means of
further contact.

Furthermore, she waves because she realizes at some level that she
cannot dominate our relation of similarity. She waves as a plea, as someone who sees that neither of us is the origin of our pairing together, of
our involvement. She waves to mean 'please, please take up what we
already have between us.' Indeed, within any appearance of our similarity with others, then, each of us also realizes that the similarity that
precedes and claims us does not take away the fact that it is only in *one*
of these bodies that each of us rules and governs, as Husserl notes. Our
similarity does not *enforce* upon us as its members the manner of our
explication of itself.

Because one still experiences distinction within the similarity, the
phenomenologist thus recognizes that *similarity* is not the synthesis or
the experience that adequately accounts for the possibility of the experience of an alien body. The woman on the street does not wave at me
simply to announce how similar we are. She waves because she wants
to say more, to someone who can say 'no' or walk away from her, even
as my hand is already responding.

Similarity therefore cannot *as such* explain the discontinuity between
the other's body and my own, the resistance to the original-copy des-
ignation. And thus Husserl is compelled further to explore the genesis
and appearance of the interrelationship that occurs across the irreduc-
ibility of both oneself and the other. What the phenomenologist discovers is that the difference that still occurs within the experience of
similarity leads to the discovery that our *mutual and symmetrical* functioning as individuals occurs as a mutual *overreaching* and eventually as
a mutual *awakening* and *overlaying*.

B. Overreaching

How do we perceive ourselves as similar when we are so separate, when the other is precisely other? The similarity occurs, Husserl finds, only as similar discontinuities. It is the discontinuities that are paired, that occur as similar.[4]

The other person as a body that is immediately a similar lived body appears as a *noema* that *exceeds* its own limits. The other's body appears as demanding that it be recognized as a similar *system* of perceiving, one that gives its own evidence of itself. The other appears as a 'there too,' Husserl says. Yet this overreaching of the alien body, this penetration of one's own sphere with its similarity and demand for equal recognition, which no other object or body on its own can do in the same way, occurs because, in one's recognition of it, one has *also enacted* this same kind of overreaching. To recognize the other's demands, claims, overreaching – this means that one's own act of perceiving must also have already reached beyond itself, reached into the other's otherness and made sense of it.

Husserl discusses the overreaching that persons enact relative to one another as the motion of pairing. In any pairing, including one's own with the other person, there is 'an intentional overreaching [*Übergreifen*], coming about genetically (and by essential necessity) as soon as the data that undergo pairing have become prominent [*abgehoben*] and simultaneously intended' (*CM*, 112). The relationship, the pair, comes about 'genetically.' That is, the relationship immediately issues into the members, who each enact its structure. The jazz group starts to play together and already from the very first practice session, certain dynamics, certain patterns of which player solos when (and in what ways), mark themselves out as the usual course. The group can work at making these patterns explicit, work at changing or varying them, but the overreaching, the way they impinge on one another and sidle or smash their ways into the centre, has already started before they can reflect on it.

On the one hand, then, the members of a pair of persons, of lived bodies, become intended by each's own consciousness simultaneously and are taken up *as simultaneous*. Each has already overreached itself and entwined itself with the other. One's entire lived body and one's ability to experience *as such* are paired with another person's – that is, both of us see the table as seen by the other; both our gazes are locked in a loving, desirous, indifferent, or angry situation of seeing each other.

On the other hand, this simultaneous overreaching can only happen in this way, in this recognition of the otherness of the other as claiming recognition, because the overreaching preserves the very limits that are being transcended. For each member, the individual-bodily limits 'overreach' each other while preserving the ability for each to experience the pairing as his or her own.[5] They are simultaneous and yet sequential, in the same way that a soloist does not require the others to stop playing, and in fact often *needs* them to continue laying down the beat or the bass line.

Overreaching names this strange mixture of unified simultaneity and individual, sequential limits (a pair is both together; a pair goes from this one to that one). Overreaching, then, is one of the descriptive terms that Husserl uses that I believe, like simultaneity and the others listed in this section, names something intuitable. That is, it names something that is both a condition for the possibility of the experience of other persons *and* a concrete experience.

In short, the experience of overreaching names this fact: people come to understand themselves and one another according to their relationships. From a long time beforehand, perhaps from the beginning of one's memory, one perceives oneself as a (paired) member of a family, or of a marriage, or of a friendship. Yet within that relationship, within that pairing, one maintains and even develops the capacity for freedom and self-reflection by virtue of the fact that the relation only occurs as something that preserves a distinction and distance between it and oneself. What one discovers in the course of relationships is that one is held accountable for the course the relation takes *as if* one were always already explicitly and completely bound within and by it – without ever fully being so. A relation, such as the family, that appears initially as *complete* coincidence and simultaneity, as the complete submersion of one's own role as a particular individual, later manifests the fact that it has always already called on one's own power (as a *separable* layer) to assent to and preserve it.[6] The relation is also what situates and preserves the members.

I argue that it is this situation of becoming prominent together and overreaching one another that is most important for Husserl's description to continue towards layers and layering. One can come to one's own self-experience (and for phenomenologists, persons can only perform the reduction to the sphere of ownness and eidetics generally) *only* if one begins *as if* in a fully original upsurge of mutual prominence and mutual (albeit implicit, perhaps regulated and graduated) abridgement of distance and perspective. This is precisely what Husserl means, I take it, when he emphasizes that the overreaching comes about 'genetically' (CM, 112). The overreaching occurs as the very genesis or origin of persons' becoming prominent together. Overreaching is coeval with persons' prominence as singulars. That is, ownness occurs only within and given the decentring and mutual relationship of oneself and others.

The description of one's experience as an overreaching, however, is still not sufficient to account for one's experience as it appears. This overreaching does not itself reveal *how* both persons do not immediately annul one another's limits completely. One has merely recognized that these limits are not destroyed because one has experienced them as having had to reach 'over' to one another. Within this overreaching, then, something remains to be discovered – and that something is the most sophisticated descriptive syntheses, *awakening* and *overlaying*.

These syntheses can be experienced in their own right in myriad encounters involving the lived body, and with them the phenomenologist can finally clarify for herself the manner in which the initial similarity and overreaching occur as both ruptures and ongoing initiations into and a preservation of ownness. The passive (awakening) and active (overlaying) syntheses display themselves in their intertwining as the basis for our mutual perception of one another as humans – that is, for co-perception as similarly embodied and mutually implicating subjects. These two syntheses allow the phenomenologist to account for the ways in which her experience of the other person is an identifiable unity of *her* experience, which by definition retains her ability to be awakened by the other person to new demands, to new meanings.

C. Awakening, Overlapping, and Overlaying[7]

The moments of any pairing, Husserl says, are more closely described as 'a living mutual awakening [*Sich-Wecken*] and an overlaying of each [*überschiebendes Sich-Überdecken*] with the objective sense of the other' (CM, 113).[8] The phenomenon of awakening [*Sich-Wecken*] is the phenomenon of the *distance* or limit between oneself and another as nevertheless founding the appresentation of overreaching similarity. The phenomenon of overlaying (*Sich-Überdecken*) is the phenomenon of the *bridge* that those involved make over their distance, a distance that the bridge (unlike the initial overreaching) nevertheless continues to bring before them in their passage over it. Overlapping (*Überschiebung*) is paired here with overlaying (*Sich-Überdecken*) as a noematic, affective pressure that motivates a noetic grasp.[9] By means of the overlapping, noematic contents that push consciousness towards a grasp of its intercorporeality, awakening and overlaying stand in a correlative relationship and reveal themselves as such, just as the bridge reveals the distance required for it to be a bridge.[10]

Awakening and overlaying are correlative by means of overlapping contents eliciting a synthetic response; that means neither awakening nor overlaying itself is sufficient to account for the experience of overreaching and similarity, for how a similarity and an overreaching with others actually come to *matter* to us. In one's empirical description of emergence from sleep to the recognition of wakeful experiences of objects and other persons, one has some evidence of the experience of sleeping as both similar to and distinct from that of wakeful experience; but the transition from one to the other happens always as if behind one's back, out of reach of one's immediate identification, insofar as one's senses operate anonymously, receptive to the affective and overlapping contents of the waking world.[11] One's emergence from ownness (or indifference) to the particular experience of particular other persons evinces a similar structure to the empirical experience of waking up from a sleep or coming to recognize overlapping family structures in the sense of one's own utterances.

The phenomenologist recognizes that the experience of another person and that person's *Leib* must have been prepared by a passive synthesis that precedes explicit identification. Like the process of waking up from sleep, which involves a kind of implicit but constant and increasing (passive) resistance on the part of consciousness to remaining in its sleeping state, the awakening to another person's lived body is an experience that the phenomenologist discovers to be possible only insofar as the other person offers constant (albeit previously implicit) *resistance* to one's own intention. One awakens to the sense 'other person' because one's consciousness cannot understand the other as a moment of itself. One awakens because one's consciousness experiences the other's resistance and is thereby called out of itself, out of its own restrictions into a wider, shared field of play.[12]

The phenomenon of awakening is thus experienced as the *limit* to one's identification of the other person. One cannot make 'one's own' what allows other people's bodies to be theirs, and this limits the extent to which one can make immediate, explicit sense of the other person and vice versa. Mutual overreaching, in other words, is experienced to some extent as the preservation of one's limits relative to the other person *by means of* their ability to challenge that limit, to wake us up.

To the extent that persons have awakened one another as noematic wholes – as bodies within a nexus of overlapping intercorporeality – persons also perform a noetic act, a mutual understanding or synthesis of identification that is active and that occurs within each person's primordial sphere. This very ability to identify with one another is what Husserl calls our 'mutual overlaying' – it is the further development of the synthesis announced in our overreaching one another.

I will argue below in more detail about the synthesis of overlaying and its distinction from awakening, but suffice it to say here that the phenomenon of overlaying is encountered as the ability to have experiences of one another within a unitary experience, to identify one another as on the same earth and in an overarching relationship. One experiences other persons never in complete isolation from oneself but always in some relation – even if that relation is largely potential, merely bodily, definitively conflicted, and so on. And the fact that the other always appears in relation to oneself, then, is the fact of overlaying.[13]

D. Conclusion

Husserl's discovery and explication of the structural, correlative, and experiential notions of awakening and overlaying comprise the most sophisticated layer in his description of the experience of the other person. When one experiences one's mutual encounter as an overlaying, for example, one sees the origin and preservation of the earlier description of the apperceptive transfer:

> As the *result* of this overlaying, there takes place in the paired data a mutual transfer of sense [*Sinnesübertragung*] – that is to say: an apperception of each according to the sense of the other, so far as moments of sense actualized in what is experienced do not annul [*aufheben*] this transfer, with the consciousness of 'different' [*Anders*]. (*CM*, 113; my emphasis)

And, although Husserl does not maintain it here, I argue in the sections that follow that the transfer of sense as egos also depends on their noematic awakening to one another. Indeed, all the descriptions of appresentation – transfer, similarity, and overreaching – come about because of the gap between the lived bodies, a gap that is ineradicable and mutually identifiable and that awakens persons to one another and to themselves.[14]

In general, pairing and mutual transfer can break off or decay whenever one's perceptual attention turns towards other things or when the characteristics of egohood disappear – as in the case of death or in the experience of what seemed human being in fact a mannequin. The pairing, which begins as a recognition of a bridge across a gap, a shared gap that allows for mutual understanding, a gap that *is* consciousness – the pairing that begins as a bridge of one lived body to another – can in fact conceal aspects of itself or fracture into a relation of oneself with another mere body (*Körper*). But this shows, then, that the authentic case of pairing is not a case of merely reaching out and intending another person as simply a mere body (*Körper*) and from there gaining access to her alienness. Essential to pairing is the unconcealing of the ongoing and co-primordial element of awakening to the other's alienness, the uncovering of a relationship that the phenomenologist cannot fully bring to explicit awareness as simply her own constitutive activity.[15]

II. Intersubjectivity as the Basis for Intuiting Essences

Intersubjectivity does more than just name the general conditions for the encounter with an alien body. It is not just the fact *that* alien bodies call for a kind of unity that must pre-exist them. It is also *how* they do so. In other words, the meaning of the term 'intersubjectivity' includes the specific *kinds* of unities that are formed by means of bodily overlaying with one another. It includes the way the conditions of experience likewise become concrete, particular stances of taking up the world and one another.[16]

For Husserl, intersubjectivity is also at the heart of consciousness's ability to intuit or 'see' essences. By means of the perspectives of other persons, integrated within each one's own perspective, each person, each subject has the ability to intuit or perceive essences on his or her own. By means of these mutually implicated perspectives, each person can anticipate, codify, and organize his or her concrete experiences in terms of the actual types and rules that function within and across them. In short, it is because each subject can apply her or his pairings with alien bodies to objects as such that essences appear immediately as what they are.[17]

A. The Functional Community of One Perception

The experience of one's subjectivity, of one's growing power of reflection, is the experience of arising as a body for oneself. However, the experience of one's subjectivity is also the experience of living with another person in a shared field of perception, a shared world of objects. Indeed, as Husserl describes the conditions of this encounter, he finds that another way to point out the mutual overlaying and awakening that occur within the encounter is to point to an operative, perceptual co-functioning: 'In other words, the two [the sense of other's body for me and the sense of the other's body for himself] are so fused [*verschmolzen*] that they stand within the *functional community* [*Funktionsgemeinschaft*] *of one perception*' (CM, 122; Husserl's emphasis). Persons co-perceive one another, and together (in mutual co-perception) they co-perceive the world as one world and their correlated perceptions as one act of perceiving.

A functional community of one perception means the following three things: both oneself and the other perceive in *similar ways;* both self and other perceive the same *things;* and each one of the pair can experience his or her own separate acts of perceiving as implicated in (or as directed by) the other's. I will consider each of these in turn. Oneself and the other perceive in similar *ways:* each has the same kind of perceiving body; each needs to move to get a better view on things, and so on. Both self and other perceive the same *things:* each experiences her or his perceptions as limited perspectives on things that require other perspectives to fulfil them. And finally, the perceptual acts of both self and other *implicate* each other: I experience the other person as a similar yet separate ego who co-perceives herself when I perceive her, who co-perceives herself when she perceives me, who co-perceives me when she perceives herself.

Each of these three components of the functional community of one perception requires the others. Ultimately, however, the third component is the foundational one. The other two, perceiving the same objects in a similar way, are possible only given our mutual implication. In other words, we see that we are similar because the very act of *seeing similarity* is shared. By virtue of mutual implication, by virtue of oneself and the other people mutually appearing together and to one another within a situation, one's experience appears always as an excess, as a yet-to-be-fulfilled system of empty intentions and fulfilments. The guarantee that it is possible to live with this excess, to recover, to interpret or to make something out of it, stands there in the already implicated person of the other.

An example might come in the experience of a national or familial tragedy. We may not know the others who also mourn or who are shaken by these deaths. But immediately on being thrown together in mourning, we seem to 'find' one another, to feel connected as ones who have lived through the same situation. We see without thinking or speaking that we have recognized the same things, even if only passively. And even if we never speak, even if we can never recover the situation in its entirety, since we did not live through it together in exactly the same place or manner – that is, even if loss is an irreducible moment of the temporal character of persons' functional community as such – still we take the other person as a route into the excessive character of that experience. Access to the other, lost faces of the shared world is what the other *means* and *exists*.

Following this example, perhaps Husserl's most concise formulation of the functional community of one perception is as follows: one experiences the other person 'as if I were standing over there, where the Other's body [*fremden Leibkörperß*] is' (*CM*, 123).[18] From this it becomes clear that the alien body has imposed the necessity of one's being involved, of being in relationship. The relationship is not something external, not an introjection. Rather, it appears as a recognizable unity-through-distance. The 'as if I were,' as a kind of subjunctive distance between oneself and the alien lived body, is not collapsed. Rather, it is always maintained. The unity with others is a unity in which one always has work to do to understand what the situation is, what it has been, what it means for the future. In any finding oneself together, the experience of the relationship is an ecstatic experience of standing outside of oneself. It happens according to simultaneous but different modes of intuition that can always be taken up reflectively. And in this being outside oneself – at least in terms of the sense the other person has for oneself – one is given to oneself as this ego who, despite ecstasy, finds the value and meaning of its own perceptions only within the relationship itself.

B. Functioning Together, We Intuit Essences

Having discovered our functional community of perception, what we find in Husserl, I argue, is that it is *because* we are intersubjective that we are able to see essences. It is *because* we are always already over-reaching, awakening, and overlaying all other subjects with our whole bodies that we can perform the activities whereby particular objects and the world in general can yield to us the essences that make possible an experience of something *as* what it is. In other words, it is *because* we already form a functional community of perception that we can function perceptually together on behalf of one another, on behalf of that community.

Returning to the example of listening to jazz music, we can anticipate the insights discussed in this section. The following examples, it is true, are ones in which I describe how I come to intuit essences about explicitly intersubjective phenomena – the identity of an artist across her music or of a song across its variations. However, although I do not start here with the intuition of an essence of 'an object as such,' I will go on to show how the intuition of all essences operates according to the logic of intersubjectivity, which is simply writ large in these examples.

The first example is of listening to the singer and pianist Nina Simone and trying to determine the essence of her music. Now I very much enjoy her songs, but if I were asked what it is that motivates that enjoyment, I would have to do a bit of work to figure that out. That work would largely include listening to her play and sing across a sufficient number of her songs, albums, moods, and so on.

In fact, as I do move from one song or album to another, I hear Nina's voice shifting. Sometimes her voice sounds to me like a muted trumpet; at other times, like a harsh wind; at still others, like a slightly out-of-tune violin. Across these differences, though, in which she seems to be a series of modifications of the same singer and artist, something grabs me. As I work to describe her impact on me now, it seems that what motivates me to like her work is that, in each piece I hear, she sounds like the particular 'enworlding' of an idea, like justice or oppression itself.[19] That is, the variations of her voice resound in me as if she and I shared an important idea, an idea that resounds directly through and as her. For me, then, the idea of Nina Simone as a whole, the idea of her jazz music as immediately bearing witness to her particular inflection or deployment of oppression and social justice through the particularity of her tenor and tremors, arises through these songs, across them, as if it were an important part of her essence as a musician. I hear her as if a particular face of justice were what she brought to and through these pieces, as if that was what I picked up on and affirmed in my enjoyment.

Another example might be to think about the essence of a particular jazz standard – say, 'Someday My Prince Will Come.' What is it that characterizes this song? What does it mean to hear it? Many great and undiscovered jazz artists and groups have played this song – Bill Evans for one, Miles Davis for another. But if we are to articulate the essence of this song, we need to listen to *all* of these variations – and they can be *quite different* from one another.

In jazz particularly, the essence of a piece does not lie shut up in the markings of the original sheet music. Rather, the standard can still sound within the variations, and sound more urgently, even though each variation is an opportunity for the artist or group to be in dialogue with that piece and with one another. How do we establish the essence of 'Someday My Prince Will Come'? By listening to the variations, by hearing through them what the song intends, what the groups do, what it and they leave open, make possible, forfend, and so on. Through the variations something happens – some grasp of what ties these variations together – that is both a particular chord progression or rhythm or key and more than these – that allows one to grasp the essence.

In both of these examples – the unity of Nina Simone through her works, and the unity of the song 'Someday My Prince Will Come' through its variations – it is clear that a functional community of perception is required and enacted in the process of describing the intersubjective phenomena being considered. I can perceive the essence of Nina Simone's music only (1) by bringing her different musical acts together so that an organizing principle of justice lost and longed for shows through them; and (2) by myself communing with her perceptions, or by acting as if I can, with what I hear of her, in the process. I perceive the essence of the song 'Someday My Prince Will Come' only (1) by allowing the variations themselves to show a communal appreciation across their differences (and perhaps because of them); and (2) by allowing my own perception and understanding of music to contribute to the bridges between them, to hear through them and with them what they are all calling for.

As I now go on to lay out Husserl's description of the intuition or experience of essences, I will emphasize the way in which other people are necessary for the intuition and experience of *any* essence, and not simply the essence of these societal, cultural, musical producers and products. What will be interesting to note is how the logic, the structure of these intuitions, is exactly the same. All essential intuition, for Husserl at least, operates as if trying to determine the essence of a person or a cultural production.

The main textual example I use here comes from section 87 of *EJ*, titled 'The Method of Essential Seeing.' Across that work as a whole, as we learned in the first chapter of this book, Husserl is concerned with the role of the pre-predicative sphere in the recognition of essences and their identification as unitary phenomenological objects. In this particular selection from within *EJ*, Husserl states that, with the multiplicity of variations that her imagination provides in the process of eidetic variation, the phenomenologist sees the development of the *eidos* as a rather organic and qualitative leap:

> In this transition [*Übergang*] from image to image ... all the arbitrary particulars attain overlapping coincidence [*überschiebender Deckung*] in the order of their appearance and enter, in a purely passive way, into a synthetic unity in which they all appear *as modifications* of one another *and then* as arbitrary sequences of *particulars in which the same universal* is isolated as an *eidos*. Only in this continuous coincidence [*Deckung*] does something which is the same come to congruence, something which henceforth can be seen purely for itself. (343; my emphasis)

I will now explicate this text in reference to Husserl's discussion of intersubjectivity in the Fifth Cartesian Meditation, focusing particularly on the terms 'transition' and 'modification.'[20]

1. TRANSITION

Essences, for Husserl, appear directly. The experience of them, for him, cannot be disputed. We do not simply see particulars and then *argue* to essences. We see or 'intuit' essences, and this kind of direct seeing or intuition of essences is a problem only insofar as we attempt to clarify how it occurs, especially relative to other kinds of intuition.

As implied in the text cited immediately above, one of the differentiating marks by which an essence appears is the kind of act that makes its appearance possible. For Husserl, the acts of consciousness, out of which an essence appears directly and in person, are called 'eidetic variations.' In performing these variations, consciousness then enacts a 'transition' from image to image, from one variation to another. Through that transition, consciousness comes to leave behind the variations in favour of a full intuition of the essence itself.

For example, in order to clarify the manner of appearance of the essence 'table,' the phenomenologist holds in mind the appearance of this particular table with regard to one aspect – its four, brown, short legs; she then varies that aspect by moving imaginatively to another, possible appearance of five, yellow, longer legs, and so on. The *fact that she can make the move back and forth* between these two appearances or variations, as well as to a multiplicity of additional variations not given explicitly in her intuition of this table here, allows her, after amassing a sufficient number of particular variations, to see each and all variations as 'arbitrary sequences.'

This change, wrought upon each particular instance, each of which is now given the sense of 'arbitrary,' occurs by means of this sufficient and uninterrupted set of consciousness's own acts. The subsumption of particular instances towards an overarching *eidos*, then, would not happen without one's ability to make transitions and to allow a multiplicity to fade into the background in favour of a new appearance, the appearance of an overarching principle of unity, for its own sake.

In light of our discussion so far, it is important to note that the appearance of the essence or *eidos* occurs because of the noematic–noetic correlation of content and act. The subject makes a noetic move in that she 'transitions' between acts of variation. She inaugurates, in other words, a flow of action, a continuity, and her consciousness maintains its unbroken focus through its movement, through the variations. This continuous motion allows her to be open towards the *eidos*, which is prepared by the manner of the variations fitting together.

Correlative to the continuous, noetic transition is the noematic sedimentation or 'belonging together.' The contents of the images respond to the continuous, purposive, and imaginative movement. They respond by giving themselves as 'modifications' of one another, as variations that join together. Out of the successful, continuous transition – indeed as the meaning of that very success – the content of each variation supports and calls for the following one. The noematic affirmation of the noetic process thereby eventually allows the subject to experience any further instances or variations as *already belonging together,* thereby allowing the rubric to appear on its own precisely because the contents and the acts correlate so fluidly.[21]

The noetic act of 'transition' and the noematic content of 'modification' are moments or concepts that Husserl also locates within the phenomenological description of the encounter with other persons. I will briefly explore the role of each within intersubjectivity in order to move towards the conclusion of my argument for this section – namely, that other people are necessary for the intuition of essences. What I will show here concerning transition are two key points: first, that the transition I perform in order to see particulars as various instances of the same *eidos* is something I am always already involved with all the time within intersubjectivity; and second, that it is because I *am* both a variation and a motion of transition within transcendental intersubjectivity that I can establish a correlation between variations and transitions in my own experience of essences.

Now, by way of anticipating objections, it is true that Husserl does not use the term 'transition' or *Übergang* in his description of *Fremder-fahrung*. I believe he does not do so because he recognizes that the experiencer cannot actually 'go over' to where the alien other person is and live her experiences as she lives them. One's particularity as this lived orientation, as the zero-point of one's own Here, is, as Husserl says, irreducible. And thus one can never *oneself* truly achieve the transition towards the other person in the way that one can move from one's own lived experience of this table to an imaginative variation.

Nevertheless, as we have discussed in the previous section, the experience of another person compels the phenomenologist towards the motion of transition – and indeed, implicates us within it – insofar as we are compelled to say that the other person appears from there 'as if I were there': '[the body of another person] brings to mind the way my body would look "if I were there"' (*CM*, 118). The sense of the subjunctive 'if I were there' thereby evokes in the experiencer the recognition of the structure of transition, even if, unlike the eidetic variation, the transition cannot actually be fully and intuitively completed in the experiencer's own consciousness. Thus the manner of appearance of the other person is evidence of a transition that cannot be fully completed yet appears *as if* it were always already completed imaginatively.

In fact, the other person not only appears as if *some* appearances of one's body had already been involved in a transition between them as one lives them here and hers as she lives them there, but also as if there were always already performed a movement or transition by one's *entire* body: 'The first-awakened manner of appearance of my body is not the only thing that enters into a pairing; my body itself does so likewise … Thus the assimilative apperception becomes possible and established, by which the external body over there receives analogically from mine the sense, animate organism' (*CM*, 118). In other words, the relationship between persons that Husserl describes as 'pairing' or *Paarung* can only appear as a unity if it is the case that one's body as such already has, within its appearance to oneself, the sense of having 'gone over' to where that other person is and confirmed their sense as an 'animate organism.' One's transition or movement from over here to 'as if I were there' is therefore a necessary movement that one recognizes as *demanded* by the encounter, as a transition that *must* already be made, even if it occurs by means of gaps that can never fully be filled in.

Neither in eidetic intuition as such nor in *Fremderfahrung*, however, can transition be a structure sufficient to account for how the appearance of the *eidos* or the other person as other comes to presence for consciousness. As mentioned already, the *eidos* appears as the *correlation* between transition and variations, as the principle for this correlation, or as the noematic recognition that appears as the simultaneous index (and transcendence) of the phenomenologist's own noetic movement. In the case of *Fremderfahrung* more particularly, it is precisely *because* the transition between the phenomenologist's self-perception and the other's perception of her *cannot* be fully completed within her consciousness that the transition shows itself to be insufficient to account for the entire sense of her encounter as a pairing and a unity. It is not the case, then, either in eidetic intuition in general or in the experience of the alien other, that the transition alone (as the motion consciousness performs) could be the content of any *eidos*.

2. MODIFICATION

In his description of both eidetic intuition and *Fremderfahrung*, Husserl asserts that the noetic transition that consciousness enacts correlates with a noematic sense of each image, variation, or person as a 'modification' of the other. Ultimately, this correlation of transition and modification leads the phenomenologist to describe an 'overlapping coincidence' in which the *eidos* appears. Insofar as the transition in each case – that is, in eidetic intuition and the experience of the alien other – occurs within one consciousness, then the two images, variations, or persons do not simply remain separate from each other. They sustain internal references from the one to the other; they appear as modifications of each other *by means of the very possibility* of moving between them.

Let us take each in turn. First, in the description of *Fremderfahrung*, Husserl describes the appearance of persons as a system of modifications:

> It [the sense of the lived body of the other person as immediately expressing their subjectivity] is therefore conceivable only as an analogue of something included in my peculiar ownness. Because of its sense-constitution it occurs necessarily as an 'intentional modification' of that Ego of mine which is the first to be objectivated, or as an intentional modification of my primordial 'world': the other as phenomenologically a 'modification' of myself. (*CM*, 115)

There he highlights that the other person appears, and could 'conceivably' appear, only as an appearance of a person who is linked through and through to one's own self-appearance. A person appears as a modifying claim on one's own self-experience, as if one had already made the move to be there where she is standing.

In terms of the second case, namely that of eidetic intuition, we have already cited the parallel description of the modifications involved in eidetic seeing in the passage from *Experience and Judgment* mentioned at the beginning of this section B. As a brief reminder, Husserl describes there a kind of *progress* from the appearance of particular images to their appearance as 'modifications' of one another 'and then' to their role as 'arbitrary particulars' that yield a new appearance of the separable *eidos* in their overlaying.

After thinking through the significance of the terminological similarities in the descriptions of both essential intuition and *Fremderfahrung*, I claim here that Husserl meant for us to attend to the process of (1) appearing as modifications of one another, and then (2) forming the *eidos* through those modifications, as a process that founds and previews what we do when we see any other *eide*. In fact, the process of modifications forming an *eidos* is directly visible as a temporal development in numerous examples from intersubjective life.

Let us take as an example the act of listening to a jazz trio play a familiar standard. The acts of transition between the soloists and the group are made by means of different registers, different interpretations of the same theme or piece. Each solo is, in its own way, a modification of the others, a taking up of them, an anticipation and remembrance of them. For the attentive listener, it is by following the transitions and by hearing the modifications as calling for one another that he can hear the whole, the essence of the group's effort and communication. In some sense the *eidos*, the true sense, of the song appears to the attentive listener only as the recognition of the solos as modifications of one another and of the original piece.

To be sure, this insight is able to be (and usually is) hidden by the skill and intimacy of the jazz group. For we often hear the group or the piece and not the motion of foreground and background of the solos, not the means by which the group or the piece appears as such. Yet an attentive listener, one who interrogates the ground of her enjoyment as she listens to the music, can attend to the layers of the music, can hear and follow its motivational structure and musical development as she encounters it.

Like the attentive listener, the reflecting phenomenologist is trained to attend to the way the *eidos* arises by means of its variations. And in attending to that development, the phenomenologist can notice that the process of intuition in which the *eidos* arises also evinces the same kind of structure as the experience of *Fremderfahrung*. That is, the phenomenologist can see, in any particular encounter with an alien other, how the appearance of the lived body of another person first stands out as an irreducible particular; and then, through a kind of transition, appears as someone similarly embodied to her, as making a similar set of demands (i.e., appearing as modifications); and then, how she and the other serve as mutual modifications, as cases within the general structure or *eidos* 'other person.'

Yet there is an important difference, one that I highlight in order to show what I take to be the proper ordering of essential intuition as such to intersubjectivity. The experience of *Fremderfahrung* is one of mutuality, of one's becoming an eidetic variation – becoming a modification – of the alien other person and vice versa. But in this mutuality it is also an experience of becoming and *owning* the shared *eidos* of transcendental intersubjectivity without having fully submerged oneself as an *arbitrary* modification.

If I recognize myself to be a variation of you, and you of me, in *Fremderfahrung*, it is not true to say that we thereby recognize ourselves as members of an arbitrary sequence for an intercorporeal, intersubjective *eidos*, which arises through us but outside of us. Intersubjectivity does not appear by our losing touch with – or distancing ourselves from – our ownness as such. Rather, the *eidos* that we are together, which we intuit directly as our community of function within intercorporeality and intersubjectivity, is, like all other *eide*, still also an *eidos* 'for' each of us in our own particular perceptual lives.

The *eidos* 'transcendental intersubjectivity,' then, has always already been formed in the same basic manner in which all other *eide* are formed – through variations overlaying one another at a distance and thereby making possible the intuition of an *eidos*. But because in the *eidos* of intersubjectivity *all* of our being and meaning is involved (and not just a particular noematic content), and because the *eidos* that we enact is one that we recognize ourselves to *be*, the variations or modifications are never fully or simply arbitrary. In other words, we are able to grasp ourselves as modifications of each other only insofar as our perspectival (and irreducible) particularities refuse simply to serve as arbitrary functions within our 'functional community of one perception.'

Given this difference, why should one note the isomorphic structure of essential intuition and *Fremderfahrung*? The answer, I take it, is that the variation in the isomorphism is itself significant. Indeed, as I will go on to argue below, the variation indicates the fact that the *eidos'* transcendental intersubjectivity is formed prior to all other *eide* and is, by virtue of its ability to provide a limit to arbitrariness, the target or goal within all other *eide*.

Let us turn now to the difference in the overlaying that operates within the encounter with the alien other person. There, in forming an essence by means of all that we are, by means of our entire embodied consciousnesses, which we see as given wholly together with the other person in *Fremderfahrung*, we function not as arbitrary modifications of one another but as relatively (more or less) *anonymous* ones. The two terms *anonymity* and *arbitrariness* mean very different things.

An anonymous person is not an arbitrary one. An anonymous donor to a university, for example, keeps an important, particular sense in their withdrawal or withholding of their name. Not just any arbitrary person could have donated this sum, and so on. Likewise, because of the sense that anonymity preserves, it is the anonymity of one another as modifications that press towards intersubjectivity that now deserves further consideration. For ultimately, it will be the anonymity of the variations within intersubjectivity that call for but also hold accountable and revise the arbitrary modifications of other *eide*. It is because we can never fully know one another within our nevertheless mutual formation of intersubjectivity, it is because anonymity is never fully dispelled, that (a) we can have *eide* at all, and (b) we must hold *eide*, on behalf of those who have not perceived or spoken yet, as immediately grasped but as indefinitely susceptible to critique.

Let us return to the example of eidetic variation in the experience of the essence 'table.' To vary the appearance of this table imaginatively and arbitrarily is to engage in eidetic intuition on behalf of the others with whom one always already forms transcendental intersubjectivity. It is to acknowledge their simultaneity, their ability actually to take up other views right now that are contemporaneous with but distinct from our own. To vary our perception of 'this here now' towards an *eidos* is to attest to the gift of the other persons' very particular, very own, powers to view what we do ... but from where they are, from the very actual and specific but largely anonymous standpoints that they enact.

However, the anonymity of the others whose powers one uses to vary the appearance of the table, even without their being present in the room with us, even within what appears as our own imagination – this anonymity does not take away their co-givenness with us as transcendental intersubjectivity. By virtue of this co-givenness, it is always possible that their anonymity could, at any moment, diminish. In fact, the anonymity of those other modifications of oneself is *in principle* convertible to personal particularity in each and every case of an encounter with alien others.

All that someone need do is to appear within our experience and introduce to us a table whose structure we had not thoroughly accounted for in our own variations. Or all she need do is point to a piece of the music or of a text in philosophy again, and highlight a word or phrase, and suddenly we realize that we had enacted a series of variations or interpretations on her behalf, on behalf of all readers or hearers of that text, which were inadequate.

Phenomenology, in other words, helps us see that in order to intuit an essence, we must be willing not only to 'take (over) a stance' but also to communicate it, to 'stand up' for it, to allow it to be confirmed and disconfirmed. To intuit essences is thus not simply to participate in the movement of absolute truth but also to participate in the tying together of truth and intersubjectivity, of experiencing absolute truth as the explicit coming-to-recognition of what always already occurs implicitly and anonymously.

To have a perceptual world, to have essences, by means of a functional community of one perception, means that within our essential intuition and our communication of that experience, anyone can, anyone must, come to check our work and to fill in concretely his or her formerly anonymous co-functioning. In this occurrence, in the efforts of the person who appears to 'check our work,' in the interruption or the resistance or the creativity of the now *less* anonymous other person, we see the always provisional status of the arbitrary variations that we pass through to grasp the *eidos*. We see how *eide* are given on behalf of the anonymous others with whom we share our structure as transcendental intersubjectivity. And we also see how they are so given only for ongoing description and communal efforts within our shared perceptual system.

The only certain *eide* are those given as the very structure of transcendental intersubjectivity itself – for example, the structure of mutual overlaying and awakening, the structure of intentionality, of the way in which the object as such reflects noetic rays, or the pattern of modifications overlaying one another and allowing the *eidos* to shine through.

And that means that most – perhaps all – other *eide* must be what Husserl would have called 'inexact' essences.

Before I leave this section on modification, let me point to a further place in the *Cartesian Meditations* where I see Husserl discussing the encounter with the alien other person as a mutual modification. There, in the description of *Fremderfahrung*, as the motor of the 'apperceptive transfer' (*CM*, 110) we discussed above, Husserl points out the 'mutual overlaying [*sich-überdecken*]' (*CM*, 113) of the sense of one's own lived body and that of the other person. This overlaying, this transfer, is the noetic and experiential indication of the noematic and synthetic unity of persons as modifications of one another in the *eidos'* transcendental intersubjectivity.

To point to further textual support for my argument here, I would highlight that Husserl also discusses transcendental intersubjectivity directly as anonymous, as concrete, and as open-ended – that is, as the very horizon of all actual and possible other persons: 'It is also clear that men become apperceivable only as finding Others and still more Others, not just in the realm of actuality but likewise in the realm of possibility ... To this community there naturally corresponds, in transcendental concreteness, a similarly open community of monads, which we designate as transcendental intersubjectivity' (*CM*, 130). For Husserl, transcendental intersubjectivity stands ready as a transcendental, eidetic 'possession' on behalf of concrete encounters, conflicts, and abnormalities. That means that, while forming itself within the pairing of particular non-arbitrary persons, intersubjectivity happens largely passively and anonymously. Intersubjectivity is therefore a sketch of our co-perceiving community that is filled in concretely by means of communicating the eidetic intuition we experience. Intersubjectivity is the way we articulate, in particular utterances, how essences appear; and because of their linguistic structure, these utterances always function on behalf of the others who inhabit one's structure too and who therefore can interpret and critique them.

Intersubjectivity is recognizable because one is always limited in one's recognition of another person's life and the relations that person has with still further other persons. These other persons, the facts of one's limitations in the face of another, always appear as demanding concrete and specific action. For it is always as an actually existing person, who arises out of anonymity as immediately attached to the world and to a particular variation on one's perspective, that one encounters another. It is for the sake of these others and their actual–possible differences from one's own that one experiences all other *eide* as the achievement of an anonymously arising, open-ended multiplicity.

Arbitrariness is thus something that each person uncovers as a useful tool within the actuality of consciousness as a lived structure of anonymity. For the anonymous person on whose behalf one intuits an essence, this shift from this perception of a brown, four-legged table to an imaginative variation of one with an arbitrary number of legs, an arbitrary colour, and so on can be performed. The other is anonymous and thus does not immediately contest this act. But arbitrariness, and its pairing with anonymity in the enactment of eidetic variation, always yields in principle to the explicit encounter with the other person, to the explicit taking into account of particular views, which check our work.

It is only because we form an intersubjective nexus as irreducible and intercorporeal persons that our anonymous standing in for one another works in tandem with our 'transcendental concreteness.' It is only because persons do *not* form transcendental intersubjectivity solely or essentially as a merely pure and abstract concept, devoid of reference to their concrete existence as these particular lived bodies, that persons can have eidetic intuition at all. And, finally, it is only because our deployment of arbitrary sequences serves to promote future communication between particular and actual experiencers that arbitrariness, and the modification structure it makes possible, appears at all relevant and helpful.

C. Conclusion

I have tried to show in this section and in this chapter that Husserl presents a description of intersubjectivity, of the experience of other persons, that implies that it is the ability of actual others to be implicated in one's own perspectives and profiles that makes eidetic variation and eidetic intuition possible.[22] In other words, I have argued that Husserl's texts provide evidence for the claim that the intersubjective community of co-perception to which one belongs serves as the source of one's project of knowing all other objects and their *eide*.

Furthermore, I have claimed that the power of this source of eidetic intuition as such lies simultaneously in the other's alien and existent *distance* from one's own perspective and in their *overlaying* with one's own sense. Were this not the case, were there not other perspectives to negotiate as simultaneously co-given and as distant, then imaginative variation, the projection of one's own standpoint into anonymous other ones, would not be possible. Were there not a play of anonymity and personal actuality in the experience of intersubjectivity, there would be no secure limit to arbitrariness and to the process of imaginative modification within one's own faculty of imagination. Finally, I have demonstrated that without both (1) implying the other anonymously, as the one on whose behalf I vary the appearance of the table, and (2) leaving open the possibility for that anonymous other to interrupt and contribute to my project of variation in a particular, alien way, nothing would appear as a 'what' with any significant content.

I will now go on briefly to discuss some passages in *Analyses Concerning Passive and Active Synthesis* that further my treatment of essential intuition in its relationship to intersubjectivity. What I will show here is the fruition of this argument – namely, the idea that essences are perceived as intersubjective stances on shared objectivity. And I will show within Husserl's isomorphic descriptions that essences are experienced as taking a stand together on the meaningfulness of the givenness of the world. I turn to the *Analyses* for this for two reasons: first, to show that Husserl took his description of essential intuition as an overlaying of modifications to be central to his phenomenology, as it recurs across several texts (including *Phenomenological Psychology*); and second, to highlight how it is precisely overlaying at a *distance* that Husserl recognizes as promoting the possibility of meaningful experiences.

In the *Analyses* (hereafter *APAS*), when Husserl discusses the *eidos* or the universal implicit in similars, he discusses it as a necessary following up of a process of overlaying as a whole. The universal is recognized through one's involvement in the relation of the variations, through one's following up of the transition of one aspect, example, or perspective into the other. It is this transition one's consciousness performs that brings to light their overlaying as producing a single, transcending unity:

> [The universal] can only first be ready for possible thematic grasping, by carrying out the activity of grasping uniform objects separately in the synthetic transition [*in synthetischem Übergang*] from the one to the next ... The direction of interest toward the universal, toward the unity as opposed to the manifold, is not that of determining the one uniform object in relation to the other being uniform to it; rather what awakens [*weckt*] interest is the One being actively constituted in the coinciding [*der Deckung*] of individually grasped uniform objects; the One is the same, and is the same over and over, no matter what direction we may pursue in passing from one to the next.[23]

The *eidos* is reached as a recognizable unity, in other words, only when the 'distance' between the variations is compatible, only when the passage from one to the other loses all trace of specific density. The 'interest' is no longer one or the other, but the fact of the 'transition' itself. In other words, the *eidos* appears when consciousness awakens to its own power of movement both as *having already* generated meaning (that of the specific or particular objects now recognized as similar variations on a theme or type) and as *continuing* to generate meaning in its very motion.

One might see in this discussion the very bodily structure of habit formation. If I, an amateur and rather out-of-practice pianist, focus on playing the piano like Vince Guaraldi does, all at once, I will surely fail. My ability to be similar to him is not going to occur by my simply desiring and demanding that my hands play what he could. In fact, I have tried to play like he does through attempting to play his transcriptions, and I have failed.

But when I both hold on to the desire to play like Guaraldi and also do the work on my own relationship to the piano and to music, allowing that desire to be like him to submerge itself in favour of the real steps of learning how to listen and to practise *on my own*, I begin to get better both at playing in general and at playing like him. Eventually, after alternating sessions of practice and listening, while not focusing explicitly or reflectively on Guaraldi's own accomplishments, I hear myself playing a phrase or a note in the same kind of style. I hear his influence on me as I catch myself playing a riff of his in another song. And then, in that moment, I notice the achievement of our unity. Something about the essence of Guaraldi is also mine.

I take this example to flesh out the role of being awakened to an essence in the overlaying of the variations. One cannot force an insight onto the way in which an essence embraces its particulars, its variations. One can only be awakened to variations that appear, as if on their own, to call forth a new appreciation of their commonality. The essence is an experience that is passively prepared by the variations one moves between. Nevertheless, the essence is new. It does not arise *as* the variations but rather gives itself *within* the continuity of the movement by which I transition from one to the other.

Indeed, Husserl explicitly describes the newness of the *eidos* when he goes on to say that the *eidos* or the One occurs only once: 'The One does not repeat itself in something uniform; it only occurs one time, but is given in the many.'[24] To experience an essence, then, is to experience its arbitrary variations, its particular instances, desiring one another, communicating with one another. But in that communication something else, something excessive, arises, which nevertheless retroactively confers upon the variations a new layer of sense.

The *eidos* 'table' occurs once. It is the same occurrence throughout all its variations, all its instances. But in that single occurrence it announces itself as 'given in the many.' This means that the essence, because it arises out of the multiplicity of instances and variations, also gives something back to them. It allows them to be inhabited by its unity; it allows their space and time of multiplicity to be held together by its singularity.

It is in this light that Husserl declares that the *eidos* depends on the particular, that the *eidos* is both a product of and the pre-existing principle of the unity of the particulars or variations:

> We encounter the universal as a novel objectlike formation ... although, of course, *on the basis of sensibility*, insofar as the activity of 'going through' of grasping the individual, of *bringing into a coinciding is necessary* so that the universal as such can be *pre-constituted*, and *then later* can become a thematic object.[25]

I sense this thing here and that one. I see flat surfaces, numbers of legs, colours. On the basis of my sensibility, I bring my experiences close to one another, allow them to overlay one another by holding them in memory or in imagination, the one after the other. In doing that, I allow 'the universal' to arise as a pre-constitution – that is, to be given as a unity that, while arising for me *after* my effort to move from one particular experience to another, nevertheless announces itself as already having been implicit in the particulars that sustain overlaying and communication.

The first time I recognize what a rock, a tree, or a classroom is, I immediately experience a retroactive refiguring of my experience. I remember former experiences, which were hazy, as instances of this *eidos*, as if it were 'pre-constituted,' always there, lying in wait for me to see that, then too, I held a rock, entered a classroom, and so on. The 'novel' formation of the essence, then, loses nothing of its novelty by being given 'on the basis of sensibility.' Rather, the novelty is precisely possible in taking sensibility seriously, in allowing sensibility to do its work synthetically.

For Husserl, there really is the possibility that what one discovers, on behalf of the distances between instances, variations, perspectives, and persons, is truly new. That is to say, in the case of essential intuition (and as it finds its parallel *Fremderfahrung*), there is

a coinciding and yet not a complete coinciding. The elements of the similarity that overlap [*überschobenen Ähnlichkeitsglieder*] (which by the way need not be separate) have a distance: different similarities have different distances, in fact, they themselves can be compared ... Nevertheless, something in common also comes to light here in the coinciding at a distance [*Deckung unter Abstand*], or as we could put it perhaps in a better way, it shines through originally as a universal.[26]

The distances between sense-experiences that communicate with one another, that sustain a relation of similarity or shared sense ... the distances between subjects who are implicated in the very ability one has to make a transition from one variation to another ... these distances are precisely the spaces in which the universal, transcendental intersubjectivity, shines through. And it shines through 'originally.' This means, I take it, that the appearance of an essence can take me, can take the *community*, by surprise.

In one of my first experiences listening to a good jazz group perform live, one led by David Braid, I heard a song with a religious title. I think the title of the song was 'Reverence' or 'Reconciliation.' And I remember being moved by the way in which the piano and the other instruments played together but not so tightly as to be like my own experience of playing in a high school jazz band. In high school, we were all playing the same song at the same time. Our togetherness was anxious and frustrating (who played that wrong note?), and our musical production was much less interesting. We were more or less worried about faithfully rendering the notes on the page. But this professional group was far more sophisticated. In their playing together there were real gaps, but the gaps did not cause them to worry. Rather, the fact that they were not all playing in the same way or at the same time or, perhaps, even playing the same thing was the point of the piece.

I remember being moved by the fact that, in their rather distant togetherness, in their motion from and towards togetherness in the song, a religious meaning was captured for me in that shared act. Somehow their distances or rhythms of solo and group play allowed the idea of reverence or of reconciliation to come through. And I remember thinking at the time that they had successfully communicated that idea in musical logic.

For Husserl, all essences occur like my experience of this religiously titled jazz piece. Something new occurs within the gaps between the variations. And, more important, this structure of novelty is preserved within the most important essence, that of transcendental intersubjectivity itself.

What it means to be modifications of one another, what it means to make transitions on behalf of one another, is never fully given beforehand. The appearance of our community is always surprising, always sustaining revision and pre-constitution. Our friendships, our enmities, our indifferences, our marriages – they are never done with us, and they always arise both as showing us their novelty, as if covering over our distances, and as returning us to those very distances. To fully appreciate the structure of human experience, to do a reverential description, is to be resigned to reconciliation as its motor. We do all come together in the process of constituting the meaning of our shared lives, but we do so by way of irreducible differences and distances that are the very push to these shared, essential, and only relatively exact and stable positions.

3 How Others Demonstrate (and Call Upon) Our Embodiment

As we have seen in the previous two chapters, intersubjectivity not only sets the conditions of an encounter with other persons but also forms the content of those encounters. Grasping the 'chairness' of a chair is in effect using the other person's body, its spatio-temporal perspective and differently situated organs, to allow the world to open into a horizon and play of object and subject, of absence and presence. Using one another's intertwining bodies, we see not just 'this thing here now' but a certain kind of whatness, a whatness that expresses the community of our bodies, which – to follow the example of a chair – can sit, pay attention, fall asleep, in short *use* chairs.

Yet the use we make of chairs, the use we make of others in order to see things *as* what they are, does not happen by means of giving up one's own self-experience. In fact, what the phenomenologist discovers, by paying attention to the syntheses at work in the experience of other people, is that the same structure of layering, of overlaying-at-a-distance, echoes within the syntheses proper to one's own body and in the relation of the ego to itself.[1]

In this chapter, then, we return home to the experience of one's own body and ego in order to show the isomorphic character of layering here as well. In doing so, we build on the insights of chapter 1, in which we noticed how our organ–object–organ movements were grounded in our pairing with other's lived body. And we will conclude here in a similar vein: namely, that the prior unity of intercorporeality is what sustains the overlaying of sensation and perception, the reversibility of one's touch organs, and the experience of one's own transcendental ego as layered and implicated in the world.[2]

I. One's Own Sensation Shows the Structure of Relations with Others

As we took note of in previous chapters, to be a body means to be an organism whose organs can turn one another into objects and can turn back into organs through the fact that the body is unified and owned. I have shown that this is possible only given that one's *whole* body is really part of a larger, all-encompassing situation of intercorporeality, which characterizes one's body as an organ that co-functions within a community of perceiving. It is because one's ownership of one's body is not *solely* a kind of privatization but a sharing of responsibility, which comes from a 'higher genesis,' that one can successfully direct one's own perceptual organs, that one can relate one to another the whole and the parts of one's bodily life.

Having said this, I should acknowledge that it is true that I have not yet cited Husserl explicitly saying that my body's own powers derive from its intercorporeal situation. In fact, given the previous reading of the material in the *Cartesian Meditations*, it might seem that I begin with a full if inadequate grasp of my own body. However, I would like now to present a passage in which Husserl comes closer to acknowledging the dependence of my bodily unity and capacities on my intercorporeality. The passage is from the third volume of his intersubjectivity material, in #24, titled 'Personal (I-like) Community with Myself as Parallel to Community with Others.' There Husserl claims the following:

> I and I in overlaying [*Deckung*] and life with life, horizon with horizon – in their 'overlaying' ['*Deckung*'] these make possible the structural formalism; they ground the overall overlaying as such [*Deckung*]. Just so I and another person. (*Husserliana XV*, 417; my translation)

There are two points I would like to note immediately in my reading of this passage. First, Husserl is claiming here that the 'overall overlaying as such' – which I take to mean both the course of communal life and the course of one's own perceptual life – is 'grounded' in or delimited by the way I overlay myself as a whole. That is, because I overlay myself as a whole, I can overlay other persons and my touching hand can overlay my touched one.

And second, in the very title of the passage, Husserl explicitly casts the descriptions of the two experiences of one's own self-identity and of the relationship with the alien other as 'parallel' – that is, as being similar both in terminology and in content. The overlaying of 'I and I' and the overlaying of 'I and another person' belong together and thus co-found the experience of community and world. Together, 'I and I' and 'I and Other' make possible 'the structural formalism' of all my experience as such.[3]

In the next three sections of this part of the third chapter, I further this discussion of the relationships between 'I and I' and 'I and another person' as grounding 'the overall overlaying as such' within human sensation and perception. To do this, I discuss the customary acts of visual and tactile sensation, noting in Husserl's texts where he describes these activities according to the logic of overlaying (*Deckung*). I then go on to consider Husserl's description of an abnormal act of sensation – namely, that of crossing and uncrossing one's eyes. It is important to consider both normal and abnormal perception, I would argue, because it is in a perceptual breakdown – or in this one of crossed and uncrossed eyes at the very least – that the movement of overlaying comes to greater prominence.

A. Visual Sensation

Let us begin to draw out the isomorphic structure or 'parallel' between self-experience and experience of the other person by describing visual sensation. What I would like to do here, in this section, is show how Husserl describes one's own perception of a red thing and how, within that perception, a certain act and content of the *sensation* of red data overlays but conceals itself in favour of the act and content of the *perception* of the thing's redness.[4] What will be noteworthy for the purpose of my argument is the way that sensation evinces and maintains itself even in its concealment.

Husserl defines sensation in Appendix III to the *On the Phenomenology of the Consciousness of Internal Time* (hereafter *PCIT*) as follows: 'We consider sensation as the primordial time-consciousness. In it is constituted the immanent unity color or sound, the immanent unity wish or favor, and so on' (*PCIT*, 142). In that same work, from the lectures of 1905, Husserl claims that a sensation – for example, a sensed (*empfundene*) red – is 'animated by a certain function of apprehension' in order to become a perception of a phenomenological object (25). And the way that sensation becomes apprehended is through a synthesis of overlaying, in which the red that one senses in the flux of temporality and the red of the thing that one explicitly intends as this or that perceived meaning function together. The overlaying of the sensation (which is not perceived) and the quality of red about the object (which *is* perceived) is the very motion of apprehension as it sees *through* the sensations to the quality.

However, this synthesis of overlaying between sensed content and perceived quality – the overlaying that enables perception proper – is *not* one that leads one to identify the perceived red (the red of a thing) with the sensed red (the immanent datum). For the sensed red does not in fact appear at all:

> If, with reference to certain phenomenological occurrences, one speaks of a 'coincidence' ['*Deckung*'] of one with the other, he must still consider that it is through apprehension that the sensed red first acquires the value of being a moment which exhibits a material quality. Viewed in itself, however, sensed red is not such a moment. One must also note that the 'coincidence' ['*Deckung*'] of the exhibitive and that which is exhibited is by no means a coincidence of a consciousness of identity [*Deckung eines Identitätsbewusstseins*] whose correlate is one and the same. (*PCIT*, 25)

The role of sensation and its ability to partake in the perception of a red thing, for Husserl, comes from its already founding the higher level of perception. From the standpoint of a perceived thing and its redness, one can move back into the layers of its composition and notice the contributions of each. But one can move back to sensation only from a distance, only within the difference that sensation bears from the always already apprehended quality of the thing.

The sensed red and the perceived red occur, in a sense, at the same place and at the same time. The red data emerge there from the thing's surface. The thing's surface is perceived there as a red one. Yet the only person who could witness the identity of the place, the shared 'there' of sensation and perception, would be the one who could see both as if from another, non-participatory third-person point of view. Only for such an external viewer do the sensation and the perception that is always already an apprehension *of* some quality appear at all to indicate their separation.

For oneself, the act of apprehension that responds to and yields the identity of the perceived red thing thus *conceals* the overlaying of the moments of perceived quality and sensed data, perceiving noetic act and sensing noetic act. And to the extent that sensation can be viewed by oneself – that is, reflectively – it is always viewed as being for the sake of the perception of the thing as this or that quality.

That Husserl continued in his description of sensation to use the notion of overlaying (*Deckung*) while calling attention to its difference from 'coincidence' by putting it within scare quotes signifies, to me at least, that this activity of overlaying is essential to the act of giving and receiving sense, or to the act of the 'constitution' of experience. Even if the layer of perception conceals the layer of sensation within its pursuit of the perceived red thing, the sense in which perception is prepared by a pressure, an intertwining with the layer of sensation, remains. And it is because these layers, sensation and perception, still sustain by means of their difference or gap some capacity to move between them – it is because of this that an ego can perform reflective analysis upon sensation, which does not appear on its own.

What I would further argue here is that sensation, precisely *because* it does not appear directly, therefore could not be something I move back towards in reflection, could not be identified as *at all* a moment of the perceptual encounter with the thing, unless the overlaying of oneself and the other in *Fremderfahrung* were already drawn from and employed.[5] An example: it is the ophthalmalogist who gives me a colour-blindness test, with its patches of sensed colours. It is he or she who comes up with a test to see if there are any *indications* as to the breakdown between the normal unity of sensation and perception. Furthermore, it is that doctor who can see the function or disease of my eye in my act of perceiving the chart on the wall. And precisely within such a medical or scientific example, it becomes apparent that it is because my whole body always already overlays the other person's body within the experience of pairing, because I am always already intersubjectively structured by means of my body's ability to be an object for the other, that there arises my own possibility to trace out the evidence of sensation within my perception of this red ball here.

I can move back to my own sensation because I take over the standpoint of the doctor. Or, to echo what we have said in the previous chapters, it is because I am a layer that enacts itself as a layer, because I am an organ whose organs can all be objectified at any time by means of the person with whom I am paired without being identified, that I can begin to analyse layers of my own acting that do not on their own come to appearance.[6]

A further clarification: Husserl in the passage cited immediately above notes that in the overlay between sensation and perception, between sensed red and perceived red, there is not a consciousness of identity. The overlaying or *Deckung* does not lead to the identification of sensed red dots and the shape of the red thing. Instead, the sensed red dots remain *different* things from the perceived red surface.

Because of this problematic concealment of sensation within perception, I would argue that their relationship echoes the relation of oneself to the other person in *Fremderfahrung*. Indeed, I would argue that it is *because* we are given together in a unity of intersubjectivity that precludes a simple identification of us together (the other person is not simply a double of oneself) – it is *because* one forms a synthesis of overlaying with other persons that is not a simple synthesis of identity – that aspects of oneself, acts of sensation and of perception, can do so as well. Or, to put it another way, it is *because* we live out the revelation of a sense of our togetherness by means of our concealment to one another and to ourselves that we can, as Husserl said earlier, 'ground the overall structure of overlaying as such' and thereby ground the relation between sensation and perception, in our overlaying of one another (*Husserliana XV*, 417).

Let us turn to further evidence of this terminological 'parallel' and 'grounding' of sensation within intercorporeality. In section 16 of *Experience and Judgment*, 'The Field of Passive Data and Its Associative Structure,' Husserl returns again to the notion of sensation, and again he describes the process of sensation in terms of overlaying (*Deckung*). This time, however, he becomes a bit more instructive as to what this notion of overlaying offers in terms of sensation itself, and he clarifies how the layer of sensation is to be found and described.

Let us take his account slowly. First, the set-up: Husserl explicitly claims that it is by means of 'an abstractive turning-of-regard' that we are able to see 'a field of sense' and to 'make this apperceptive substratum itself [*Unterschichte selbst*] into an object' (*EJ*, 73). Because our abstractive regard is *successful* in recognizing the layer of sensation, Husserl argues, that indicates that sensation is itself an activity of synthesis, an activity of *receiving* colour-data – in this example, as striving towards the meaning of a perceived quality of an immediately and explicitly intuited thing. Sensation is a pre-intentional activity, a passive synthesis, which nevertheless has the structure of intentionality about it.

Husserl goes on further to discuss how, within a particular act of sensation, 'a particular element in the [sight-]field is raised to prominence in such a way that it *contrasts* with something; for example, red patches against a white background' (*EJ*, 73). The sensation of the red is already passively or pre-intentionally noted as standing out against the white. This occurs because, within the sensation, one notices passively that the red moments of the sensed red stand in a relationship to one another of greater intimacy, and their overlaying with one another is different from the relationship of contrast to the white patches that form the background.

As Husserl says, the red patches 'blend without contrast' with one another 'certainly not in such a way that they flow over into one another [*ineinander überfliessen*] but in a kind of blending at a distance [*Fernverschmelzung*], in which they can be made coincident with one another as being similar [*sind miteinander zur Deckung zu bringen*]' (*EJ*, 73–4). The red patches from one point to another against the white thus are not sensed as 'within' one another but rather 'with' one another, and they are 'brought' by virtue of our passive powers of recognition to overlay one another as striving to 'blend' across the 'distance' brought about by their separation, by their distinctness.

As Husserl goes on to add, if the patches of red really are completely alike, then they are sensed as 'repetitions' of one another and are sensed as in 'completely perfect coincidence [*vollkomener abstandloser Deckung*]' (*EJ*, 74). If the red patches are only similar to one another, and not completely alike, then 'a kind of coincidence also takes place, but it is only partial, being subject to the simultaneous opposition [*Widerstreit*] of the unlike' (*EJ*, 74). In sensation, then, the overlaying between moments of red (or another colour or sound-data, etc.) can either be without distance (*abstandlos*) or through distance and conflict (*Widerstreit*). That which promotes the identity of a perception – in this case, the perception of a red circle on a white page – can therefore be more than one kind of sensation, depending on the consistency of the colour data. And therefore a continuous act of sensation can deploy one of several kinds, or perhaps more than one kind at once, of overlaying.

To give further evidence of the argument for sensation's being founded in intercorporeality, I now cite the following passage. It further develops both cases of sensation under consideration – that is, the sensation of overlaying at no distance and the sensation of overlaying that incorporates conflict. In both cases, Husserl notes that they 'affect' the ego:

[T]hese syntheses of coincidence, whether it is a matter of coincidence in undifferentiated blending [*der Deckung in unterschiedsloser Verschmelzung*] or of coincidence together with the opposition of the unlike [*der Deckung unter Widerstreit des nicht Gleichen*], have their own affective power [*affektive Kraft*]; they exert a stimulus on the ego which makes it turn toward, whether it obeys the stimulus or not. (*EJ*, 76)

This power of affection,[7] of sensation as a process of the object's standing out and motivating the 'turn' of the ego, is what Husserl describes as the process whereby 'the intentional object in its directedness towards the ego attracts the latter more or less forcefully, and the ego yields to it' (*EJ*, 77). Sensation in its self-concealing syntheses of overlaying, therefore, has a purpose. By forgoing its own appearance in favour of perception, sensation allows us actively to turn our attention, to focus on the 'call' or the agency of the object, to the 'directedness' that the object bears to the ego.

Within a description of sensation, then, Husserl shows how the overlaying of the sensed contents, even ones at a distance with one another, are preparing for perceptual responses to the object's own activity within the intentional relation. As sensed, the object is awakening; as sensing, I awaken.

In fact, just as in *Fremderfahrung* we notice our mutuality both as overlaying and as awakening, so too in his account of sensation Husserl notices explicitly not just the structure of overlaying but the event of awakening as well: 'The accomplishment of the turning-toward is what we call the being-awake [*Wachsein*] of the ego ... To be awake is to direct one's regard to something. To be awakened [*Gewecktwerden*] means to submit to an effective affection' (*EJ*, 79). Describing sensation, then, Husserl finds a unity of overlaying that immediately awakens consciousness to a larger, more sophisticated relationship, one of intentional, active, and explicit directedness out of a pre-predicative, passive, and implicit unity.[8]

To conclude this section, then, I reiterate that the activity and structure of sensation, as well as its relation with perception, enact an echo of the activity and structure of *Fremderfahrung*. Furthermore, Husserl has intimated as much when he claims that sense-data united in the now of consciousness 'are those in conformity with affinity (homogeneity) and strangeness [*Fremdheit*] (heterogeneity)' (*EJ*, 74). It would be impossible for one's own body to manifest this self-concealing structure, it would be impossible for sensation itself to deal with what is alien, with 'strangeness,' on its own. How can a passive act of sensation, which is different in principle from an explicit perception of strangeness, handle, or 'conform' to, both 'affinity and strangeness'? The only way that sensation could do so, the only way in which it could form its self-concealing unity with perception, is by means of always being in debt to one's whole 'corporeal schema,' which, as we have shown, is always already engaged, even if only by its implication, outside the sphere of ownness with the alien other person.[9]

B. Touch-Sensation

If we move now from visual sensations to tactile ones, we see Husserl describing the overlaying at work there in an even more explicit sense. For when we touch with our hands, there is no sense in which a geometrical or full 'coincidence' could name the activity we engage in. Instead, there is always a gap between the finger or the hand and that which it touches. As we follow his description of the type of overlaying at a distance that is at play in sensations of touch, the most important passage of Husserl's work, at least for our purposes, will be *Beilage XVIII* of his third volume of intersubjectivity material titled 'The Manner in which the Lived Body [*Leib*] constitutes itself as *Körper* and as *Leib*, Insofar as the Manners of Its Constitution and External Thing-Constitution Are Paired' (*Husserliana XV*).

There Husserl speaks explicitly of how parts of my touch field (say of my finger) are moved by me in order explicitly to overlay moments of the touch field (say, the surface of a tactile object). Husserl phrases this as follows: 'To the piece of the touch-field "finger-point" X belongs a particular kinesthesis and groups of combined kinestheses; its performance of touch is that this piece X can be brought to overlay [*Deckung*] with each piece of the touch field and thereby can be laid out [*aufgelegt*]' (*Husserliana XV*, 296; my translation). As within the visual sensing of red data, within tactile sensing there is also an activity – namely, the 'kinesthesis' of the touching movement. In this peculiar motion, the active 'laying out' of one's touch field (the deployment of one's fingertip or hand) is simultaneously, as in visual sensation, the process of turning toward, of being passively receptive to the outline of the object, to its call.

However, there is a peculiarity internal to touch that is important for our discussion. In visual sensation, it is the sensed contents that one experiences as 'overlaying' one another. But within touch, the overlaying involves oneself more directly, as it involves both the data and one's own organs. The fingertip overlays the keys as I type them, and I sense their blocky smoothness as my finger contacts them.

Because touch occurs by means of the object's direct, explicit contact with the lived body, Husserl also mentions in the same discussion that 'in touching we have doubled-data, each with its own extension in the sense-field and its objective place in an overlay ['*Deckung*']' (*Husserliana XV*, 298; my translation).[10] The sensed data that appear across my finger's touch-field, in other words, both appear to be *on me* at this precise point *and* appear to be at the place on the object that they overlay. When typing, for example, the 'doubled-data' I sense with my hand would be the following: I feel the data of smoothness of the keys at the place *on the keys* where my fingers touch them; I feel the same data, the smoothness, *on my fingers* at the tips of them. The data are on the keys and on my finger. In some sense, they are the same data – they are that which promotes my perception of the keys' 'smoothness.' But the sensed data are clearly given simultaneously – that is, they are given twice and given differently, one according to the unity of the keyboard, one according to that of my finger.

One might anticipate here that the direct overlaying of touch onto objects, its doubled currents of significance, is what will serve to ground the possibility of all the other senses to engage in intentional perception. For in straightforward, normal visual sensation, I do not see the red of the object both there in the object and here in my eye. And in normal hearing, I do not hear the timbre of the violin both there in the concert hall and here in my ear. On the contrary, in visual and auditory sensations, I am, as it were, prepared by the acts of sensation to be lost in the perceptual sense of the object. In vision and hearing, I cannot, as in touching, immediately turn my sense organ into an object and sense the doubling of the sense-data or the noetic and noematic moments of my object-directedness.

But it is possible to touch one's eyes and ears and nose and tongue. And through this possibility, it is possible to retain the significance grasped with these senses as one's own, as mattering and occurring within this body, within this consciousness, as well as there in the object.[11]

Husserl describes this power of touch to assure oneself of one's entire body, to ground all one's other courses of sensation, through the power of touch to inaugurate a kind of *reversibility*. That is, because the touching organ must actually contact and overlay the object, touch-sensation does *more* than unite the two localizations of the touch-data – there on the object and here on the touching organ. In addition, touch deploys the further possibility of uniting its own *reversibility*, the possibility of *keeping together* and of *moving* back and forth within its *own senses of itself*, from the hand as organ to the hand as object:

> We find always and originally in the most original touch-experience, which *produces* the lived body as *Körper* and as *Leib*, a functional being-with-one-another of the touching and touched organ, and with that a *possible reversal* so that the touching can become the touched. With this *reversibility* occurring, there arises the *possibility of reversal* even of the function of the pair of sensations as *self-overlaying* [*sich deckenden*]. (*Husserliana XV*, 298; my translation and emphasis)

The sensation of the fingertip as *Leib*, the sensation of the fingertip as *Körper*; the right hand touching the left, the right hand being touched by the left – these possibilities of reversibility occur at the very moment that touch begins. To touch, in Husserl's description, is to 'produce,' to enact the 'functional being-with-one-another,' the dual resonance of *Körper* and *Leib*. And it is to enact this community, this dual resonance, these overlaying senses of the fingertip as organ and object – it is to enact this overlaying as a correlation to the 'doubled data,' to the preservation of the dual system of their localization.

Touch as a continuous openness to how touch-data are both on the object and on the fingertip occurs because touch is 'like' what it touches. Its openness occurs because the overlaying with the object –the 'functional being-with-one-another' of the 'doubled data' – maps onto the 'self-overlaying' relation that is internal to touch. However, because of this correlation – because the overlaying with the object maps onto the self-overlaying of the fingertip as *Leib* and *Körper* – the agential character of the object remains preserved.

To touch is to remain open to the 'possibility' that the reversal could happen because of the object touched. The object may assert itself within my fingertip, passing over it as too hot or too sharp to sustain a continuous appropriation of its data. In a certain moment, I suddenly sense my fingertip as in pain, even before I may perceive it as injured, and I pull it away. And thus, by virtue of the touched thing keeping its own localization within those doubled data, by virtue of my ability to sense the heat or sharpness there in the thing, the fingertip's self-overlaying of *Leib* and *Körper*, as that which prepares to meet the thing, is never fully within one's own control.

Furthermore, the 'self-overlaying,' which the touching fingertip deploys in meeting the doubled data, allows for the 'possibility of reversal' not just of its own senses of *Leib* and *Körper* but of those of the entire 'lived body.' In order to begin to touch, in order to be vulnerable to the object, the fingertip has moved to the foreground of the whole 'lived body.' However, by moving to the foreground, by its insertion into the world and its vulnerability, the fingertip has also committed the lived body as such, which remains in the background, to the possibility of reversal by the very thing the fingertip explores. What I am touching could always 'respond' – that is, it could explode, could burn me, cut me, caress me, and so on. And in so doing, the object could touch me in places on behalf of which my fingertip acts.

To touch with any part of the touch-field thus immediately 'produces,' commits, deploys, or brings to light the character of the *whole* lived body, of the *Leibkörper, within* the fingertip or the hand. To touch is immediately to touch on behalf of the whole, with the logic of the whole. And each touch indicates that the synthesis of the whole touch-field, the reversibility of *Leib* and *Körper,* as well as the reversibility of a differentiated foreground and undifferentiated background, is involved in overlaying the object.

To return to the argument of the whole book: the reversibility of touch concretizes one's *a priori* involvement in intercorporeal structures. The act of touching with my fingertip on *behalf of* the whole body shows that I sense only because I have always already been given the wholeness of my body. But that wholeness is the gift of intercorporeality. I touch because I am always already a touchable *Leibkörper* for the others with whom I am (at least anonymously) co-given.

In other words, I foreground and touch with this reversible organ, this fingertip, because I already have access to how my whole *Leibkörper* functions as both organ and object. I deploy my fingertip on behalf of my whole lived body because my whole is always already living out its total reversibility.

In touch more than in vision, then, the parallelism and the relation of founding between *Fremderfahrung* and sensation is writ large. As we have seen, in Husserl's description of touch sensation, the following come to prominence: first, there are doubled data of touch-sensation, a pair of localizations; second, in the act of touching, the functional 'being-with-one-another' of *Leib* and *Körper* supports the possibility of their reversal; and third, a touching organ such as the fingertip arises as a touching organ out of a relatively undifferentiated touch-field, out of its anonymous relation to all the other moments of my touching body. The same structures always already occur within *Fremderfahrung,* and,

I argue, they prepare for the possibility of touch. Witness the following: first, in any pairing with the other person, I am given as a *doubled* set of localizations, as both my irreducible Here and as my sense of being 'as if I were there'; second, I am given as together with the other but also as *reversible*, insofar as I can be acting or acted upon, insofar as I can pursue a shared project, act out of my own sphere, or come to appreciate hers; and third, I am given to myself and to others only within a structure of *anonymity*, out of which I and the others can always become personal and active organs of our 'functional community of one perception.'

C. Abnormality: Crossed Eyes and the Overlaying of Whole Senses

A further experience Husserl describes, which I think offers additional evidence that he saw intercorporeality as founding sensation and perception, is that of crossing and uncrossing one's eyes or fingers. This example is one of an experience of abnormality, where the previous two sections dealt with normal ones. However, in this account, an additional kind of self-overlaying as a self-concealing comes explicitly to prominence. And, within the movement we enact from crossed to uncrossed eyes or fingers, we can see how sight and touch operate in the same manner as essential intuition does, that is, by perceiving a single unity by means of the convergence and submersion of variations. This similar operation would further attest to the absolutely thoroughgoing unity of consciousness as embodied, as it would help claim that there is nothing of one's own that is not also already a deployment or echo of intercorporeal, intersubjective life.

Here is the relevant passage:

> If I cross my eyes, or if I cross my fingers, then I have two 'things of sight' or two 'things of touch,' though I maintain that only one actual thing is present. This belongs to the general question of the constitution of a thingly unity as an *apperceptive unity of a manifold of different levels* which themselves are already apperceived as unities of multiplicities. The apperception acquired in relation to usual perceptual conditions obtains a new apperceptive stratum by taking into consideration the new 'experience' of the dispersion of the one thing of sight into a pair and of the fusion of the pair in the form of a continuous overlapping and convergence [*einer kontinueierlichen Zusammenschiebung und D e c k u n* g] in the regular return to the former perceptual conditions. (*Ideas II,* 66; Husserl's emphasis)

The first thing to notice in this passage is that it describes how, in the process of an abnormal movement, one apprehends the way the normal sensory act conceals its own 'levels' or 'multiplicities' in favour of a straightforward access to a single object. That is, if to see or to touch is normally to see 'thingly unity,' as if in a one-to-one correspondence between myself and things, what this abnormal crossing and uncrossing of the eyes reveals is that I have this apparently normal, continuous experience of sense through having reckoned with, unified, and concealed a 'multiplicity.' Within the crossing and uncrossing of organs, it becomes apparent that to sense is thus not a simple act at all. Rather, this example reveals that sensation is the complex process of taking in at one glance a number of noetic and noematic 'levels' or layers. To sense is, furthermore, to 'apperceive' both the separation of those layers and the propulsion that they have towards a further unity.

In this abnormal motion of which we are capable, we experience how a 'new apperceptive stratum' or layer occurs by means of the abnormal act. The 'new stratum' in question is the possibility of intuiting or witnessing the 'overlapping and convergence' as such, the experience of how the multiplicity passes into the unity that we normally sense directly.

Let us clarify. By means of this abnormal motion, which one can always do for oneself, one experiences (directly) the conditions for normal vision. In performing it, we see that in normal vision, organs function together without competing, without being capable of turning one another into mere bodies, mere pieces of flesh. They allow one another to *pair* together such that the nature of their differences recedes in favour of a common project. They act much as whole persons do within a friendship or a community that is well-established and just.

By means of this open experience of crossed eyes, however, we also see directly how, at any moment, by means of accident or of freedom, the experience of the duality of one's eyes, of one's participation in a process of dispersion and fusion, can come to the fore. What does the recognition of this latter possibility, the possibility of experiencing the separation and dispersion of organs and objects – what does this mean for us? What does it offer? It offers at least two opportunities: first, it gives us further insight into how our vision differs from and unites with our touch; and second, it helps us understand how important it is that our vision evinces the same structure as our essential intuition.

Let us take up these opportunities one at a time. We begin with a further examination of the relationship between vision and touch. As we have just seen, touch is defined by the *reversibility* of the touch-organs, a reversibility that serves as the condition of their directly contacting and overlaying one another and the world. However, what defines vision is not reversibility but rather the *simultaneity and co-constitution* of the self-concealing sight-organs. This example of crossed eyes gave us evidence that not only do the *qualities* of sight-objects overlay one another in vision (e.g., red with red in the sensing of a colour patch), but so also do the objects *themselves*, as well as the separate visual acts and fields.

This insight into the way that vision, too, deploys the structure of overlaying within its acts also makes further comprehensible the way in which sight and touch can relate to each other. We have already shown that because of their openness to touch, the eyes can be continuously located within my own lived body as organs in which I live and govern. I can at any moment touch my eyes or rub them and confirm to myself that my eyes are openings of my body onto the same world that I touch. However, I rarely touch my eyes. And if I *had* to touch my eyes all the time in order to unite my seeing with the rest of my senses, I would never see clearly.

What we now see, however, is that, because vision is thoroughly operative as a self-overlaying system, vision and its field of objects as *wholes* have always already united with touch and its field as wholes. Indeed, it is the consonance of their structures as wholes that allows me to be assured of their togetherness from the beginning. And it is this assurance that allows touch to locate even the distantly appearing objects of vision as part of my lived bodily experience:

It becomes a *Body* only by incorporating tactile sensations, pain sensations, etc. – in short by the localization of the sensations as sensations. In that case the visual Body [*Leib*] *also participates* in the localization, because it coincides [*sich ... deckt*] with the tactual Body, just as other things (or phantoms) coincide [*sich ... decken*], ones which are constituted both visually and tactually, and thus there arises the idea of a sensing thing which 'has' and which can have, under certain circumstances, certain sensations (sensations of touch, pressure, warmth, coldness, pain, etc.) and, in particular, have them as localized in itself primarily and properly. This is then a precondition for the existence of all sensations (and appearances) whatsoever, the visual and acoustic included, though these do not have a primary localization in the Body. (*Ideas II*, 158–9; my emphasis)

What is essentially reversible – that is, touch – is therefore compatible from the beginning in its structure with what is simultaneous and non-reversible – that is, sight. That my eyes can be touched or felt simultaneously as moments of my touch-field is a given fact. But what maintains the eyes when I am not touching them, when I am not alive to the way they feel when I am viewing something, is that the very means by which they see 'fits' the means by which I touch.

In fact, as this passage shows, the relation between vision and touch as *wholes*, between the lived body as visible and the lived body as tactile, is echoed in the experience of things. The experience of a keyboard, for example, is one of sight and touch throughout. This could be, Husserl implies here, only because sight and touch bear an internal relation, actively grounded by touch but also internally deployed by sight. Touch grounds vision. But vision *extends* touch. Or, to put this another way, it is because the entire senses of sight and touch overlay each other, because the simultaneity of the eyes and the reversibility of the hands are deployed together, that a thing can be 'constituted both visually and tactually,' as having layers that appear at the same time as one acts, by means of the same relation that touch and sight enact.

But if the self-overlaying of the entire senses of vision and touch is the 'precondition for the existence of all sensations,' it is also true that this overlaying, of the body with itself, has its own pre-condition. In talking here about the precondition of the body's self-overlaying, we are now moving away from this last passage and returning to take up the second opportunity mentioned in the discussion of the preceding passage. In other words, we are now turning to discuss how important it is that our vision evinces the same structure as our essential intuition.

Perhaps a reminder from the passage previously cited is in order. There, in his description of moving from crossed to uncrossed eyes, Husserl describes the 'dispersion and fusion' of the doubled sight objects as an appearance of coming together as a 'pair' and returning 'in the form of a continuous overlapping and convergence *einer kontinueierlichen Zusammenschiebung und D e c k u n g]*' to the previous unity of the appearing as of *one* thing of sight to the eyes.

This description of the way in which the separated sight things yield a single experience is almost exactly parallel to the description of pairing in Husserl's account of *Fremderfahrung* and to the description of an essence arising out of variations within eidetic intuition. In all three cases – that of the sight-things, that of the pairing of lived bodies, and that of the *eidos* arising out of variations – what is fostered is the possibility of a higher-level unity arising by way of layers that position themselves over one another.

What I have argued throughout the book, and what I also argue in this chapter, is that the parallelism of the descriptions arises only because of an experienced relationship of similarity between the registers. That is, my whole argument really boils down to the claim that Husserl describes these different cases in the same terms because they really are *given together, implicated within one another*. If I am right, then the pairing with the other person, with the other lived bodies within intersubjectivity, is what makes possible the pairing of senses (sight and touch) within one's own lived body and the pairing of sight-objects within one's visual sensation of the one thing. If I am right, the ability to *see* two together is possible because I *exist* as two together, because I always already exist within a 'functional community of one perception.'

Further support for this claim, for the grounding or implication of one's own experience within the intercorporeal one, comes in yet another part of Husserl's description, cited above, of what occurs within the experience of crossed eyes. As we have seen, there he mentions that the very experience of the doubling of the sight-things 'belongs to the general question of the constitution of a thingly unity as an *apperceptive unity of a manifold of different levels* which themselves are already apperceived as unities of multiplicities.' I would like now to draw out more from that sentence.

To 'constitute' or recognize or be open to a thing in any way, in any act of intuition, whether sensory, perceptual, or essential, means to be open to 'apperception' as a unity that has 'different levels.' Each level or layer is itself 'already apperceived' as a manifold. This means that 'the general question' of how things come to mean what they do for us is not capable of being answered on one level, one layer alone. We are rather referred *by* the current level to others.

This means that sensation cannot appear to me as simply a self-delimited act of my being open to or gathering together these particular data. Rather, the act of sensing and the data that I sense are always already moving towards my perceiving. In addition, at any moment, I deploy explicitly or foreground one of several types of sensing (visual, tactile, auditory, etc.), all of which are themselves nested within a lived body that comports itself to them in the same manner as they do to their noematic objects. The 'living out' of sensation as itself a multiply layered event is what lends credence to the argument that sensation emerges out of a prior, transcendental structure of intercorporeality.

Considered on its own, how could sensation move beyond itself? How would the eyes 'know' to function in such a way as to enact the structure of pairing? On their own, sensation would not press forward;

the eyes would not work together. Only if the eyes received their 'logic' from the whole of oneself with others, of one's body within a community of apperception, could the eyes enact their own community of
structure. Furthermore, only if sensation and bodily organs appeared
within a nested structure of levels *founded* by intercorporeality – only if
vision both originated from and moved back towards intercorporeality
– could sensation, perception, essential intuition, and any other mode
of intuition organize themselves and map onto one another.

And here, finally, is what we can recognize as the second opportunity offered by the example of crossed eyes. In Husserl's description,
especially in his discussion of the sight-things returning to a kind of
'overlapping and convergence,' the logic of visual sensation is in fact
structurally similar to that of essential intuition. How important is that
fact? It is so important that we can say that it is only by virtue of that
logic's similarity that we see essences as 'things themselves.'

For Husserl's account of the seeing of essences to work, for us to
agree that we see essences directly *in the same manner as other types of intuition*, our grasp of essences must somehow echo or call up to mind the
way in which every other act of intuition works. If we grasp essences
through variations, and if we do so directly, we must witness that same
pattern in sensation, in perception, and in our own life as an essential
subjectivity, as the transcendental ego. Not to be able to do so, not to see
the consonances among essential intuition, perception, and sensation,
would mean we are unable to relate essences to embodied life, unable
to reconcile the life of the body and the life of essential subjectivity.

Or, put differently, what this all means is that, for essential intuition
to appear at all, it must appear as fundamentally linked to the processes
of seeing and touching that allow us to pay attention to the variations
that push towards essences as such. Essences that would be grounded
in any other logic, essences that would by definition be unable to be
communicate with the structures of our embodiment, would not appear and would not matter to us.

There is a reason, then, why Husserl describes sensation, perception,
essential intuition, and intersubjectivity as evincing the same structure,
the same bodily and erotic structure, of *Deckung*.[12] And that reason is
this: he discovered that consciousness was thoroughly embodied; he
discovered that the levels or layers of one's experience moved towards
one another; and he found that the experience of things themselves sustained this description of them. After all, like Socrates returning to the
symposium of his friends from his solo discourse, it is only in experi-

encing and deploying essences as intrinsically linked to bodily intuition that one is motivated to continue moving back and forth, from the
natural to the transcendental attitudes.

II. The Ego as Synthesis of Overlaying and Analogue

In chapter 1, we discussed Husserl's description of the transcendental
ego, even within the sphere of ownness, as having its own body. And I
argued that this body appeared within the sphere of ownness because
the ego is always already engaged with other people's bodies. Indeed, I
argued that it is only because our consciousness as such is intertwined
with the bodies of aliens that our consciousness is also intertwined with
our own whole body.

In the previous section of this chapter, in its analyses of visual sensation and tactile sensation, I have attempted to show how other persons
are always already implied (and present) within one's own acts of sensation as such. To that end, I also reiterated how sensation relies on a
notion of the whole body, one that is given only by means of *Fremderfahrung* and intercorporeality.

Here, I want to show that even the features of the ego that appear
least bodily, particularly its essential character as the locus and power
of recognition, bear the trace of the alien other and of the layering structure of one's own body. It is not just that the transcendental ego has a
body; it is that the transcendental ego's structure is thoroughly isomorphic with and recalls the layers of bodily synthesis.

A. The Ego as a Self-Overlaying

Within the descriptions of the second volume of his *Ideas*, Husserl
claims that the pure ego is in fact not something in addition to the acts
of consciousness. Rather, the pure ego appears as the very organization
of the 'media,' of its lived experiences:

> [T]he pure Ego exercises its pure 'functions' in the acts of the multiformed
> cogito … [T]he Ego cannot be thought of as something separated from
> these lived experiences, from its 'life,' just as, conversely, the lived experi-
> ences are not thinkable except as the medium of the life of the Ego. (*Ideas
> II*, 105)

Lived experiences do not add up to the ego, as if one had to amass a number of them before one were an ego. The ego 'exercises' itself 'in the acts.' As the acts' own organizational structure, the ego is immanent to the very acts of consciousness, inseparable from them. And the ego is experienced directly in its own right, as the centre of the life it lives, the life that matters to it.

Husserl is clear, as his description continues, that the pure ego appears. But he also notes that as it appears, it appears in its own way. According to Husserl, then, the ego sets the terms of its appearing:

> [E]ach and every cogito, along with all its constituents arises or vanishes in the flux of lived experiences. But the pure subject does not arise or vanish, although in its own way it does 'step forth' and once again 'step back.' (*Ideas II*, 109)

'Each cogito,' each particular intentional act, appears on its own, and it does so as tied immediately to the structure of internal time-consciousness and the flux that generates it. This means that these intentional acts, as well as the entire lived experiences constituted by them, have a duration. But the ego does not have a duration in the same way as do its acts. It steps forth or back in a way peculiar to itself, since the very flux of temporality, the way in which the lived experiences themselves flow and endure, *also* matters to the ego.

Lived experiences appear, therefore, because they permit and call for a unity that cannot be divided from them but that appears 'in its own way.' This style of the ego, this 'own way,' is the marker of the ego's difference from the acts in which it lives. And, like the lived body and like an essence, so too the ego appears as a surplus to the lived experiences, a surplus that has its own way of 'stepping forth' in one's life, *as* one's life.[13]

However, the ego, in all of its character as surplus or excess or singular style of appearing – in all of that, the ego is still responsible to its lived experiences. It 'cannot be thought separately' and thus must continuously acknowledge its debt to its experiences as those events wherein it lives and moves and has its being. The ego is what it is precisely as a facilitator of the experiences in their relations.

If I have returned after going to a night of listening to live music, I find that I am humming a few bars or that a piece of the music calls up a sense of joy or sorrow in me. If I reflect further, I can be amazed at how 'in the music' I was, how I almost seemed to forget myself, and how now, as I step forward as a witness to myself and my experiences, these events and the experiences that arose within them are now becoming reasserted as part of my life, part of a course of learning to appreciate jazz or solitude or inclinations in myself. I 'step forth' again into my own life as the way in which the previous experiences mattered and continue to matter in my life. And this life itself, as centring in my ego, is itself a kind of lived experience that embraces all of the events and bodily activities that go on within it.

When I find myself reasserting, organizing, and describing my experiences, though, it is not as if I was somewhere else while the music was playing. I was literally 'in' the music. And my ability to reflect upon experience is the proof that what characterizes my 'I' is an all-embracing grasp, even if one of 'stepping back.' This all-embracing grasp, for Husserl, is described in a now familiar way:

> [T]he Ego is the identical subject functioning in all acts of the same stream of consciousness; it is the center whence all conscious life emits rays and receives them … The coincidence [*Deckung*] of all acts in the numerically identical Ego-center lies on the noetic side. (*Ideas II*, 112)

The ego thus is 'identical,' is something that arises as a synthesis of identity, only as the overlaying (*Deckung*) of intentional acts.[14] Just as the essence appears within the overlaying of its variations, and the body appears by means of the overlaying of hands or sensory fields, the ego appears by means of it acts themselves, the 'one' that they situate as their very condition of possibility *as* acts.

B. Self-Overlaying Ego as Analogon of the Lived Body

It should be clear now that my argument throughout this book is that the structure of overlaying within every major facet of self-experience gets its motor from, while also making possible, the experience of being paired with other lived bodies within *Fremderfahrung*. And indeed, that the structure of overlaying is at work in the ego's self-experience is something we have discovered in the previous section. I will now demonstrate how Husserl himself described the self-overlaying of the ego as analogous to the self-overlaying structure of the lived body. Husserl's discovery and description of this analogy thereby makes it possible for me to go on to show that the experience of one's own body and one's own ego are called up for the purposes of participating within transcendental intersubjectivity.

The relevant passage, again, comes from the second volume of the *Ideas*:

> The structure of the acts which radiate out from the Ego-Center, or, the Ego itself, is a form which has an *analogon* in the centralizing of all sense-phenomena in reference to the Body. In absolute consciousness there is always a 'field' of intentionality, and the spiritual 'focus' of the attention 'directs' itself now onto this, now onto that. (*Ideas II*, 112; my emphasis)

The very 'structure' of the acts and their relationship to the unity, the surplus of the 'ego-center,' is 'analogous' to the structure of the body. The body has its fields, and consciousness has its own as well. The body has the capacity for synaesthesis, for a central regard that unites tactile, aural, and visual experiences as experiences of the same object. So too the ego has its 'focus' and ability to 'direct' and unify itself.

As we recall, the 'form' of the body's centralizing structure was that of a self-overlaying (*sich decken*) of the sense fields. This included the overlaying of the touch-organs with the surfaces of their objects, and it extended, by means of the touch-organs' capacity, to the organs and ultimately the objects of other sense-fields. The 'form' that Husserl must have in mind in the passage currently under discussion, then, is the way that the layers of ego and of body press towards their higher unities by means of preserving and deploying both their differences and interactions.

Indeed, shortly after talking about the ego as bodily analogon, Husserl does appear to admit directly that the form common to ego and body is just that of overlaying. He does this by describing how the overlaying of thing and subject is an overlaying of profile and orientation:

> If we take the field of thing-objects which appear to the senses, and which are given in an orientation, then the coincidence [*Deckung*] with the 'Ego-orientation' becomes understandable: the processes of adaptation (my movements) pertain to the constitution of the thing, and, parallel with them, I always grasp more of the thing. (*Ideas II*, 113n1)

According to this, the layers of any perceptual experience are at least two. First, there are the profiles or *Abschattungen* of the thing. And second, there are the perspectives or orientations that the ego takes by means of its bodily 'Here' on the thing perceived. The unity of the noematic profile with the noetic, oriented ray of regard is seamless. The profile of the object, its sight- and touch-appearance from here, over-lays the possible movements one can make as one's body. The 'ego orientation' thus can be a relation of overlaying with profiles because the orientation 'participates' in the body's Here.

This means that not only does the ego have an *analogous* structure to that of the body, as if there were two distinct structures that shared some commonality. Rather, this also means that the overlaying proper to the ego *derives from* and is *immediately involved with* the bodily self-overlaying. The ego is made to intend, perceive, and consider things *by* touching them, *by* turning them over, and thus the ego *must* have the structure that the body has, while preserving its possibility for more independent activity.

The analogous structure of overlaying in body and in ego is therefore a peculiar and intimate one. Their relation does not permit them to be taken simply as independent of each other. However, their relation also does not enforce the experience (or the appearance) of the ego simply as immersed in the body. Rather, the analogy or correlation of noetic acts and bodily capacities is what makes it possible for the ego to overlay the world *and* the body, to gear into the world in ways that are not simply what one might call reflexes. Not only can one touch a thing, but one can also touch it differently and constitute it differently, depending on how the ego steps forth or back within the very unity it shares with the body. The 'adaptation' of one's movements to reflect a changing ego-orientation, and the success of one's sense-experience as validating that change in ego-orientation, shows that the structure of the lived body and the ego are complementary.[15]

III. Transcendental Ego's Body Is the Life of the Life-World

In the previous two sections of this chapter, I have shown that the body and the ego are both characterized by a process of self-overlaying and that the analogy of those two leads to an overlaying of ego and world. I will now argue in this section that the body of the transcendental ego as already transcendental intersubjectivity is the entirety of what Husserl calls the life-world.

In the *Crisis of the European Sciences*, Husserl claims that the life-world appears as living, as a kind of organic whole. This claim, coupled with his general discussion of the life-world as embracing both the pre-scientific and the various sedimented layers of the senses of consciousness and its objects, seems to me to suggest that Husserl holds that the transcendental ego constitutes the life-world as the changing, developing, and expanding *way* in which the objects of experience can call out to and intertwine with the ego, can draw the ego into a mood, and can even serve as the ego's memorial cells.[16] And to constitute the life-world as the *way* objects matter is to constitute it in an analogous manner to the lived body, since the lived body too appears as the very way in which particular objects come to hold meaning for consciousness, as graspable or visible, and the extent to which they appear as such.

To say that the life-world is alive, that it has agency, then, is not to claim that the life-world in any significant way opposes or is completely concealed from the transcendental ego. Rather, the organicity of the life-world and its sustenance of our objects suggest a peculiar kind of intimacy with transcendental consciousness. Indeed, I will argue that it is only as primordially (and thus intimately) united with the life-world (as intimately as one is united with one's own skin) that the transcendental ego could (re)constitute itself as objectified. Only as a human being who confronts her or his world in *greater or lesser* degrees of intimacy, who moves along various 'trade routes' marked out by bodily organs and the things that overlay and contact them, can a transcendental ego pre-constitute a priori structures that have concrete relevance.[17]

A. Life-World as Pre-scientific and Concrete Totality

In explicating Husserl's discussion of the life-world, and in making the argument that I am attempting here, however, a significant problem arises. This problem, made especially salient by commentators like Donn Welton, is this: Husserl in the *Crisis* appears to have two notions of the life-world: one is of 'a pre-scientific experiential world,'[18] and the other is of 'a totality' and a 'concrete whole, which ... encompasses the multiplicity of particular worlds.'[19] If this is true, then it makes more problematic the claim that the transcendental ego experiences this life-world as a whole and further experiences this whole as its own flesh. However, and following what I take to be the general tenor of Welton's three chapters in *The Other Husserl* that deal with the life-world, if the life-world is experienced as the flesh of the transcendental ego, and if this flesh is in fact the network of activities of the ego's syntheses (and its self-alienating, self-returning constitutions of its correlates), then the problem of Husserl's two life-worlds disappears.

The life-world does in fact *appear* to the phenomenologist as *both* pre-scientific, experiential world *and* the encompassing concrete universal of all particular worlds. However, these are moments or aspects of the appearance of the same life-world. It seems to me that the life-world is neither one of these two options without the other. Using Welton's distinctions, I thus argue that seeing the world as the flesh of the ego allows us to discover the manner in which what is 'epistemic' in Husserl's characterization of the life-world as the pre-experiential 'horizon' for the possibility of science is in fact tied to what is 'ontic' in the 'field of action and thinking' that characterizes the life-world as concrete universal.[20]

I arrive at the evidence for this last assertion by noting the experienceability of the life-world as flesh. That is, I begin from the experience of the lived body and then note first, how the *notion* of the life-world grounds such an experience as its *condition*, and second, how the *experience* of the life-world goes some distance towards showing that this notion of the life-world appears (and could only appear) in *an analogous way* to the lived body's appearance. I will now cite what I take to be a critical example.

My experience of my lived body is that of a pre-scientific unity of life that nevertheless allows me to incorporate scientific habits of self-reflection into my very experience of myself. As I grow up, I learn not to fear the doctor and not to feel too comfortable in my body but to develop an internal 'searchlight' for disease and to go to her every time I feel a certain way. How can this experience of progressively sensing my embodiment according to science be achieved?

This experience can be achieved only if the entire life-world itself is already lived by the transcendental ego as the condition for its lived bodily experience. The life-world thus *must* appear as both the transcendental ego's object-like horizon waiting for constitution (pre-scientific, immediately simple and unitary) and as its subject-like field actively guiding that constitution (sedimenting, mediately multiple, but referring backwards and forwards towards an overarching, synthetic whole). The only way, in other words, that it makes sense that my lived bodily experience could develop in these ways is if I am bound up with the world, the whole world, as a transcendental constituting consciousness in a similar way to the way in which my same consciousness is bound up with its own lived body – a body that is given to me not only as a whole but also as a kind of whole that only becomes *more explicit in its wholeness* through incorporating my ways of living it.

The life-world *must* serve as the condition for my becoming conscious of my body differently, but how do I experience the evidence for

this 'must'? The evidence, as I see it, comes through the very experience of intersubjectivity. As I come to be able to take on more than one
perspective at a time, to overlay perspectives onto one another, and
to emerge as a newly constituting human being who bears a new relationship to what is pre-scientifically his, I experience an *increase* in
my experience of world. This experience of *increase* is not merely an
experience of quantity growing larger but an experience of the very
qualities of ownership and involvement. For within this experience of
increase, I also experience a shift in how I identify myself; no longer
am I simply the person or the child who stood and lived within the
pre-scientific world, for example, prior to my first encounter with the
doctor. I now own myself, I relate to myself, as a medically sensitive,
harmed, channelled, and improved being Yet the ownership, the self-
identity, that I am does not simply let go of the pre-scientific self, either.
I still own, I still am, that pre-scientific person, too, even within my new
medical self-ownership. Granted that experience becomes typically pe-
ripheral, but that does not mean that it is gone – perhaps I still am that
pre-scientific person as a particular, vague, reluctant experience of loss,
of prior innocence, of childhood's indifference towards certain bodily
parts, and so on.

One might say, then, that my world 'opens up,' becomes 'shaken,'
and becomes 'familiar again' through my experience of relating with
others and through my putting into play a way of concealing former
layers of self-awareness or meaning without losing them completely.
It is the very experience of things being unsettled but becoming reor-
dered, of things being revealed by means of concealing others according to a new, pluralized perspective, that brings with it an experience of
the life-world as a whole as in some manner my own flesh. As I 'settle
with' the doctor's new and medically sensitive gaze, I appear to pass
from one world into another, and it (this new medical world and all of
its correlates) becomes embodied *in my own gaze*. It is this experience
of the world being opened up and reclaimed successfully by means of
concealed yet preserved past experiences that points beyond itself to
the totality of the life-world as being my own flesh, as sustaining me
as I pass into and through the relationships I discover with others. I
experience my world as an original and as a totality, and I experience
the one by means of the other.

In other words, just as the transcendental ego experiences its life-
time as self-constituting flux, the same ego experiences its life-world as
self-constituting sedimentation into and preservation of its original. Or,

to put it another way, the experience of the life-world is best evidenced in the experience of trust and familiarity being restored. The self-constituting flux of time meets the self-constituting stability of world.

It is important to note that this very experience of the life-world as an experience of *sedimentation and preservation* is not an experience of alien relations out there in the world that only get transferred subsequently by means of an act of thinking to myself. The analogy I want to point out between my body and my flesh, between *Leib* and *Lebenswelt*, is not experienced *as an analogy*, since when I begin to be initiated into these (medical) mysteries I am a child who does not realize explicitly his capacity to think in analogies. And I am particularly not aware of how I become sensitized to disease by my ability to take over the perspective of an adult doctor. Rather, I experience the other views, the linking of perspectives, the changing of my own view into a 'searchlight' directly. My experience of the world is immediately an experience of myself as well. The 'pairing' in which I engage the doctor is really the experience of the world of medicine and the world of my own self-experience overlaying each other. It is the experience of the world as such, as separate layers, coming home to me as my single world, as the world through which and in which and on which I live.

The life-world then really is the experience of the necessary reclaiming of my total flesh: that is, only if my point of view on my body was always already able to become the perspective of the doctor and of science as such *because I equally was those mediated views transcendentally since all the objects and perspectives that those views constituted were my own familiar flesh* could I learn to feel myself immediately and empirically in those ways.[21]

B. Life-World as Alive

According to Husserl, the life-world is what we have as '*einer geistigen Gestalt*' (*Husserliana VI*, 115), as a style or as 'the unity of a living organism [*eines lebendigen Organismus*]' (ibid., 116/[E113]). To the question of whether the description of a life-world truly (and not simply metaphorically) appears as a *Gestalt* or an *Organismus*, I believe Husserl to have answered in the affirmative.

To experience the life-world as something non-living would be to experience the transcendental ego as non-living. To constitute itself as alive, the transcendental ego needs to constitute itself as having a history, as having been the same whole that now had its hand as an organ and now as an object. But without the life-world *itself appearing* as historical, as organic, the correlates or acts or layers of sense that the transcendental ego entrusts to that world would be preserved without any internal organization, without the character of historicity as such, and thus the transcendental ego could not itself retrieve those historical acts *as historical.* That the life-world does appear as historical, as the very ability of things to retain their references to life and historicality, is shown in that one can *accidentally* dig up *any* archaeological site and immediately experience the objects found as historical. Any experience 'in the world' hearkens back to the life-world; any experience of the life-world must be that of organicity.

In addition, to argue that flesh has no place in the ultimate self-constitution of the transcendental ego is to take away, as I argued earlier, the means by which one could understand how that transcendental ego could become objectified in particular human subjects. And to do that – to take away the comprehensibility of the relation between the transcendental ego and the particular humans who claim it as their own – is to commit Kant's error, that is, to 'distinguish this transcendental subjectivity from the soul' (ibid., E118) in such a way as to leave philosophy for myth.

In order to prove that the transcendental ego has its flesh, then, I will argue that the life-world is more than metaphorically alive. To constitute the life-world is to recognize that the life-world is pre-given as the foundation of all objective meaning; yet as pre-given, it nevertheless builds itself up anew as the particular experiences of world, as 'objective' truths that multiply *in order to return us to a shared experience.* The life-world is something that means to us a kind of agency; we experience it as 'pulling' 'all of science … along with us' into itself (ibid., E130–1). It builds itself; it pulls us – the experience of the agency of the life-world suggests that it is experienced as alive.

The life-world's organic agency, in fact, and its ability to both ground our activities and contain them, is what allows us to be alive *qua* objectified or *qua* human subject. Much as we are aware of only one of our organs or limbs at a time in conscious focus, we are also aware of only one of our vocations, one of our life-projects at a time. The life-world is the flesh that preserves the other projects of our embodied subjectivity that we deposit there for the time being. The life-world is the flesh that we 'entrust' with our own as human beings.

As a husband or colleague, I cannot sit down to write a paper. Rather, those projects must recede at least for a while into the background in favour of the project of writing as a scholar. Even the 'vocational interest, whose universal subject matter is called the life-world,' has its time, Husserl says, a time when other vocations are bracketed or fade into the background (ibid., E136). The possibility to foreground and background one bodily organ or one vocational interest for another, the possibility to *direct* our entire human body, our entire natural subjectivity now in this way (as mother or brother) and now in that way (as professor or researcher) depends for its possibility not simply on the operational structure of our lived body or *Leib*.

Pursuing a vocation is precisely the putting into play of this *entire* body, this *entire* subject in a particular manner. The question becomes, however, how the total experience and mobilization of our body is possible if we are never given it *as a whole* in *adequate* self-evidence.

Yet the experience of my body is given to me as a whole even if not adequately. And I do have the experience of being able to change directions quite easily. Therefore, since any vocation requires the notion of our body, our subjectivity as a whole, and since this whole is not given adequately in any moment of time, the only way to make sense of our ability to change directions or projects is to recognize how we already constitute our body as a whole that itself is being foregrounded and backgrounded thanks to some larger organism, some larger bodily whole. In other words, in order for our *attention* as subjects to *move* back and forth, we must have already recognized that the world makes room for us, sustains us, that we are in it as members are 'in' a family, as a beloved is 'inside' of my body, my thought, my heart – even more intimately than that.

We have a body as a whole only insofar as we (the human, natural egos) cede full rights to its constitution, only insofar as it is also constituted in relationships, in families, in cultures, in a world, and in a universal subjectivity that entwines itself in us. We take on projects and push others into the background only insofar as we already claim that our own flesh is a much more complex affair than what is immediately apparent.

To write a paper now is to foreground one project with the co-experience of having faith that the other projects I also care about do not *thereby* die but remain secure. My friends will still call me, my wife will walk back to the room a few hours from now, and so on – these concerns or projects do not appear to be in danger of being erased solely by my sitting down to work. To act with the whole of my subjectivity in one particular way is implicitly to acknowledge the way the world maintains the other directions of my constitutive acts, just as the body maintains my eyes when I am focusing on listening to the music in my headphones, and so on.

To turn our attention, as Husserl suggests, to the life-world as such a guardian of our own constitution is to gain a further insight into the very process of correlation between things and our syntheses. The life-world is the confluence of things and syntheses that stand 'in an insepa-rable synthetic totality which is constantly produced by intentionally overlapping [übergreifende] horizon-validities; and the latter influence each other reciprocally' (ibid., E145). To constitute the life-world, then is to constitute the whole of ourselves-with-things; to constitute the life-world is to see, perhaps for the first time, the life of the whole in which we are implicated.

Just as an organism is a unity of its own organs and systems, mem-bers and acts, so too is the life-world. It is not a 'totality' if by that word one means an adequately grasped and closed set of meanings. How-ever, it is a whole, given as such just as our body is, not as simply an ideal object, not as simply *any* kind of object. Recognizing the whole of the life-world as a correlation of our ultimate subjectivity makes clearer why the 'naive faith' in the world as preserving whatever projects we are not currently engaged in is not immediately a misguided optimism. The life-world is just the flesh in which our human flesh is free to sub-merge itself (as our memory deposits itself in concrete objects) in order to return, when we switch directions, to another position that continues to matter to us.

Just as *we* are movements, unities of kinaestheses responding to things, and just as *things* are unities of adumbrations responding to our movements, so too the whole of our constituting life responds to this life of the world and this world responds to us. Ultimately, the life-world is entwined with the life of the transcendental ego. There is *one* life, *one* flesh, that of universal subjectivity. Yet the constitution of the life-world as the one flesh of intersubjectivity equally demands imme-diately that it be experienced as a living whole that confronts its unifier as another kind of living thing, a body that confronts an ego as its own, since it is *through* the experience of the *multiplicity* of monads that the life-world comes to be experienced as such.

C. *Life-World as Life of Intersubjectivity*

Having suggested how the life-world displays an organic agency in general, I will now go on to talk more specifically about the particular ways in which the life-world demonstrates its organicity. First, I will restate with Husserl what the life-world is *not*. The life-world is more than the *lebendigen Horizonthaftigkeit* of our particular acts in the natural attitude (*Husserliana VI*, 152G). It is more than this horizon that makes possible the life of the subject as having now this and now that experience of particular objects and vocations. The life-world is more than 'a single indivisible, interrelated complex of life [*Lebenszusammenhang*]' (149E; 152G). The life-world is not simply a horizon or a complex.

These remarks about what the life-world is *not* make sense, life in the natural attitude makes sense, our ability to change from one vocation to another makes sense, only if the experience of the life of the life-world is much more than a simple attachment of the word 'living' to rather abstract ideas like 'horizon' or 'complex.' The life-world is not alive from without; it is an organism, which the transcendental ego lives as its own from within. However, given the transcendental *epoché*, the life of the life-world is also not necessarily anything like the idea of life in the sense of the natural sciences. The transcendental notion of life and the notion of the transcendental ego's body both *precede* the natural-scientific concepts and *ground* them.

Husserl begins to describe the notion of life that the life-world *is* when he says that 'our exclusive task shall be to comprehend precisely this style [*Stil*], precisely this whole merely subjective and apparently incomprehensible "Heraclitean flux"' (*Crisis*, 156E; 159G).[22] A style, a flux – a flow that is not random but one that would 'push us on to inquire into new correlations inseparably bound up with those already displayed' (159E) – this is the beginning of the description. But the life-world's agency is more than an external force that moves us from experience to experience as singular subjects. The life-world lives as the very sustenance of our mutual interpenetration. Its *internal* agency displays itself as the internal links between subjects.

The life-world is alive insofar as it makes us aware that what we perceive is already perceived by others. The experience of this life-world's own life then is the experience of an *internally regulated* flow and style that compel us towards one another as co-subjects, the flow and style that make things elide any one person's full grasp. The life of the life-world is the life that allows a thing to appear but at the same time to remain a thing 'which no one experiences as really seen, since it is always in motion' (*Crisis*, 164E). We become aware of the life-world as having an internal determination, as being itself alive, through the way in which it compels us to see our own internal determinations, our own extensions into the lives of one another.

The life-world's life is experienced as the life that sustains the phenomena that occur *between* ourselves, the life of the 'between' that most of the time gets immediately and concretely constituted as the 'separate' life of intimate relationships, families, and societies. Each experience of a relationship appears to us as having a 'life of its own.' Each relationship appears as having a kind of agency that we belong to, that we help to flesh out, but that we do not singularly or perhaps even together necessarily control. We experience the life-world as that which is responsible for these separate lives of our interpenetration, responsible for their very appearance, for the larger notion of their 'higher level personality' or life. The life-world is alive in the sense that it 'organizes' us, compels us towards, sustains or challenges our relationships with others. This is why the life of the life-world is not given adequately to us in the natural attitude; the life is only viewable from the standpoint of the whole of the transcendental ego, the one that is already intersubjective.

Agency, flow, style, internally regulated organism – these are the words that can be used to describe the life-world. These characteristics reappear in particular ways in the experience of things and of one's own lived body. My own body and any other experienced thing each appears, each in its own way, as 'an index of its systematic multiplicities' and 'a harmonious flow of manners of givenness' only because I recognize the world as the flow of flows, the index of indices, only because I am fundamentally a transcendental ego that recognizes itself as a correlation between subject and world, between subject and other.

The life of the life-world that is also my own as transcendental ego is never simply that of an organism plugged into its environment, an environment on which and in which it equally thrives and suffers. Rather, the life of the life-world is that of an organism that *is* its environment, that is at once both the condition for the possibility of that environment and the direct production of it. Only such an experience of life could then be separated into two terms, organism and environment, that stand to face each other. Only such an experience of life could be separated into different subjects, into subjects and objects, with the subject discovering just how *demanding* other subjects and objects can be.

The life of the life-world is intersubjective and layered; it is a life in which 'all the *levels* and *strata* through which the syntheses, intentionally *overlapping* [*übergreifende*] as they are from subject to subject, are *interwoven* [*verflochten*] [and] form a universal unity of synthesis' (*Crisis*, 168E; 170G; my emphasis). The life of the life-world is an overreaching (*übergreifende*), an interweaving. It produces the very possibility of this lived body here to overlay other bodies, other things, and to identify them. The life of the life-world is at once the life of all of us, of intersubjectivity, and also the life that is accessible only when we see that we form, together, a kind of universal subjectivity, a subjectivity that we own (much as we own our family, our university, our country) only by also being produced by it as its particular layers.

The life-world has its own time, just as each of us lives through our sickness or health in a particular way. The life-world also has its own space: 'the world is a spatiotemporal world; spatiotemporality (as 'living,' [*lebendige*] not as logicomathematical) belongs to its own ontic meaning as life-world' (*Crisis*, 168E; 171G). The life-world lives its own time and space. And it does so as the universal subjectivity that is interwoven in and correlated with it.

Only if I live, on the one hand, as a human *within* and *on* the organism of the life-world, only if I, on the other hand, *also am* the whole transcendental subjectivity that *is* its world as *its own flesh*, does it make sense how my own experience of my anxiety appears as conflicting with the experience of the 'objective' space and time of a flight from Chicago to Italy. The relationship between my experiences of objective time and of my own personal lived time indicates the relationship between my own lived time and that of the life-world. My own lived time (this personal anxiety) as this person here and now in the plane is made possible by an experience of time that embraces all human relationships, that is lived on behalf of all consciousness, even the 'objective' one. My ability to experience the fact, even within the throes of my anxiety, that she lives this flight differently than I do – she can sleep! – is possible only if an experience of time on behalf of the whole of intersubjectivity is possible and given. The transcendental ego lives the time of the entire life-world as its own. Hence, I can make changes in my own lived time, can work through my anxiety, can let her ability to sleep calm me.

Only if the life-world is an original organism does it also make sense that I have a lived experience of space that conflicts with the objective one. My own body sustains ever-new experiences of its own synthetic unity (this toe hurts when I walk too far for the past two days) and of its relations to others (physical proximity and intimacy with a spouse is never simple and never finished being described and delimited even if the size of the apartment never changes). This ever-new experience of lived space – the experience of the airplane as not a number of square metres but as a prison or a bedroom – is possible only if my experience of my lived space appears as conflicting with my experience of objective space and of the lived space of others. But again this experience of conflict presupposes an experience of space that is the unity of these separate spaces. We, as the transcendental ego, do not simply have space or time as a 'program' in our ego; rather, we live it as an experience that embraces all modes of space. We live the space and time of the life-world.

As an internally regulated organism, as a separate experience of time and space, the life-world sustains and then takes up our experiences into itself. In a sense it is the perfect organism in that it feeds on what it has yielded. Indeed this transcendental life, this life-world, only feeds and expands or changes according to self-defined limits: 'But however it changes and however it may be corrected, it holds to its essentially lawful set of types, to which all life and thus all science, to which it is the "ground," remain bound. Thus it also has an ontology to be derived from pure self-evidence' (*Crisis*, 173E).[23] As the ego's flesh, the life-world is not without limits. Yet the ego must still discover those limits as if for the first time.

Although the life-world is experienced as an organism, although it has an ontology of its own, still the life-world only appears as such because it is *limited by the transcendental ego's original activity*; only as delimited by the transcendental ego as its correlate can the life-world be experienced as itself alive. The life of the life-world is therefore not that of a foreign organism; it is that of a unity of ourselves, our deepest functioning 'yes' to the entirety of experience insofar as it can appear as our own lives. Any difference the life-world presents, then, is a kind of self-alienation – one that is addressed by our coming back to experience it. Hence, the life-world is an organism that appears on the one hand as one's own (transcendental) life yet appears *qua oneself as this person* as a separate, ongoing experience.

Ultimately, I claim that the body of the transcendental ego just is the life-world. Its flesh is just as surely its syntheses and correlations, its flow and style, in the same way that Archie Bunker's body extends to the chair in which he habitually sits (as evidenced in the uncomfortable glances Edith and Gloria give to Mike when he sits in it). However, this argument needs to be further developed by showing *both* how one moves from the lived body to the life-world *and* how one moves back from the life-world to the body.

D.   Leib *and* Lebenswelt, *A Unity of Habit*

This section returns us to the characterization of the life-world as alive. This will enable me to to close this section and this chapter with a discussion of how Husserl's path towards the life-world is one of habituating oneself.

In division IIIB of the *Crisis* (*Husserliana VI*) Husserl discusses how the relation between psychology and transcendental phenomenology, and thus the relation between the natural attitude person and the transcendental one, is one 'of the alliance of difference and identity' (205E). That relationship, the alliance of difference and identity, is exactly what one could use to describe the relation between organs and systems in the body, between an organism and its environment, between persons in an intimate relationship. And indeed, Husserl makes it clear that any activity the transcendental ego can perform, such as looking from above at the life-world as a living whole, must be located again 'in a psychological internal analysis'; in other words, the transcendental ego's acts and insights 'would be apperceived as something belonging to the real soul as related in reality to the real living body' (206E).

The transcendental ego and its intertwining with the life-world must reappear as the relation between soul and body. It is in this sense then that the transcendental ego has its flesh, is related to its flesh. Not simply, not just as I am living out my own body here and now in the natural attitude, in the writing of the paper. But in such a way as to constitute the entirety of what appears as in a sense my own, as close to me as my body is. That the transcendental ego and its insights would have to be an appearance in my own soul–body relationship must mean that the transcendental ego is not foreign to flesh, is not a mythical *logos* that has nothing to do with what it encounters. Rather, there is a notion of flesh, an experience of it, that the transcendental ego has that is translated into embodiment: 'everything that has newly flowed in is now concretely localized in the world through the living body, which is essentially always constituted along with it' (*Crisis*, 210E). The world and my body, Archie and his chair – these co-constituted unities of experience are only possible as together because the transcendental ego has its transcendental flesh already within it. But even more – the insight I have into the life-world now gets translated into a new kind of lived bodily life.

To live in appreciation of the life-world as the foundation of the concept of my own life as this organism here writing the paper means to have to act in particular ethical, relational ways. To know that I do not kill my relationships necessarily by sitting down to write does not mean that this particular time of writing is not poorly chosen. The life of the life-world that sustains all my other projects is a co-constituted life, one that does not maintain itself from an individual standpoint in the natural attitude. Relations, cultures, societies – these and the projects and insights that are part of them – are alive and relevant to transcendental subjectivity only insofar as that transcendental ego is immediately also this and that person, their embodied lives, and the structures of pairing that bind them together. Grasping the structure, the experience of the life-world as such, makes demands on me to re-evaluate the experiences of life as particular phenomena, each with *its* time, space, flow, and so on. Grasping the life-world re-energizes the issue of life in the natural attitude.

As we have seen, in order to recognize the life-world, one first has already had to move in a bodily manner. But the motion that acquires a world, a motion that acquires a skill like phenomenological description, cannot be arbitrary; it must be a developed motion, a habituated one. Indeed, the motion by which one learns to grasp the life-world and its relation to the ego is quite similar to the motion by which one learns to play a sport or a musical instrument: 'anyone taking the phenomenological attitude first had to learn to see, gain practice, and then in practice acquire at first a rough and shaky then a more and more precise conception of what is essentially proper to himself and others' (*Crisis*, 248E). To learn to see the transcendental ego is to have to learn the rules of a new embodiment, a new set of habits. To learn to see the life-world, one has to learn how to be that ego on its own.

And it is very difficult to learn phenomenology, as it is to learn how to play jazz piano like Bill Evans or Oscar Peterson, because the insights are not analytically 'derived from common experience' (*Crisis*, 248E). There is nothing in the common prejudices or the common language that can prepare us for the way in which we are *always already* with other persons, with things, and with the world in order for anything to appear at all. To speak of the mutual internality of all subjects in transcendental intersubjectivity is to speak of an experience of flesh, of embodiment that is simply incomprehensible to a person whose vocations are solely those of family member, worker, or friend. To speak of this mutual internality as a universal subjectivity is to speak of an experience of an organicity that is not a fascist state (not a 'We' that *only claims* to do justice to individuality). To speak of the life-world is not to speak of an organism by which the transcendental ego objectifies itself as individuals that are merely to be its organs.

Rather, the life-world is in us as intersubjectivity: 'In the concreteness of transcendental intersubjectivity, in the universal interconnection of life, the pole, or rather the system of poles which is called the world, is contained as an intentional object in exactly the same way that any intention contains its intentional object' (*Crisis*, 262E). *The flesh of the transcendental ego* is *our flesh*. Not our flesh in the sense of an abstract essence of the normal, human form; not our flesh as simply this particular human body or that one. But the transcendental ego's flesh is just the way that I can be 'in' the music, be 'towards' my death, be 'bothered' by the cars in the street, be 'practising' basketball. Just as I can have my own intentional objects, which are at once the objects of my culture and body that co-determine how I 'have' them, so the world is something that the transcendental ego has by virtue of its universal possibility of allying difference and identity, its possibility of alienating itself from itself as its own kind of embodied, habit-forming subject in order to recover itself in its having of the experiences as such.

My *whole* being as consciousness appears as encompassing and being encompassed by a world as its flesh. Insofar as my consciousness encompasses the whole world, I can immediately identify myself as the transcendental ego as transcendental intersubjectivity. Insofar as my consciousness is located within the world that it embraces, I identify myself as a variation or instance of the transcendental ego among others. Both senses are true at the same time, however, and my sense as a variation or instance immediately refers back to my sense as the whole, and vice versa.

Because I am a variation on the world-constituting ego while being that ego, I can *modify* any of my existing perceptions and give it the function of a variation and thus grasp, in immanence, a certain *eidos*. Because I am not just this body as ending at my fingertips and toes, because my flesh is the whole world, because the world in a certain sense is 'my oyster,' then a particular oyster, a basketball, a person, my sneezing, this book can become 'my whole world.'

4 Conditions of Overlaying – Time-Consciousness and Whole–Part Logic

In the previous three chapters, we have seen how Husserl describes the layers of subjectivity at work within the experiences of intersubjectivity, essential intuition, bodily structure, and egoic life. Central to the description of each chapter has been Husserl's description of the unities involved in terms of overlaying (*Deckung*). But in each of these preceding chapters, an important discussion has been deferred. What has been deferred, and what we must now address, are two important conditions for these experiences – the conditions of internal time-consciousness and of the deployment of the logic of wholes and parts.

This chapter therefore has two sections. In the first, we examine Husserl's description of internal temporality in order more fully to account for the whole structure of overlaying at stake in sensation, perception, and the experience of the alien other person. The particular textual examples used in this section come from the collection of Husserl's writings on temporality titled *On the Phenomenology of the Consciousness of Internal Time* (hereafter PCIT or *Husserliana X*).

And in the second section, we examine the description of the logic of wholes and parts in order to make fully comprehensible the originality of Husserl's description of *Fremderfahrung* and intersubjectivity. Our focus for this material is on the Third and the Sixth of Husserl's *Logical Investigations* (hereafter LI) or *Husserliana XVIII* and *XIX.*

At the completion of this chapter, the consistency of Husserl's employment of the notion of overlaying, which occurs through every aspect of the subject's experiential life, should be fully evident. And with this consistent focus, we should be prepared to move on to discuss Husserl's anticipation of the concern with alterity and distance that has characterized later Continental thought.

I. Time-Consciousness

In the *Cartesian Meditations*, when speaking of intersubjectivity, Husserl attempts 'to draw an instructive comparision' between the way the alien is recognized by and connected to me and the way my experience of the past and the present relate to each other:

> Somewhat as my memorial past, as a modification of my living present, 'transcends' my present, the appresented other being 'transcends' my own being (in the pure and most fundamental sense: what is included in my primordial ownness). In both cases the modification is inherent as a sense-component in the sense itself; it is a correlate of the intentionality constituting it. (*CM*, 115)

Within this 'instructive comparison,' upon which Husserl only somewhat elaborates in the subsequent discussion of the *Cartesian Meditations*, one can begin to see two helpful possibilities for our discussion in this current book.

First, it would seem that within the passage just cited, Husserl has already identified an isomorphism between time-consciousness and *Fremderfahrung*. Both involve important 'modifications' of oneself that are able to be experienced on their own terms. And these modifications, presumably *because* they can be experienced as such, both 'transcend' and 'inhere' within the sense of the experience itself. Following up on this isomorphism, then, and looking to see whether time-consciousness too is described in terms of overlaying (*Deckung*), could be quite fruitful.

Second, if the isomorphism is really constituted in terms of overlaying, it might be that time-consciousness provides more than an 'instructive comparison' with intersubjectivity and pairing. Rather, the isomorphic structure of self-modification might indicate that time-consciousness is called into play, not merely by Husserl's argument, but *ontologically* by the pairing of self and other. One would experience time, if that were true, as the *gift* of being intersubjective; one would experience time in order for oneself to *be* the proper kind of contribution towards the on-going discovery of the meaningfulness of pairing (*Paarung*).

A. Overlaying and Time-Consciousness

Edmund Husserl's description of the consciousness of internal time (i.e., the time that passes as the life that I live, the time that makes pos-

sible my awareness of objects and others) involves his careful description of the 'now,' the 'living present,' or the moment. As we experience
and live the present moment, Husserl says, this moment of time does
not fundamentally appear as a measured portion of an objective time –
say a 'second' as if it were divorced from the rest of the members of the
series pertaining to a 'minute.' Rather, time is lived, and fundamentally
appears, primarily as interconnected moments insofar as each moment
is a shifting marker that is attached from within itself to the past and to
the future.[1]

For Husserl, the interconnection of moments is produced by, and
works to constitute, a flow of lived time, such that within the present
moment one can remember or anticipate both intentional objects and
one's lasting relations to them. Within the flow of lived time, the appearance of the 'now' or the moment is repeated at each moment as the
same and is at each moment passing away and renewed by the emergence of a new 'now.' On the one hand, then, the moment, the 'now,' is
in a sense never whole and entire to itself; it is, instead, always passing
away and always arriving. On the other hand, the 'now' also maintains
itself as an ever-renewing, self-modifying structure, despite never being by itself on its own terms.

To hear a melody at a jazz performance is to pursue the melody
across its moments, its notes – and I can experience myself allowing
each note played 'now' to pass away in favour of the whole melody,
which one anticipates according to the laws and customs of this form of
music. Each note, each now of the perceiving of this note, passes away
in order to let the new ones flow harmoniously with the older ones.
Each moment is thus different from the others. Yet there is not only
alteration happening, the moments do not simply make way for one
another. Rather, the making way of one note to the next occurs so that
the experience of the whole melody is possible, and this means that the
continuity from one note to the next is not only presupposed but also
heard.

The continuity itself is heard because one does not just hear the separate notes but rather experiences the fundamental identity in terms of
form from one moment to the next. On the one hand, each new moment, as an iteration of 'now,' is the same as each other one. On the
other hand, my experience of time is as a flow, in which each now is integrated with, bites onto every passing and every newly arriving now.
Thus, the moments of my lived time support a structure that allows me
to notice both that each now passes away and that each now maintains

me along a single path. It is this identity through difference that I deploy in order to hear the same song across the different notes.

To put this another way, this self-maintaining, self-modifying structure of the moment (such that we could ever say 'In this moment, I feel excited about listening to this trio') comes because of its passing, because it is also continuous with (or is being bitten by) the 'just past' and the 'just future.' The 'bite' of the past into each moment is what Husserl calls the process of retention, the way that consciousness holds onto the now that is just past. The 'bite' of the future into each moment is what Husserl calls the process of protention, the way that consciousness launches itself, through the now, on the way towards the future.

In terms of a lived experience similar to the experience of hearing a melody, we could also take the act of typing. Each moment of my typing this sentence here both holds onto the previous sentences and words and also anticipates what comes next, what needs to be said before the period is placed. This 'holding on,' though, is not done explicitly. I do not focus explicitly on either the moment as such or on the syllables or the separate words already accomplished or yet to come when I type or speak. I simply act – I type, I speak the idea, the sentence. Because I can act in such a way in this moment, because I can act in a way that holds onto the just-past and the immediate future, *without attending* to the way I do that, my consciousness is free to employ its own passivity in favour of an explicit awareness of particular, complex, and intersubjective phenomena.

Passively, I retain and I expect what comes next, or what came before, in the sentence in order to remain within the experience in a fluid, continuous way. I 'make sense' in what I express here in this sentence because my consciousness of internal time is what I deploy on my behalf to retain, without my thinking about it, the words that have preceded and the words that come after this one. This ever-renewed deployment of retention and protention on behalf of my active, concrete grasp of particular meanings, this construction of a flow within my specific experiences, allows each word now to be one I can relate more explicitly, in more active recollection and anticipation, to a more fully developed grammatical sequence and meaning.

1. RETENTION

Within his discussion of internal time-consciousness, Husserl spends a great deal of time describing the notion of retention, the way the 'now' bites onto the 'just past.' This is because retention, that which preserves the now in its transition into the past, is difficult, though not impossible, to experience on its own. And as a passive form of remembering, which Husserl calls 'primary' memory, retention is the necessary bridge between present experience and 'secondary memory' or acts of recollection.

The ego does not necessarily have to attend to its operations in retention. In the case of typing, speaking, or listening, if I do attend to the process of retaining each syllable or note, I am in danger of losing the flow of the whole. However, I can always turn to the way in which retention works, as in the case of paying attention to the syllables in speaking. And it is in this attentive regard that I discover that, when I allow primary memory to work towards the preservation of the form and content within the ever-renewed now, it functions so as to form a 'law of modification':

> Every actually present now of consciousness, however, is subject to the law of modification. It changes into retention of retention and does so continuously. Accordingly, a fixed continuum of retention arises in such a way that each later point is retention for every earlier point. (*On the Phenomenology of the Consciousness of Internal Time* and thus *Husserliana X*, 31)

Through retention, every now is modified. And the process of modification is continuous, reflexive, and total:

> [E]ach later retention is not only continual modification that has arisen from primal impression; each is also continual modification of all earlier continuous modifications of that same initial point. (31)

Retention thus allows the modification of each now, each impression of an object – say a tone – to pass harmoniously into the next and to retain its meaningful references to that new act of perceiving, that new unfolding of a melody or sentence. But all of this modifying, though continuous, does not translate into an indefinite power of memory or attention to the past. Rather the opposite.

Retention, although continuous and total, founds or supports only a limited access to the particular experiences it makes possible. Retention indicates, in other words, the limits to the temporal field and to the act of memory that focuses on the objects that appear as retained.

In the following passage, I turn with Husserl to examine the way in which retention supports the recognition of my temporal field as limited. What is interesting to note here is that Husserl discovers within the structure of temporality an isomorphism with visual perception and a shared overlapping (*Überschiebung*) or 'moving over' of the field of the objects that temporality and vision constitute:

> [T]he melody has run its course and silence has ensued, then the perception's final phase is not followed by a new phase of the perception but simply by a phase of fresh memory, which in its turn is followed by another phase of fresh memory, and so on. Thus a pushing back into the past continually occurs. The same continuous complex incessantly undergoes a modification until it disappears; for a *weakening*, which finally ends in imperceptibility, goes hand in hand with the modification. The original temporal field is manifestly *limited*, precisely as in perception's case. Indeed, on the whole, one might dare to assert that the temporal field always has the same extension. It *moves*, as it were, over [*verschiebt ... über*] the perceived and freshly remembered motion and its objective time in the same way as the visual field *moves over* objective space. (*PCIT*, 32E/30G; my emphasis)

As Husserl argues, a melody ends. And we cannot explicate whatever happens next within the particular melody, within the retention of the notes we have just heard. Perhaps after the song is finished at a concert a friend of mine leans in to say she is going to get a drink and asks me what I want. This conversation is of course not fluidly implicated within the melody, even if the flow of time maintains its retentive structure continuously. I might try to draw out the links between her voice, the character of her movements to bring drinks and my memory of the song, as if poetically determining how the song impacted the manner in which she leaned over and spoke to me. But in doing so I would quickly strain the link between the melody and the new motion. The melody ends, and other things begin.

To preserve the perception of the melody, I then need to turn to 'a phase of fresh memory' and away from my perception of the concert hall or bar. In contrast to the melody or the act of remembering my hearing of it, retention as such, the motor of my time, does not stop. It retains the melody, my relation to the melody, and the time I am taking to remember it. In so doing, retention is indifferent to the content that it supports, and in its process of ongoing modification, it 'weakens' my relationship to the melody and even to my own project of remembering my hearing of it.

Retention thus is both the preservation and the weakening of my experience. It is the preservation of experience since only by retention can I hear the notes passing away into one another. It is the weakening of that experience in that retention is passive, an anonymous moment of my anonymously produced flow of time, and it thus cannot on its own preserve the personal significance of what it modifies. Retention as a passive process makes possible my active remembering, my taking a stand within retention to focus on that melody, but it retains that in the same way as it retains everything else – by moving it towards the back.

If it is true, though, that 'weakening ... goes hand in hand' with retention's supportive founding of experience, then this means that my 'temporal field' is also limited. And it is limited in two ways. First, my overall sense of my time, of my life, is limited to the extent to which I can actually 'move over' my field. Insofar as my retention pushes everything back towards imperceptibility, I cannot 'move over' more than a certain stretch of time. After a few hours, my power to remember the melody and the situation of my hearing it becomes a bit less strong – more has happened in those hours. After a few days, I have to reach much further back into the flow that has continuously emerged, and my 'reach' is much shorter from the perspective of the experience to be remembered. And so on.

Second, and more important for us here, my temporal field is limited insofar as my attempt to hold onto the melody that passed *itself takes time*. It is not just that my life as a whole continues and that the melody is pushed back further and further as a result. Rather, retention must continue to push back the memory *even as I remember it*. And thus what retention makes possible, a flow that can grasp itself as the flow that it is, also works to undo that flow's relation with itself by its very acting.

A further part of this comparison that Husserl 'dares to make': He compares the limitation of the temporal field to that of the visual one. In doing so, I think he means to point out that both fields allow me to focus on objects, a picture or a melody, only by *reducing* my perception within the corresponding field to the space or time of the object. To see this picture or this tree here is to direct my eyes to move over the room or landscape in a certain way, and ultimately to forsake landscape or room for the spatiality of the picture or the tree. In seeing this picture in the museum, this tree in the yard, I come to restrict my visual field to the frame of the picture, to the outline of the tree. I thereby push into the background, or see past, the things around them.

The temporal field, Husserl argues, operates in 'the same way.' To hear the melody is to move over *its 'objective' temporality*, to 'hear' the time it takes. I restrict my temporal field to its time. To hear the melody is thus to deploy my internal time-structure in such a way as to push to the background the other temporal experiences that could come to the fore. To hear the melody is to ignore the coughing in the audience; it is also to move over my temporal field in such a way as to 'see past' my upcoming plans, my friend sitting next to me, my traumatic childhood experiences. To be 'in' the music is to occlude, to push towards a weakening, the other defining moments of my lived time.

Two final thoughts on this comparison: first, it is important to note that time-consciousness operates for Husserl in the general *way* that vision does. This passing over as the motor common to both suggests that time-consciousness makes vision possible and that subjectivity is thoroughly embodied, since even its most abstract structures indicate community of form with explicitly bodily structures. Furthermore, the comparison of the movement of vision to the movement of time also indicates that, just as vision can only see within the current horizon and must *move* in order to see the things occluded by the ones currently in view, so too does time-consciousness. Time-consciousness then has a field that embraces all the other fields, in which certain objects both suggest and occlude others.

Second, and following from this point, it is important to notice the character of one's relation to temporality as limited and yet as more than one can comprehend. One discovers retention and its simultaneous preservation and weakening. One discovers it as one's own and yet as not something one feels directly responsible for. This suggests that time is given through an anonymous process of being drawn out of oneself, into a time that means more than we alone can know by ourselves as the persons we alone are.

Such a recognition, of one's time as involving oneself in further significances, bears a very real link to bodily perception. In each of these fields, too, one is given a perceptual sense – a pair of eyes and their abilities, for example – as an inheritance, and as an opening. A child already opens onto the adult she or he will become. And the very character of vision is to see the horizon as simultaneously holding back what is still implicit and as offering an opportunity for further view, for sailing beyond in order to see more.

Actively to take up a temporal experience, then, is already to have agreed to retention as one's own process. It is to have reconciled oneself to the fact that memory and the preservation of any experiences that arise temporally only occur by that very remembering occurring *in time*. I remember only by agreeing that the object gets its time only as something I 'pass over' and leave behind. I have time only as I have a body – as something that acts but also weakens and dies.

2. RECOLLECTION

My passive motion of retention, the very foundation of my internal time-consciousness, emerged as a structure of modification, which supported an 'overlay' of my temporal field in memory. Now we will turn to an examination of that active motion of recollection itself. What we will see is the even more explicit way in which Husserl describes memory as an act of overlaying (*Deckung*).

Recollection builds upon and overlays retention as primary memory for Husserl. It is the way that I can explicitly remember, in an active way, the melody I have recently heard, as my friend goes to get refreshments. I live in the act of recollection in a very different way than I live in retention. I give recollection to myself. I am given by retention to myself.

Considered in itself, recollection, by contrast, does not evince the same structure as retention. Instead of modifying the now by means of its 'bite,' recollection re-presents the past moment before me once again, as a kind of echo of the original experience of living it: 'the running-off of a melody in *recollection* represents a 'just past' but does not *give* it' (*PCIT*, 42–3). To recollect a melody is thus to enact a structure of modification and connection with the present now that is a kind of re-presentation. Recollection is a kind of *doubling* or pairing of two distant nows.

Recollection, the recollection of the melody while my friend goes to get us drinks, places within the now a past now, a past duration, a past object, for me to live through again, as if in witness to myself:

> Recollection, like phantasy, merely offers us re-presentation; recollection is *as it were* the same consciousness as the act aimed at the now [perception] and the act aimed at the past [retention], the acts that create time – *as it were the same*, but nonetheless modified. (*PCIT*, 43)

Recollection thus allows me to remember a melody, a sentence I have typed, by my explicit act of attending to it, by my ability to bring within the present moment a whole stretch of the past of my own experience. And recollection can do this by means of its ability to allow me to live both in the now (as the one who remembers) and, to some degree, within the past (as if I were simply back there, listening to the melody again in that moment).

As one might anticipate after having studied Husserl's account of pairing in the Fifth Cartesian Meditation, the subjunctive mood to this relationship of the past now within the present one is quite important. I can live both in the now of remembering and in the past now of myself hearing the melody directly because the two 'nows' preserve their distinctness within their being given together. In fact, their distinctness in their being given together lies in the *manner* of their givenness: 'This now is not "perceived" – that is given itself – but represented. It represents a now that is not given' (*PCIT*, 42). In other words, I simultaneously live two different I's that are mine directly, the one within the other, but not in the same way.

The 'I' that does the recollecting is given directly to itself. I inaugurate the process of recollection with *this* I. The 'I' that is recollected, the one that listened to the music, is not given directly to itself. It is given 'as if I were there.' Thus, in the synthesis of recollection, whereby I have the past I given within the present I's act, I cannot live to the same degree in each. I recollect by maintaining the distinction in givenness and the unity between the past-I and the now-I (and the now-I has all the power).[2]

In fact, the process of recollection works because I submerge the difference between my present-I and my past-I (for the most part) within the course of the recollection; I submerge them in favour of the melody or the sentence or the experience. In other words, within recollection it is not with the past-I that I appear to dwell but with the past-I's experiences. Within the appearance of recollection, it is 'as if' there were only one I, only one stream. Indeed, the only marker that this is not quite the case is the quality of the recollection itself, which marks itself out as unoriginal, as different from perception, and as being about something that happened to me before.

When my friend returns with drinks, for example, she can ask me if I had seen our mutual friend enter the bar. Though I had been turned in that direction, I admit that I had not, so attentive to the recollection had I been. For it is as if I had been living, directly, in the past.

Indeed, as often happens, I can make a habit out of living in past experiences. I can recollect an experience multiple times. Perhaps the melody I heard that night was a particularly pleasant or gripping experience. Perhaps the friend who got up to get drinks continues to be particularly meaningful to me, and so I remember that night, which might have been our first shared concert experience, and, in the repetition of the act of recollection, the whole evening is charged with even more significance, including and especially the melody.

Years go by, and I remember the melody again, and her with it. What happens then, in terms of recollection, as I return again and again to that act, to that content? How do the recollections themselves relate to one another and to the original lived experience in which the melody was originally given to me as a meaningful unity? Husserl explores this relationship by means of familiar terminology:

> I can, however, undertake a reproduction in 'coincidence' [in 'Deckung'] with this 'result' that is being pushed back [zurückschiebenden 'Resultat']. Then the past of the duration is given to me, given precisely as the 're-givenness' of the duration simpliciter … I can relive the present, but it cannot be given again. If I return to one and the same succession, as I can at any time, and identify it as the same temporal object, I produce a succession of recollecting experiences in the unity of an overlapping [übergreifenden] consciousness of succession. (PCIT, 45E/43G)

To recollect is thus to add layers to my internal time-consciousness by means of my own power. In recollection, 'I can' do something; I can 'lap backwards' (zurückschieben), and thereby I can overlay the motion of retention, the passive 'pushing-back' of my lived time. Recollection is a capacity of my freedom, then, insofar as I can come to overlay, to be 'in coincidence' (in Deckung) with the continuous retention of the 'I' that was. In my act of recollecting, I add layers to my lived time.

As I repeat the process, I 'produce a succession of recollecting experiences,' which arises now as a meaningful unity in its own right. Whereas before I was the person who had and could recollect this experience, I am now the person who has done it, and who intends to do it again. I am now the person to whom the multiplicity of recollections matter as such – as in the slogan 'We Remember' or 'We Will Never Forget.'

As Husserl says in the following passage a bit more explicitly, this free production[3] of a succession of recollections is possible 'only through a coinciding [einer Deckung] of the reproductive flow with a retentional flow' (PCIT, 52E/50G). Only in its repeated 'overlay' with segments of its lived time, only in the repetition of its active 'flow' overlaying the passive one, can the repetition of a recollection also become a 'succession.' In its repetitions, recollection thereby follows the direction of retention. Recollection does not merely separate out the significance of the melody or the night; recollection 'flows' with it.

But recollection does not simply 'follow directions.' Recollection also *directs* retention, asserts my freedom to insist that retention operate just here on my self-produced moments of remembering. In repeated acts of remembering, then, each memory of the melody and of that night is something I intend to have a purchase on the other, repeated memories in order to build towards a characterization of the one who remembers this time fondly or well. Each time I remember it, say after the friend has died or gone out of touch, the succession allows me to feel touched with sorrow – as the previous memories of that act while she was still alive or still 'with me' carry the mood of a former happiness or intimacy.[4]

My internal time-conciousness itself, then, in recollection and in the creation of a succession of recollections, builds on itself, constructs a life. In the process, the consciousness of time as 'an overlapping consciousness,' as a flow that overlays itself, matters to me in particular ways, and the 'mattering to me' is now retained as a new layer. In the fact that I can *only* overlay my previous consciousness or experiences, there is something of the 'pushing back' of retention. There is loss of intensity, references, and so on – after all, I can only remember *as if* I were there again. But there is also, within that loss, within the doubling of my flow, something of preservation.

Recollection, by means of its internal differences from perception, thus provides the only route to the preservation of perception and to the impetus to return to it and to draw more meaning out of it:

> Every memory is reiterable not only in the sense that an unrestricted number of *levels* [*Stufen*] is possible but also that this is the sphere of the 'I can.' Each *level* [*jede Stufe*] is essentially an activity of freedom (which does not exclude obstacles. (*PCIT*, 46E/44G)

Our subjectivity, our relationship to our past experiences, is thus layered, multilevel. And we create those levels by means of our continuity between the now and the acts of memory. We remember. We forget. And we forget in order to remember, in order to allow the passing of the experiences to support our freedom to forge links anew between them and the now of perception.[5]

What is required for recollection is the ongoing perception and retention of sequences of objects, which are linked by passive syntheses of similarity or likeness. The notes in the melody are different yet are perceived as belonging together. This is possible, Husserl says, and it is possible to remember them together in the meaningful unity they present, only if the manner of their relation does not explicitly announce itself as a separate act of explicit regard:

> If we have in succession unlike objects with like prominent moments, then 'lines of likeness,' as it were, run from one to the other, and in the case of similarity, lines of similarity. We have here an interrelatedness that is not constituted in an act of contemplation that relates what it contemplates ... Only the similar is truly 'comparable'; and 'difference' ['*Unterschied*'] presupposes 'coincidence' ['*Deckung*'] – that is, that real union of like things interconnected in the transition [from one to another] (or in their coexistence). (*PCIT*, 46E/45G)

As we have just seen, the overlaying of past-I and now-remembering-I is possible, but it is possible only if their 'differences' are 'presupposed' as compatible, only if their unity is prepared for by a passive coming together of what is fundamentally capable of the same kind of relation. By the same token, we now see Husserl asserting that only if the contents of perception themselves form a unity of overlaying, one that not only incorporates but marks out their 'differences,' can the remembering consciousness in its own self-opposition or self-differing return to them as the meaningful whole or wholes they are.

In light of this isomorphic relation between the logic of the 'I' and the logic of the object, then, we now see the following: the ongoing perception of similar objects is possible only if I can navigate their differences in the same way that I do the differences I bear to myself. Only if I can locate the notes' 'differences' within an overarching unity of 'overlaying' can I hear the melody as a melody. In short, only if I bear within me the logic of melody can I hear one.[6]

3. FLUX OF INTERNAL TIME

What enables me to be a simultaneously retaining and recollecting I, and an overlaying of recollection and perception, is the fact that I am not just acts of retaining, perceiving, and recollecting that somehow join together without my unifying them. Rather, recollection happens because 'the representational flow is a flow of experiential phases that is structured in precisely the way in which any time-constituting flow is structured, and which is therefore a time-constituting flow itself' (*PCIT*, 53). Recollection works, in other words, and it overlays my past and present I's, because it enacts a whole flow of temporality that is itself retentive and protentive, that overlays my present flow with my past flow as fundamentally similar to each other. At bottom, retention, recollection, and perception are compatible because what I am, in addition to retention, perception, and recollection, is an ongoing flow or flux of internal time that constitutes itself. And as it constitutes itself, I allow for myself to mediate myself.

As Husserl describes the way in which the flow of consciousness appears to itself, he notices the 'double intentionality' of our consciousness:

> There is one, unique flow of consciousness in which both the unity of the tone in immanent time and the unity of the flow of consciousness itself become constituted at once ... Our regard can be directed, in the one case, *through* the phases that 'coincide' [*sich 'deckenden' Phasen*] in the continuous progression of the flow and that function as intentionalities of the tone. But our regard can also be aimed *at* the flow, at a section of the flow. (*PCIT*, 84–5E/80G)

The overlaying of phases of the melody or of a single tone that continues to resound can give an object within the flow of our internal relation. But by means of our attentiveness to the object, by means of the fact that these overlaying qualities or objects *matter* to us in the ways that they do, we can also grasp the flow of time that we *are* all by itself. I am enjoying hearing a melody and I hear through the notes that overlap the whole. But I can also turn to my enjoyment, to the duration of the time that the song is taking as enjoyable. The *Deckung* of the notes thus makes it possible to have both the object and myself as content. Although Husserl does not say this here, it seems important – without an object, we would have no access to our temporal flux as such.

Without the possibility of attending to or 'aiming at' the flow, I could not notice retention and protention as such. Without aiming at the flow, I could not see the mechanism of overlaying that operates *from the beginning* as the way in which I anticipate or negotiate differences within an overarching grasp of wholes. But how would we know when our regard attends to the flow successfully? What does it mean to grasp the flow of internal time without being caught up in the contents that arise within the flow?

This is a difficult question to answer. And I am not certain that I could do more than Husserl does above to assert the perceptibility of the flow by shifting one's regard from the contents that are flowing by to the flow itself. However, as an example of the subject's ability to attend to the flow of internal time itself or to 'a section of the flow,' I would like to offer the experience of sitting and watching a waterfall.

This example has the benefit of being like Descartes's example of the wax – that is, it is an example of a relatively simple object that immediately yields an intuition of the concept under discussion. The wax is something that in melting shows a concrete example of a thing losing its qualities, and it helps us move towards the recognition of how the idea 'identity' or 'object as such' is produced by the mind alone. In describing the experience of the waterfall, I can attend to it as a flow, and thus point towards the kind of visibility of the flux of internal time.

On to the example: I remember a specific visit to a state park where I first realized that, depending on how I looked at the waterfall, the pace and pattern of the flow appeared differently. There appeared at least three speeds to the flow of the waterfall, depending on how much (or which part) of the fall was within my focused attention. If I focused on the waterfall as a whole, while allowing the different, individual streams or currents to pass unnoticed into the background, I saw it appear in one way, at one speed. If I focused on a section of the waterfall and attended to the way that section flowed over the rocks, I saw a second speed, somewhat slower, appear. And if I attended to an even smaller portion, perhaps the smaller drops as they continued to fall over the precipice, I experienced a third sort of flow. I found that I could move back and forth from one experience to another, seeing how the sight of the whole and the sight of the sections were given together but given as very distinct patterns.

Within the experience of the waterfall, it was possible for me to see an event, an object, that was itself made up of flux-like phases. And I could attend to the way in which those smaller phases overlaid one another and formed a whole rushing cataract. Or I could attend to sections of the flow. That is, I could attend to the phenomenon of the falls or to the phenomenon of the falling.

The experience of the waterfall in this multivalent way, Husserl would argue, comes from my own character as a flux that constitutes itself multivalently. It is itself a clue to how I can attend 'through phases of overlaying' to objects and to how I can attend to the flow of the phases themselves. Just as I can be given, can experience, a waterfall without necessarily being given, at least immediately, the phases that comprise it, so too I am given to myself as a unitary, intentional immersion in the world, without being given to myself, at least immediately, as the passive structure of flowing that supports that immersion.

If Husserl's claim were false, if I could not attend to the flow of internal time that I am, could I see the flow of the waterfall as such? Even if the answer to this question is not clear, Husserl does assert that behind each foregrounded view of oneself, behind each specific and concrete immersion in one's lived time or life, it is possible to see a rather basic, bare structure of flow, of flowing unity that makes possible the sense of me as a former child, a present and future philosopher, a parent, and an aging body. In other words, just as I could allow the whole waterfall to be in the background in order to see the moments that comprise the manner of its falling, so I can allow the specific contents of the way I pass into my past, present, and future intending of objects to pass into the background so that I can see the structure of overlaying that comprises and supports every specific grasp of myself.

And in fact, unsurprisingly by now, Husserl in *PCIT* expresses the tie between the experience of the object and that of the flux in terms of overlaying. We can attend either to the way the phases of the tone overlay one another within the flux or to the flux itself because the flux is itself a structure of *Deckungseinheit*:

> There extends throughout the flow a horizontal intentionality that, in the course of the flow, continuously coincides with itself [*in stetiger Deckungseinheit mit sich selbst*]. (85E/81G)

The way in which we approach our own whole temporal field, the way in which the temporality that we are flows within us, is itself an overlaying. Our openness to our own temporality, our recognition of its givenness as our very life, is a 'horizontal intentionality,' and this intentionality is a series of phases or of acts, which overlays itself. This overlaying series matches and supports the way that the phases of the object, the meanings that it gives us within this same flow, overlay one another.

We do not *mean* to be, at bottom, a flow. We are not conscious of giving time to ourselves. But that does not mean that we are not a flow, and it does not mean that we cannot catch ourselves in the act of being the passive synthesis of overlaying.

It is true that within the flow of internal time, we can never witness ourselves fabricating it, as if we were children trying to catch a glimpse of Santa's elves. When we grasp the flux to the extent that we can, we do not sense our personhood, our name, 'in the act,' an act that occurs in us and that we perform on behalf of ourselves as named. Nevertheless, the *anonymity and passivity* that we encounter in our own self-constituting flux is also perceived immediately as *for* the named and active person that we are. The flux appears as for the layers of sense that it supports. Thus, our grasp of the flux shows it to be an anonymous yet owned synthesis of time.

We own the flux by way of deploying it and by looking at it from within it. On the one hand, we look through the flow towards the object; on the other, we can look back towards the flow itself. In other words, whatever the flow of internal time is, it noticeably sustains and gives space to 'two inseparably united intentionalities, requiring each other like two sides of one and the same thing' (*PCIT*, 87). More concretely, we hear the melody as it flows. And we enjoy or hate it because the melody both means something on its own and makes something of our life, of the time it takes to listen to it.

In short, Husserl says the following about the flow in terms of overlaying:

> this prephenomenal, preimmanent temporality becomes constituted intentionally as the form of the time-constituting consciousness and in it itself. The flow of the consciousness that constitutes immanent time not only *exists* but is so remarkably and yet intelligibly fashioned that a self-appearance of the flow necessarily exists in it ... The self-appearance of the flow does not require a second flow; on the contrary, it constitutes itself as a phenomenon in itself. The constituting and the constituted *coincide* [*decken sich*], and yet naturally they cannot *coincide* in every respect [*sich natürlich nicht in jeder Hinsicht decken*]. (*PCIT*, 88E/83G)

The flow of internal time exists as me – and it cannot be doubted. It creates my ability to 'self-appear' as the flow mattering to itself. Because I flow, I appear to myself *within* that flow, *as* that flow. Yet I cannot 'coincide in every respect' with the flow that I am. The 'prephenomenal, preimmanent' character of the flux stands out. It is 'older' than my 'immanence' or ownness. It is produced by a 'me' that is intersubjective, or at least anonymously undifferentiated.

The inability I experience of fully overlaying the flow, of fully owning it personally, is important for our next section. The anonymity of the flow is owned as a unity of overlaying that preserves its difference from my personal, intentional life. It 'cannot coincide in every respect' and thus, at the heart of what I am as a flowing life, I have a gap, a spacing. The self-constituting flux that I am allows anonymity within the heart of personhood, and as such can support and respond to the anonymity of the alien other, with whom I pair at a distance, at a gap.

The flow of consciousness supports a relationship of overlaying of itself with itself. The flow supports the 'coming to life' of my personality. For at any moment, I can take stock of my life; I can become awakened to the way I live my time. This means that for me, as for anyone else who lives a life, overlaying is active even in its passivity; it is transitive. My life carries me along until I come to take stock of it. Thus, insofar as it names the direction of life, *Deckung* occurs for every living thing as reflexive, as *sich decken*.

The flux that I am thereby, in its transitivity and reflexivity, supports my ability to appear always already to myself as having a life, a time; the flux that I am also, though, propels me forward insofar as the significance of the life that I already am is yet to be discovered or explicated. The whole of my life, insofar as I cannot overlay it completely, is therefore mine as a project, an ethical and personal one, because the very course of it, of its very flowing, is never fully 'coincident,' never fully within my view.

Sometimes, when a favourite song no longer moves me, I may experience my life not going well. I may feel angry or puzzled, especially if I had habitually felt that listening to this song had put me in a good mood. As many of us try to do when our lives are not going well, I might then try to reflect on myself as a whole, and I could very well be unable to do more than notice that my life seems to be 'passing me by.' The habit of allowing the song to define my life, to set the tone for my life's flow, dissipates, and I have to take an active account of the way my life is moving.

Within that responsibility, however, is the recognition that I am not necessarily capable of reorganizing my moods, my flow, by myself. The song mattered because I shared its significance with someone. The song mattered because other people wrote or played it, because I heard it on a radio in a car, because the song signified a relationship with a world, with music, with meaning – in short, because it gave itself to me within a certain time of my life and therefore gave itself to me in such a way that it called for a timely, particular response.

As I heard the song in its connection to my own anonymous flow, I took up a stance towards it in enjoying it. That task, which my desire and my enjoyment immediately reflected, was to reorganize my life by way of confronting my anonymity again. That song gave me the impetus to shape my 'prephenomenal, preimmanent temporality,' to inaugurate a sequence of connected phases of recollecting the song and the time I had in hearing it. The song allowed me to deploy my character as flow in creating a flow that could appear within me as my immanent life.

At the heart of the existence that I am as an experience of internal time-consciousness, as an anonymous yet personally concretized flow, then, is a kind of self-doubling and, by means of that, a kind of openness to the anonymity of others and to their products, such as songs that appear as if arbitrarily on a car radio on a long trip. My anonymity, in other words, allows me to share time just as I share embodiment. And though I cannot overlay my flow of lived time in every respect, and though by means of the flux's anonymity I am concealed from myself, nevertheless, in this self-concealment, discoveries are possible, pairings are possible. And they come to the foreground.

Another song arises in a different situation, and my life, which is not going well, can become, at least in that hearing, like a momentarily righted ship. As I slide into a mood in light of the song, I sense that in the hearing of it, other people have shown that their time, their lives, can mesh together with my own. That melody enacts the structural flow of subjectivity as such; and furthermore, by doing so, it offers an opportunity for me to erect my own stances within and towards it. In such an example, my time, my life, then, shows itself to be not just mine; my time in listening and enjoying the song shows itself to be shared and intertwined with that of others.

B. *Temporality and* Fremderfahrung: *Other Person as a Memory of the Future*

Having shown to what extent Husserl describes time-consciousness in terms of layers and of overlaying, and having indicated the link to others within time-consciousness by means of the anonymity of the self-constituting flux, I would now like to argue for what I believe is implicit in his 'instructive comparison' cited at the beginning of this section. I would like to probe further, in other words, the similarity between the way in which the other person is within my experience and the way in which the memory is within my experience.

As we have shown in the discussion of pairing in *Fremderfahrung*, the other person confronts me as a modification of myself for which I cannot fully account. I perceive the other person, even strictly anonymous others, *as if I were there.* Yet while I do so, I also simultaneously realize that I can never actually go there where they are and perceive, at that moment, what and how they perceive.

At first glance, then, there is good reason to allow Husserl the 'instructive comparison' between memory (or recollection) and the other person. When I recollect, as we mentioned above, I double my consciousness *as if it were the same* while still being different in terms of the way it relates to the givenness of the remembered experience. That is, the modification that memory presents is like that which the other person utilizes, and both modifications occur as a self-modification in the subjunctive form – *as if I were there.*

However, there is a limit to this comparison. In memory, as we saw in the consideration of the flow of internal time, the modifications are bound together within my own prephenomenal, preimmanent flow of time that constitutes itself. Thus, the 'I' that I was and the 'I' that I am as remembering are ones that my own flow unites. I thus reckon with their differences *by existing them both.*

When we turn to the other person, however, the gap between us, the gap between 'constituting and constituted,' is something that not only I live. The gap is something that also matters to the other person. She also lives the differences between us, and in her own way and from her own orientation. I can never go over there and recognize, through a kind of horizontal intentionality, the doubled, sustaining unity that binds us together as *my own act.*

In fact, given the limitation on the instructive comparison between memory and *Fremderfahrung*, it might be more accurate to say that the other person confronts me not in the way that my memory of the past transcends my perceptual now but in the way that my experience of the future transcends my now. The other person confronts me, I would argue, as a *memory of the future.*[7]

This is something we have argued above in terms of essential intuition – namely, that the overlaying with the other person and her viewpoint on what we see is what we actuate as if we were there in order to perceive the essence of things. We return to that claim here in order to argue that the structure and self-overlaying of internal time-consciousness as anticipation is what makes sense of our experience of the other person and of the world as objective and essential.

Let us take as an example the act of attending and listening to a concert together with a friend. Perhaps within the shared experience of the concert, I begin to anticipate discussing it with her afterwards. In that anticipation, perhaps I feel a bit anxious. For when I attend to the music as my friend hears it, when I attend to my friend's act of listening, I recognize that she is hearing this group in a way different from mine. She plays jazz well, and she has studied it for years. I am only beginning to listen and to play. So I anticipate her 'perspective' on the music as one I may have to work to understand. Even more, as I anticipate our possible conversation about the music after it has finished, I remember the future, I anticipate it, all while listening in the moment. In my own sense of the concert as shared, I chart out a future for the significance of this music because she announces in her very being there with me a plurality of views to come, views I do not yet have but could come to have.

In this example, my experience of the alien other person as a memory of the future reaches into and focuses my attention on the fundamental opacity of my self-constituting flux of internal time. The way my experience of the concert flows, and the way my life as a series of habits of listening and describing flows, become issues for me. My unity of intentional life and self-constituting flux is dis-covered, and I sense the way that my time, my life, could have been and could become different in order to communicate with her.

Insofar as I strive towards what I perceive to be the way the other lives her time, her flux, by developing habits of listening and explicating music, I attest to the possibility of living time the way she does. Through my anxiety or interest, I pursue the way in which we might, as Aristotle notes, become other selves to each other within a shared life. Within the gap opened up by my friend between my actual habits – between what I have actually done with my time – and the implicit richness of anonymity of the flux itself, which by virtue of its anonymity sustains more than any one concretized way of living – within that gap, I pursue a convergence. I want to be able to speak with her, to share her interest and significance.

In a shared experience of the concert, then, we overlay at a distance, without the overlaying allowing either of us simply to turn the other into an intentional object. We bear, in other words, the same kind of relationship to each other as we each bear to our own flow.[8] And the coming together of persons is the hope, the enactment, of a shared life, a shared set of commitments. To be friends is to make and have time for each other.

But there are many times when I share experiences without being worried about how my experience will coalesce with that of others. I listen to the concert not just with my friend but with many others whose relation to this band or to music I do not know at all. In my relationships with all of those attendees, the relationship which supports us, the relationship of pairing, of intercorporeality, of intersubjectivity, as much hides itself from view as announces itself. Yet it would be wrong to think that, in its anonymity, our pairing fails to announce itself.

Even as anonymous attendees, we can see through the activity of listening together, through the phases of the concert as a public event, the way in which our perceptions of one another and of the world are given. Whether enmity or friendship, love or indifference – whether linguistic and customary or emotive and unusual – the relationship, like the flux, always sustains a horizontal intentionality of its own. It is implicit in the very perception of publicity, of a crowd, of the act of listening to music *as* music.

And in whatever way, and to whatever extent, we perceive the relationship with other persons itself, which can always be fraught with obstacles, we can also see more of the flux of internal time that we exist. My life matters because it also matters to others. My time is mine because I take *this* stand on my life, a stand that is situated by means of others' stances. In those other stances, other persons, transcend and inhere within my lived time in a way that calls to mind, that affirms or challenges, the way I do.

Let us return briefly to Husserl's discussion to flesh out how the other person engages my pre-existing flux while first giving me a sense of lived time. As a reminder, the flux is anonymous and self-constituting. The flux supports recollection but does not itself recollect. I recollect by means of my own flow of time. I recollect in order to make sense of my life, of my flowing subjectivity.

When recollection occurs, when I perform it, says Husserl, it 'is not expectation, but it does have a horizon directed towards the future, specifically, towards the future of what is recollected' (*PCIT*, 55). This means that, broadly, I recollect – or I explicitly remember – in order to do something with the significance of that memory. I recollect for some reason. This also means, more particularly, that as I remember, I lay out, from the perspective of the fully remembered event, each phase, each moment as it turns into the next. To remember is to anticipate the fully remembered experience, to take up a position of the act of remembering from the future accomplishment of it. Recollection thus harnesses the overlaying structure of the flux and directs it. But how is this harnessing and directing possible?

The way that recollection directs itself towards the future of its completion and of its significance occurs only by means of the other's temporal transcendence of me. For the other person's alterity is what I experience insofar as she or he lives his or her life there, as a flow and as an interpretation of internal time that *precisely because it flows* cannot be unproblematically or simply claimed by me.

In the example of going to a concert with a friend, I am aware that she has a life, that it is a self-constituting flow. I am also aware that she cashes out her life in her own way. This is why I am drawn to her, because the way she lives her life attracts and impacts mine. But even if my friend tells me everything about what she perceives in the music we have just heard, she will still escape from me. I cannot turn into her, or double her lived experiences as my own, simply by attending the concert with her and listening to her speak about it afterwards. For when she talks with me afterwards, when she tells me what she hears, the very flow of her life removes her from my grasp.

The chances are good that, in her act of talking with me, things in her own mind could become clearer, both about the music and about me. Perhaps she will become bored with me in telling me about how she listens; or perhaps she will become energized and see in her explanation a greater significance of music, of me, and so on. Her alterity thus sets in motion both the sharing of time as such, the sharing of the self-constituting, anonymous flux, and the impossibility of fully sharing it.

The reason her alterity sets all this in motion is that in each deployment of her self-constituting flux, she also interprets it and thereby prevents me from using her anonymity to get her personally within my grasp. She always presents herself to me as something yet to be, as someone yet to be known. The act of her mattering to herself is never fully deployed and always suggests and promises more than it offers.

What is noteworthy, then, in the way I experience another person, is the fact that the other person never appears simply as a duplication of an anonymous time-constituting flow. Rather, the other person is a duplication of the flow of time as immediately also a *lived whole*. And precisely by this duplication, by the duplication of time as lived, the other and oneself form a relationship of two lived times – each of which is perceived as a modification or variant of the anonymous flux that each one exists both on one's own *and* together, through all their particular duplications and differences.

If I were not an internally differentiated, overlaying unity of time flows – perception, recollection, expectation – I could not make sense of the other person's duplication of that. If the flux did not sustain multiple glances into it, if the flux did not sustain a variety of ways of taking it up, the other person would never be able to enter my perceptual sphere. But if the other person were not also doubling that flux by means of an entirely separate yet co-functioning lived time structure, if the other and myself were not capable of entering into a more or less anonymously co-functioning relationship with me of overlaying while preserving difference, how could I have a future in any specific, concrete sense? How could the future that Husserl says 'is something just as original and unique as the intuition of the past' (*PCIT*, 59) matter at all to me without others?

The answer is that it could not. The future, my future, could not mean anything specific to me without others. It is only in being confronted by the variation in lived time that time could concretize itself meaningfully at all. My 'having' a self-constituting flux then is insufficient for lived time. The other person is the one who marks out the future as something to be remembered, something to move towards. The other person thus provides the support for my flow to matter to itself, to transcend itself while inhering within itself.

In an hour, I have to take our baby for a walk in the stroller. Tomorrow, I have to have the full manuscript to the editor. Next year, we will have enough money to pay for an important renovation. In moving towards plans with other persons, which I must enter into if I am to continue perceiving our lives together, I find myself developing a sense of who I am, of my responsibility, and of the way in which the shared projects give shape to the way I live out my time, concretize my internal flow.

My time matters to me, I have a future and thus move through life as a life, because it is not the only way of living time, and because, by myself not being the only one, others can co-habit time with me. When I recognize myself as being with other persons, I find that my life is possible only as a variant within a system of co-variants. I live this life because it maps onto the lives of others in particular ways. I live this life because it is committed through the variants of other persons to a shared life that locates my own significance within a greater one that I can desire, as a life more interesting, attractive, fuller, and pregnant with purpose.

My friend can see that my life is going badly, or see that I interpret it that way. She can turn on the radio, interrupt my thoughts, contribute to my bad mood or to its lightening. Our baby can cry, be restless, and make demands. A look from my spouse at tax time can galvanize guilt over the way I have handled money and time. All of these experiences can happen because when I see another person, I see myself and I see the other, I see our lives as marking out futures together, futures that reach as if already united, as if backwards into our present. Through the other person, I commit to the future and thus to seeing our shared subjunctivity, our 'as if we were there,' made real as a task, a demand to launch my entire life, my entire lived time, towards myself, towards her, towards the world.

II. Transcendental Phenomenology as Problem of Wholes and Parts

We have discovered the way in which a description of overlaying (*Deckung*) characterizes time-consciousness, and we have argued for how this structure, like the structure of judgment and subjectivity as such, is doubled in the encounter with the alien other person. In so doing, we have claimed both that one's internal time-consciousness is a gift from (and is meant to become adequate to) one's intersubjectivity and that one's future is supported and ensured by means of the direct co-perception of other persons and of their self-constituting temporal flux.

This whole argument has been an attempt to return to the conditions of experience as such in order to show how thoroughgoing the relationship of overlaying is and how deep-rooted the organization of intersubjectivity is within the ego. In this current section, we will finish the last part of our journey back to the conditions of experience – namely, a return to the logic of wholes and parts, which must be available to us if we are to experience (a) ourselves as wholes, (b) ourselves doubled in the persons of other people, and (c) the relationship of pairing, which, as Husserl intimates in *Cartesian Meditations*, situates us within it as the wholes that we each are.

The path that this section takes is through a rereading of one of Husserl's early and most important works, his *Logical Investigations*. What the reader will not find in this section are numerous passages from Husserl's texts on wholes and parts within the familiar terminology of the previous chapters. Husserl simply does not often use the cognates of *Deckung* in the Third *of his Logical Investigations,* which is where his discussion of parts and wholes can be found. However, there are two things to say about this conspicuous absence.

First, I intend to show that Husserl's description in the Third *of the Logical Investigations* of the different kinds of parts, and the wholes they are capable of forming – that these descriptions are insufficient to account for the whole of the pairing or intersubjective relationship that he moves on to describe in the *Cartesian Meditations*. Thus, it does not matter that he does not describe them in terms that relate to the Fifth Meditation. In this line of argument, I therefore follow Bertrand Bouckaert's lead in his article on intersubjectivity within the *Logical Investigations*.[9]

Second, I can show here evidence that the notion of overlaying (*Deckung*) is indeed one that Husserl recognized as essentially important throughout the First and the Sixth of the *Logical Investigations*. Having done so, at the close of this section of the chapter I can suggest that what Husserl began to see is that the human person lives both roles, both kinds of parts, and that the whole that one forms with another alien person is in fact the whole that situates one's simultaneous role as layer, and thus situates the very logic of wholes and parts. It is the whole of pairing, I will claim, that is the ground of logic, to which all logic answers and strives.

Before moving to Husserl's discussion of wholes and parts, then, I will now provide some evidence that the notion of overlaying was at work for Husserl in the *Logical Investigations*.[10] This will in part demonstrate a continuity between this work and his *Experience and Judgment*, which was cited in the first chapter.

Husserl's deployment of the notion and experience of overlaying (*Deckung*) in the *Logical Investigations* comes largely within his consideration of evidence. He is concerned with evidence particularly in the First Investigation,[11] which seeks to describe the relationship of intention to expression, and in the Sixth Investigation, which seeks to describe the relationship of intention to its intuitive fulfilment.

In this brief introduction to the current section, I will use material from the Sixth Investigation. There, Husserl, in a consideration of a wish to the perception that might fulfil that wish, describes the relationship between imagination and perception, the coming true of the wish, in this way: 'both enter in unity into the character of an act of identifying coincidence [*identifieirenden Deckung*]' (*LI volume 2*, 216). What occurs in that 'identifying coincidence,' which Husserl also calls at times a fulfilling overlaying (*erfüllenden Deckung*), is that a 'meaning is fulfilled by an intuition that fits [*conforme*] it' (ibid., 217).

What Husserl means here by emphasizing identification and fulfilment is that the intuition of a wished-for reality can actually come to fit the wish, such that it is possible to 'see' the 'fit' itself. A wish would not appear *as* a wish if it were not open to being fulfilled, and therefore changed, by that which it hopes for. To put it another way, to wish is to be open to being 'confirmed' in experience.

But wishes are not the only experiences that are governed by a notion of evidence that brings to light the structure of overlaying. All experiential evidence brings this same structure to light. In section 39, discussing the experience of self-evidence, of the givenness of something *as* what it is, Husserl notes that there are in fact multiple kinds of overlaying at stake in an experience of 'this is, or this as, that.' In noting the distinctions within the overall experience of self-evidence, Husserl thus anticipates in the *Logical Investigations* his discussion of the *noesis/noema* structure in *Ideas*, and he separates out a noematic self-evidence that is immediately perceived, immediately given to view, from the noetic evidence produced by a synthetic act in which the self-evidence appears as true, as evidentiary.

For the Husserl of the second volume of the *Logical Investigations*, the (noematic) self-evidence is the 'agreement of subject with predicate, the suiting of predicate to subject' (264). The (noetic) synthetic evidence is the 'form of the *act* of self-evidence' (264). As such, the acts within consciousness produce, mediately, the following correlation:

> the total coincidence [*totale Deckung*] of the meaning-intention of our assertion with the percept of the state of affairs itself, a coincidence naturally achieved in stages [*eine Deckung, die sich natürlich schrittweise vollzieht*]. (*LI* volume 2, 265)

Self-evidence is achieved as the 'total coincidence.' Self-evidence is the way the object appears as if it has both called for and supported the judgment I make. Self-evidence is the 'natural' cohering of subject and predicate, as in the immediate intuition of this as a table or that as an Ellington song.

Synthetic evidence, by contrast, is the correlation to this experience, the effort required to allow our 'meaning-intention' to fit the 'percept' of the object as such, without which self-evidence could not appear as self-given. Synthetic evidence is what has happened as an effort of one's own, which supports and participates in this total overlaying. But synthetic evidence, our acts as they overlay one another on the way to the perception, occurs only in 'stages.' This difference in kinds of evidence is significant for our purposes here.

What I would like to point out, as a way of maintaining the relevance of the passages from the Sixth Investigation, is that phenomenology as such is a kind of investigation of immediate, noematic self-evidence by means of an effort at rehearsing, of re-visioning the noetic stages that are always already, if not immediately intuitively, involved. For example, in straightforward perceptual experience, I see this blossoming ornamental cherry tree as beautiful. I see this immediately, in self-evidence, within the pinks of the flowers and their profusion in the myriad, bending branches. I do not explicitly or reflectively go through 'stages' of noticing this branch and then that one. I do not sense the way in which my orientation, my attention, and my noetic acts refer back and forth to the noematic senses. Instead, I see the beautiful tree.

Yet as a phenomenologist moves through and describes the experience, he or she can show how the layers my experience can separate into those of subjective response and of objective call. The phenomenologist shows that the perception of the beautiful tree is in fact a response to a call that has already engendered within me the coming together of various, effective layers of my own sensory and emotive experience. In fact the immediacy of the tree *means* the overlay of moments of my internal flux, of my perceptual life – an overlay that happens in stages, in the layered engagement of my memory and anticipation, in order to prepare and found and continue this experience of the beautiful tree here and now.

What Husserl offers in the Sixth Investigation is the way in which self-evidence always involves or refers to 'natural stages' or layers. And he emphasizes how the passive reception, the passive synthesis of my experience, 'this tree is beautiful!', also involves a history of activity – a synthesis of overlaying. What is important to remember, however, is that for Husserl, the reason we need to be phenomenologists in order to see this is that the activity of my synthesis fades into the background in favour of the new immediacy of the phenomenon 'the tree as beautiful,' which moves us and announces itself as self-given.

As we think through the implication of this distinction between self-evidence, self-givenness, or *leibhaftig* appearance on the one hand, and synthetic evidence on the other, and as we think through the method of phenomenology that utilizes this distinction, we can now return once more to consider pairing and *Fremderfahrung*. Within his description of pairing, Husserl is able to isolate the layers that have gone into sustaining the immediacy of our togetherness.

In his descriptions, despite the immediacy of our self-evident grasp of other persons and of our being together in our visibility or tactility for one another, we see that we have always already been at work, preparing this recognition. In light of the discussion in the *Logical Investigations*, then, we can see how Husserl's description of *Fremderfahrung* in the Fifth Cartesian Meditation is a kind of geological expedition, one that uncovers, within the immediate experience of alien other persons, how we have always already synthesized our bodies as layers, and how we have already apperceptively transferred our subjectivity, our temporality as doubled – as if behind our backs. What we can read together in these two texts of Husserl is how he has shown that the unity of persons arises as a seamless unity *both* by means of the layers that we are and by means of the gaps between us.

Indeed, this finding of gaps within overlaying, this possibility of pairing across irresolvable distance and difference, was not new to the Husserl of the *Logical Investigations*. Even there he describes overlaying specifically as making sense even of conflict:

> In every conflict there is, accordingly, in a certain fashion, both partial agreement and partial conflict. Our attention to objective relations should have revealed these possibilities since whenever we can talk of coincidence [*Deckung*], we can talk about correlated possibilities of exclusion, inclusion, and intersection. (*LI volume 2*, 213)

Furthermore, to return to the notion of self-evidence, it is clear that for the Husserl of the *Logical Investigations*, even what appears as full agreement, signified by the copula *is* as in the perception 'this tree is beautiful,' occurs by means of gaps or differences.

As he says concerning self-evidence in section 39, the way in which someone can identify the subject and predicate of an experience is never a full fusion of the one with the other. Rather,

> even where total identification is predicated, the two 'beings' will not coincide. For we must observe that in the case of a self-evident judgment ... being in the sense of truth is experienced but not expressed and so *never coincides* with the being meant and experienced in the 'is' of the assertion. (ibid., 264)

The beauty of the tree, experienced at once and immediately, matters to us. As we respond to that beauty, as we speak about it or hold it within our hearts, we introduce ourselves into the relationship between predicate and subject, between beauty and the tree, and as so introduced, we deploy our own sense of overlaying at a distance in order to match and confer meaning on the tree as giving its beauty to us.

For us to experience is for us to have to take ownership of what calls us. But most often what calls us does so from within, in principle, a shared experience. As owned by each and shared with others, experience then reveals itself to be given to us as both immediate *and* mediate, as calling for our further explication and expression.

Perhaps we see the beauty of a tree, but another person walks up and asks why we are gazing at the tree. 'Because it is beautiful,' we would likely reply. 'Why do you see it that way?' they might ask. And, like Kant in the *Critique of Judgment*, we are thereby enjoined to do more work to describe how what appears immediately to us as beautiful *must* in fact appear in just that way.

In turning to address the other person, we realize that, while the tree remains immediately beautiful for us, we have also already 'worked it out' to be so, and we now need to rework our previous efforts. Moerover, we discover in doing that work that we have more to say, we recognize more about how we took the tree to be beautiful in the previous perceiving act. Turning to the other person and laying bare our synthetic evidence, the way we took the tree to be giving itself *as* beautiful – well, this just gives us more to contemplate regarding the connection between the self-givenness of the tree, the way in which it participated in the appearance of its beauty, and the way in which we participated in the overall synthetic experience and utterance.

As I now move on to speak about the logic of wholes and parts in the Third Investigation, I will move by means of the kinds of parts articulated there back towards the whole that pairing represents in the Fifth Cartesian Meditation. What I hope the reader has gained from this current discussion of evidence is the necessary preparation for this move. We have shown that each person can synthesize immediacy and mediacy, that each can recognize the intertwining of self-evidence and synthetic evidence within a single experience. We did this in order to show that this kind of synthesis, this kind of recognition, calls for a reappropriation, a re-visioning of the kind of whole that consciousness is. We did this, in short, to show that the structure of evidence of any sort could only be experienced and deployed by a consciousness that is itself united by being part of a larger structure of overlaying and fulfilment, within a whole of wholes.

I can perceive a beautiful tree immediately. I also come to see how that is only possible within unification of a multiplicity of profiles, of branches, of trees, and of concepts. I perceive the beautiful tree only on multiple levels at once – perceptual, valuing, aesthetic, and so on. My immediate perception is thus something I experience *as a self-given tree* only within real synthetic effort. I see that what it means to experience a tree as beautiful is to be given a chance to explore how that tree and how I are both given not just immediately but also mediately. It is towards one's mediation that we now turn.

A. *Founding* (Fundierung), *Moments, and Pieces*

In the Third Logical Investigation, Husserl recognizes the relation of *founding* (*Fundierung*) as essential to an *a priori* phenomenological account of wholes and parts.[12] Founding is a law of essence that pertains to all wholes. And each whole appears because it contains 'an *A* [that] cannot as such exist except in a more comprehensive unity which associates it with an *M*' (*LI volume 2*, 25). Wholes – that is, unities of one's experience – are produced when their parts enter into foundational relationships. This means that the whole as the unity of *A* and *M* is not a unity because of the action of some 'form of unity' external to *A* and *M* themselves; rather, if one looks at the *A* closely, one sees the way that it calls for the *M* in its very essence, in what the *A* is. The *A* in other words *belongs to M*, or *A* needs *M* for its supplementation.

The notion of *Fundierung* is not an exact one; it does not give at one stroke the specific and concrete enumeration of all types of parts or all the possible combinations of parts. It does not provide an exact and fully intuitive witnessing of the manner in which a particular whole is formed, of how founding occurs in each case. But that does not mean that founding is non-intuitive. Rather, the intuitability of founding occurs through a backwards or retrospective glance.

For Husserl, foundation occurs in two different ways, according to the two different kinds of parts. In one way, the relationship of foundation is such that 'moments' or non-independent parts provide access *through* the perception of them *to* the whole. The moments themselves do not stand on their own. In another way, the relationship of foundation is such that 'pieces' of independently recognizable parts cohere with one another *within* the whole, which can be perceived too.[13]

Husserl's own description of wholes and parts occurs as the following: 'By a Whole we understand a range of contents which are all covered [*umspannt*] by a single foundation without the help of further contents' (*LI volume 2*, 34). The foundation of the whole, the way that the unity of the whole arises, can happen in one of two ways: 'This can happen in that all these contents are immediately or mediately founded on each other [*ineinander*] without external assistance, or in that all together [*zusammen*] serve to found a new content, again without external assistance' (*LI volume 2*, 34). The first kind of foundation, which is that of the parts being implicated 'in one another,' is something that Husserl describes as a foundation of interpenetration (*durchdringen*); the second kind is more of an aggregation of parts external to one another (*ausser einander*) (*LI volume 2*, 34–5).

To clarify the kinds of wholes, Husserl distinguishes between the kinds of parts as a piece and a moment: a piece is 'independent relatively to a whole W'; and a moment is 'non-independent relatively to W' (*LI volume 2*, 26–7). The moment is an abstract part, that is, it cannot be recognized on its own without one's grasping it immediately as implicated in the whole. An example of a moment would be the reddish brown colour of the table. The pieces, however, as in pieces of a broken table, are recognizable as separable and as being able to be put back together into the whole table. Moments are interpenetrating; pieces are aggregated.[14]

To continue with the example, a perceived table appears because it has what Husserl would call 'moments' of colour. These colour-moments, *both* in their continuity with or similarity to one another within a certain range *and* in their discontinuity with different moments of colour, have formed or 'founded' the perception of a coloured extension – namely, the whole table on the horizon of this living room and its rug, and so on. But it is not the colour-moments but the table and its unified surface that appear first and straightforwardly; the act of founding and the moments of colour themselves appear retrospectively, indirectly or secondarily in the context of an already perceived thing-horizon structure.

Indeed, Husserl speaks about the perception of colour and surface in the Third Investigation directly, and with reference to a cognate of *decken*. He claims that discontinuity and difference arise only because the colour qualities, for example, attempt to 'cover over' one another and in so doing introduce the possibility of recognizing the distance between one colour (and ultimately one thing) and another:

> It is at the spatial or temporal boundary that one visual quality, e.g., leaps over [*überspringen*] into another. In our continuous progress [*Übergang*] from spatial part to part there is at the same time no continuous progress

in the covering [*überdeckenden*] quality: in one place at least the neighboring qualities are finitely (and not too minutely) distant. The same holds of a discontinuity in phenomenal order. Here not merely qualities, e.g., colours, achieve separation, but whole concreta set bounds to one another, the visual field is split up into parts. The colour-distance [*Farbenabstand*] in such a context of 'covering' [*Deckungszusammenhange*] – without which there can be no talk of discontinuity – also wins separation for the 'moments' bound up with it, the covered spatial parts of our example. These could otherwise not be free from the fusion. Spatiality necessarily varies continuously. A piece of such variation can only become separably noticeable and primarily emphatic in consciousness, when a discontinuity is provided by the covering [*überdeckenden*] moment, and the whole concretum which corresponds to it has thus been separated.[15] (*LI volume 2*, 16)

Within the perception of visual wholes, then, discontinuity enters in. The visual field is something we constitute such that moments of colour can be set off against the background of different colours, which we do not focus on. The distance of the colours of the wall, against which the table stands, from the table matters. As Husserl says, the whiteness of the wall 'wins separation' for the brown of the table, and the process of 'covering' so crucial to the moments of the table in their unified brownness depends on the difference from the wall.

The point of recognizing the isomorphism between the relationship of founding within a coloured surface and the relationship of pairing with other people should become clearer in the following passages. Suffice it to say here that the other person and oneself function as mutually founding unities, that we enact the relations that we perceive between pieces and moments. This logic is in keeping with many of the arguments of this book, which strives to show that we experience or 'see' what we 'are.'

B. *Towards* Fremderfahrung, *Wholes Containing Both Moments and Pieces*

The question for this entire section is what kind of whole one's relationships with other people are and what kind of whole one's own consciousness is. I argue that one's body and relationships are precisely the kinds of wholes that employ *both* kinds of parts, both modes of foundation, in their peculiar, concrete totalities. Furthermore, I claim that this dual sense of foundation is precisely what prevents one's embodied consciousness from becoming simply a piece of an aggregate or an inextricable moment of some sort of undifferentiated communion. Because of this dual foundation, then, one is ultimately the act of moving back and forth from one's own body to one's relationship, from piece to moment, from fusion to distance on behalf of the empty presentation of the total relationship, on behalf of the *beyond* of the relationship itself.[16]

To prepare further for this argument, I now return to the Third Investigation, where Husserl acknowledges that some wholes can involve both kinds of foundation:

> The same whole can be interpenetrative [*Durchdringung*] in relation to certain parts, and combinatory [*Verbindung*] in relation to others: the sensuous, phenomenal thing, the intuitively given spatial shape clothed [*bedeckte*] with sensuous quality is (just as it appears) interpenetrative in respect of reciprocally founded 'moments' such as colour and extension, and combinatory in respect of its 'pieces.' (*LI volume 2*, 35)

Husserl acknowledges that a single whole can support both moments and pieces, but he does not acknowledge that the two types of foundation could occur within the same part. The moments of colour and extension interpenetrate in order to provide a unitary apprehension of the table's covering (*Bedeckung*). But the pieces of the extension itself, the legs and top of the table, for example, are combined within the same whole. The pieces and moments are *not* the same parts of the table.

In fact, for the Husserl of the *LI*, the same parts of a recognized object could never be implicated in both relationships of foundation at the same time with one another: 'It is an analytic proposition that pieces considered in relation to the whole whose pieces they are, cannot be founded on each other, either one-sidedly or reciprocally, and whether as wholes or in respect of their parts' (*LI volume 2*, 41–2).[17] This would mean that there could not be the *same part* that combined itself in an immediate (covering) and mediate (combinatory) way with *another (similar) part that was present in both relations*. But from his discovery that one object can contain the two types of foundation, and his thesis that the same part cannot be connected to another part according to both relations of foundation simultaneously, we can move to describe *Fremderfahrung* as a different kind of phenomenon.

I would argue, as is perhaps obvious from the above, that his later descriptions of *Fremderfahrung* and intersubjectivity work to clarify or to expand his treatment of founding here in the Third Logical Investigation. When we consider all other wholes outside of the pairing of one's lived body with another, outside of intersubjectivity, we find that no whole can be experienced as having the same parts functioning at the same time as moments and pieces. That perceptual law sets up no contradiction, however, with Husserl's description of *Fremderfahrung* as a relationship in which *one and the same part* (oneself or the other person) appear *both* as 'interpenetrating' and as 'combining with' the other *similar* parts of the *same* whole.

No other intentional object doubles all of me, all my subjectivity, all my intentional objects, all my body. While one is looking (in the above-cited text) at a table or a piece of furniture, one is looking at a noematic object in the terms that it is given – as a partial, adumbrated index of my noetic acts, as an object that eludes me without evading me. Within the perception of a table, therefore, one can see only the difference between the relationship of interpenetrative covering and the relationship of combinatory fusion that the object 'table' embraces, the difference between the parts that the table combines and those that the table compels to appear as interpenetrating. But when Husserl acknowledges the experience of intersubjectivity, he discovers unities of one's experience (human relationships) that involve *oneself* in both kinds of foundation at the same time and to the same parts.

In *Cartesian Meditations*, this awareness of oneself as both moment and piece becomes possible through the following descriptions. One experiences oneself as a moment insofar as one always already experiences the other person within a mutual pairing; there is 'a living mutual awakening' and 'a mutual transfer of sense' (*CM*, 113). There is no dogmatic or metaphysical primacy of self or other; rather '*ego* and *alter ego* are always and necessarily given *in an original "pairing"'* (*CM*, 112). In other words, one experiences an encounter with another person as an enactment of a moment-relationship, one that makes a claim on oneself as an interpenetrating part of something larger than oneself.

But one also experiences oneself as a piece insofar as the encounter always occurs bodily, insofar as 'I, as the primordial psychophysical Ego, am always prominent in my primordial field of perception' (*CM*, 113) or insofar as the sense of the other person still is something that one recognizes 'as an "intentional modification" of that Ego of mine which is the first to be Objectivated' (*CM*, 115). One retains a sense of one's separateness, then, in the encounter, and one sees that the relationship with the other person is a kind of combination of pieces of one's experience, *as if* one had doubled oneself sensuously and claimed the relationship on the basis of adding two separate lived bodies together.

Let us take up again the example of looking at the beautiful tree. When another person comes to ask me why I am looking at the tree, I feel an immediate pressure to respond. The world is given as shared, as is the tree, as is my own experience of it. They are asking about my activity, my gaze, and the meaningfulness of these. I am given, therefore, in their very entrance into my perceptual field, as bound up with other people and as having to respond (saying nothing and walking away is still a response and an acknowledgment).

In the other's interruption of my experience, I am therefore recognizing myself as a *moment* of a larger whole. I cannot maintain my own current all by itself. I must act, speak, or question.

At the same time, though, the question of the other and the attestation I might give as to the tree's beauty ('Really? You can't see this overflowing blossoming tree as beautiful? Why is that?') both show that I am also a separable *piece*. My interpretation matters to the other person, or else she would not have asked.

In fact, her very question to me shows her to be a moment that also simultaneously enacts her distance. Her question announces her as the one to whom I must respond, the separable and yet united one whose question requires an answer from one like her.

This example shows how the overlaying or 'covering' that Husserl discovers within the structures of *Fremderfahrung* is a process that one embodied consciousness performs with another embodied consciousness *as a whole*. All of one's perception, all of one's moments within that perception (even 'moments' in the sense of one's lived time), and all of one's pieces (including the separable words or abilities of perception and understanding that arise) are paired with and overlay those of the other person. The unity of this pairing is therefore something one discovers as a unique unity, as something that one both recognizes for oneself and on one's own only because it appears as a pre-given mutuality. Pairing, as the enactment of a dual founding, thus prepares us for any and every other kind of whole, every other kind of object, which can never hope to deploy the entirety of our engagement in intersubjectivity.[18]

C. Seeing the Dual Roles within a Dual Whole

I will now take up and defend the argument I have just made about dual roles. If the description of *Fremderfahrung* is to remain consonant with the Third Investigation, and if the logic of wholes and parts is exhausted in the earlier work, then it should be the case, I argue, that the pairing of oneself and the other person works to situate and energize the relations of wholes and parts. It should be because consciousness can *perform* the roles of piece and moment that it can *identify* them elsewhere.[19]

One problem that might stand in the way of seeing the consonance of Husserl's two accounts is the kind of whole that intersubjectivity is. Intersubjectivity as such, described in its initial and founding layers with the description of *Fremderfahrung*, is a unity of activity that is open-ended and that immediately presses towards specific, concrete instances.[20] In the case of a friendship or an enmity, we experience it as always having begun some time ago, as having a character that is only partially determined by oneself, as relying at least partially on a series of perceptions that the other person never quite communicates to oneself, and as having a future that will take it who knows where. In short, intersubjectivity is a kind of whole that can never be fully defined by the parts that make it up, a whole that can change, change utterly.

The kind of whole, then, that is an interpersonal relationship, formed in the pairing of bodies – this kind of whole is unique and bears an internal connection with the flow of lived time. Husserl points to the fact that the flow of internal time constitutes itself passively and so makes possible my own self-relation as the horizontal intentionality that grasps it. Like the flow of internal time, the pairing and intersubjectivity that we exist with one another also make possible one's self-relation as an active, concrete, reflective, and meaningful one. In the relationships we bear to one another, the relationship itself sediments itself for our subsequent, reflective regard. The intersubjectivity that we already are, then, constitutes each of us by virtue of its reappearing *to us* as a prepared, noematic unity within our lives. This essential relationship that embraces us, like the flow of lived time, does so by virtue of each of our intentional capacities to witness, to 'have' or to 'bear' this essence concretely in the formation of particular relations, relations that occur themselves as there in the flesh, as offering themselves to reflection, as affecting the specific course of our emotional life, and so on.

As a whole that produces itself as an object for its members, which it also founds, the relationship of intersubjectivity also thereby fosters each member's taking up of the dual roles of piece and moment. Within my particular friendship with him, I now find that it is going badly because I have been out of touch. A study of jazz piano with her is something, by contrast, I find to be going well because I strive to put into practice what my instructor teaches. In each case, the whole is a con-cretization of intersubjectivity as such. As such, it can spur each person in the relationship to recognize the possibility for its development only insofar as each *can* take responsibility for the specific, concrete relation-ship itself – for the whole – that they live within and that situates them. Each relationship has its plans, and it has its time. We can answer to those plans and to that time – or not – on the basis of the *manner* in which the relation enacts the logic of wholes and parts and encourages or shuts down our capacity to move back and forth between our dual roles.

If the whole relationship I bear to others is to grow or at least sus-tain itself, a necessary, though insufficient, condition of that growth and sustenance is that I take full responsibility as both a dependent and an independent part. If the whole is to grow and sustain itself, then I must move back and forth between two perceptions of the whole – a perception of a whole outside of me, and a perception of a whole within me. And I must do so in an organized, engaged, and purposive way. The logic of wholes and parts, then, can become consonant and remain consistent with *Fremderfahrung* only if that logic can admit two occur-rences: first, that the same thing (oneself) can be both a piece and a mo-ment within a relationship with other persons; and second, that there be the very real possibility of developing actual interpersonal relation-ships that involve persons who *could* pursue one another and their own dual roles by means of a shared project of regular reflection.

Indeed, lived experience bears out the claim that this logic can in fact admit these changes. I do directly experience, within my relationship with others, my two roles. First, I experience myself as an independent piece, as a person who is to reflect on and negotiate the relationship. And I also experience myself as a dependent moment, as a person who can only offer something according to the terms set up beforehand, who can offer a very limited content to the other members and to the relationship itself, which exerts its own pull.

And I experience how those two roles of mine are possible within the experience of the dual structure of the relationship itself. In seeing myself as independent, as reflective and active, I experience the whole relationship as something within my consciousness. In seeing myself as dependent, I experience the whole relationship as outside of me, as that which sustains the two of us as the faces of its own unity.

A jazz group makes music together. The soloist moves from the background to the foreground and back again. I am entranced by the

smoothness of the transitions, the way that the movements and har-
monies appear to synthesize together so well. They really know one
another; they really work well together. But they work continuously at
that. The performance grows out of difference, conflict, contrast, and
practice.

D. From Vacillation to Unity

Any straightforward relationship in the natural attitude experiences
conflicts because the very ability to live straightforwardly and well in
the relationship presupposes that one can (and sometimes must) *conceal*
from oneself one's ongoing role as a part of it. One enjoys the presence
of another person, thinks that things are going well, and in so doing
forgets to take explicit account of his or her tastes, or the other person of one's own. We get comfortable and assume that we are independent parts only, who can meet without making demands on each
other. Or one rests within a common project, which seems to situate
both persons, and one presupposes that any independent differences
in approach or goal will 'work themselves out' as they arise. This assumption or enjoyment is part of the process of having relationships,
part of the concealment that is as necessary as the concealment of one's
specific sensations allow for the apprehension of a perceived object. But
whatever one conceals can (and usually should) also resurface.

One cannot live only in one role, piece, or moment and expect the
relationship to handle 'whatever comes.' The relationship has already
marked out two intertwining but competing demands for each member. It is in this sense that the reflection that conflict might engender can
help clarify the value of the project and the status of the relationship.

Insofar as those involved in the conflict can use phenomenological
insights – that is, insofar as those involved can apply the insights of
playing a dual role of piece and moment in *any* human relationship – it
could be resolved well. To choose to listen to the other person, to hear
why he or she does and does not want to quit the shared project, to
assert oneself as a piece of the relationship but to limit one's assertion
so as to provide the other person time and energy to respond – these
choices in fact can make it clearer in what ways one appears as separable from the other person and in what ways one appears as bound
through their acts to a common view of the world. As one continues to
work out the communication of each person's roles as piece and moment, as separate contributor and as interdependent or already com-

mitted member, one *could* become free to develop one's responses in more sophisticated ways.

I emphasized that phenomenology opens the *possibility* to conflict resolution. It does not ensure it. Some relationships may come to appear as fundamentally shutting down the opportunity of each member to grasp herself or himself as both piece and moment. Some relationships simply begin and maintain themselves as a kind of entrapment, which might at best offer themselves as springboards from which to pursue more mutual, phenomenologically appropriate ones.

Nevertheless, if one pursues the description of both roles, the perception of the dual whole, within one's relationships, it seems guaranteed that one would become less likely to vacillate uncritically between one's role as piece or as moment. One would be less likely simply to blame the other person as the culprit and to treat oneself simply as a piece, as a separable part of a simple contract between atomic individuals. One would also be less likely to see oneself as 'having nothing to say,' as being compelled to take on the project simply because one felt like a simple moment, because one never felt like one 'had a say.'

There is an important benefit, then, to the taking up of the logic of parts and wholes in this way. With the articulation of the relationship as a whole through conflict, and with the application of insights in phenomenology such as the *dual role* one plays as both piece and moment, one can see that, in fact, one is always already *beyond* the role as piece and moment by living both of them. One is already moving towards greater self-governance in the very initiation of the relationship itself as a dual whole.

Phenomenology thus opens up an ethical future for one's concrete life. If one learns with others how to connect being a piece to being a moment, if one learns how to connect the whole as transcendent to the whole as immanent, then the basic structure of pairing can become a meaningful, concrete structure of good, regular, and open-ended relations. The connections within the relationship itself will allow not for vacillation and conflict but for each person to act and to perceive on behalf of a purposively oriented 'functional community of one perception' (*CM*, 122) that was always ready to come to the fore.[21]

To work on one's part–whole relations in any particular interpersonal relationship is to develop one's capacities to work on all of one's relationships. One might experience the fact that 'this relationship ended badly' or 'I should have ended it long ago because he wasn't taking me seriously.' If one combines these recognitions with the phenomenological reasons for the appearance of these remarks in one's understanding, one becomes better able to anticipate types of relationships in which one's role as a piece, as a separable part, or as a moment, as someone to be appealed to in order to take up a common project, are over- or under-emphasized.

One becomes able to know the form of a relationship that is *good* for oneself, that treats others and oneself as the complicated wholes that they are, and that works as sustaining both the ability of each person involved to act on behalf of that relationship while at the same time requiring that such action be clearly delineated and sanctioned through ongoing, mutual periods of reflection and candor. Such success is possible because the insights of *Fremderfahrung* are essential while also being immediately particular – that is, existential. The unity of oneself as a whole, then, is precisely one's ability to put one's dual role to work with and for each other and for the sake of the relationship.

Conclusion:
On to 'Other' Things – Husserl, Continental Philosophy, and Ethics

In the *Logical Investigations*, Husserl defends the way in which phenomenology describes its objects: 'The descriptive concepts of all pure description, i.e., of *description adapted to intuition immediately* and with truth and so of all phenomenological description, differ in principle from those which dominate objective science' (*LI volume 2* or *Husserliana XIX*, 15; my emphasis). I would like briefly to offer such a defence of the descriptive concept of overlaying (*Deckung*). Such a defence would begin with a clarification of how overlaying might provide evidence for being 'adapted to intuition.'

Albert Johnstone offers such a clarification of phenomenology's descriptive concepts when he argues that Husserl uses 'nonsymbolic, nonlinguistic, noncultural concepts' to break what had previously been a circular discussion of the existence of other minds.[1] These concepts, Johnstone argues, occur in the awareness of one's own body, in perceptual recognition of objects or faces in a crowd, in the awareness of one's spatial location and the perception of material objects (90–1). Although Johnstone has not argued this specifically, I believe that the notion of overlaying (*Deckung*) is successful because it is such a nonsymbolic, descriptive concept.

In this concluding chapter, I pursue what *Deckung* as a nonsymbolic, descriptive concept allows a phenomenologist to discover. And what I conclude is that the notion of overlaying can lead to the formulation of a rigorous, responsible ethics.

The chapter has three sections. First, I demonstrate how, in some passages from his *Analyses Concerning Passive and Active Synthesis,* and in some of his work in the third of his *Intersubjectivity* volumes, Husserl deploys the use of 'overlaying-at-a-distance,' particularly in his description of pairing. This obviates, I argue, the notion that Husserl is concerned solely with the coincidence of self and other.

In the second section and third sections, I trace out the reading of Husserl by Maurice Merleau-Ponty and Emmanuel Levinas, respectively. Merleau-Ponty holds on to a notion of overlaying while rejecting that of coincidence. In so doing, he uses French terms that suggest his attempt to be consistent with Husserl's description within the *Cartesian Meditations* while also broadening intercorporeality to new experiences of flesh. Levinas maintains the notion of coincidence while also relating it explicitly to a kind of insuperable distance or height of the Other, thereby moving from Husserl's phenomenology to an explicit revaluation of ethics.

On the whole, this chapter attempts to launch the reader towards an experience of later Continental thought as anticipated and inaugurated by Husserl in a very positive way. It was Husserl's identification of overlaying as a synthesis that made possible more contemporary concerns about alterity, absence, and difference.

I. Overlaying-at-a-Distance

In this first section, we will now take up some representative instances in which Husserl deploys the term *Deckung* within the *Analyses Concerning Passive and Active Synthesis* and the third of his *Intersubjectivity* volumes. First, by way of contrast, however, let us note how Husserl describes in the *Analyses* the experience of a fusing *without* distance in the hearing of a single, self-same tone:

> The unity of the tone is dissolvable idealiter into tonal phases. These phases have unity through successive fusion in accordance with temporal continuity; this fusion can only be made possible as unitary in the flux of continual temporal becoming if the data meld together in a materially relevant manner *without distance* [*abstandslos*] continuously from phase to phase. (*APAS*, 188, my emphasis)

Given this distanceless fusion of phases, it would seem strange that consciousness could distinguish 'idealiter' – or in terms of its own processes of abstraction, the phases – from one another. How is this ideal separation of such intimately united phases possible?

The separation is possible, I argue, only given one's implication within a pairing with the other person. It is the distance from the alien, which is a distance I cannot cross but which nonetheless effects the very pairing itself, that I learn reflectively to deploy within the phases of my own experience of self-identical objects.[2] As bearing the distance of the other within my experience of myself as paired, I can turn to my fused experiences and look at them with new eyes. It remains for us to show how Husserl supports this argument in the texts mentioned above.

Indeed, one of the clearest places where Husserl begins to make this argument that experience unfolds its layers by means of *Fremderfahrung* is in the third volume of his intersubjectivity writings. There, in a piece titled 'The Being-Dependent of All Existents, Especially of All Transcendental Subjects on Myself and Then of Myself on Them,' Husserl describes the experience of seeing a pair of trees as the recognition of overlaying at a distance:

> For example, next to one tree appears another tree, and in similar manners of appearance. Thus I cannot be conscious of them in any other way than as 'both' together, as a pair. From the one to the other as thus appearing goes an awakening and a type of *Deckung par distance* to the other and vice versa.' (*Husserliana XV,* 26; my translation)

A pairing, as we know from the *Cartesian Meditations,* is what occurs when an 'awakening' and an 'overlaying' occur reciprocally and move across the distance between the individuals. Unlike the phases of the self-same tone, the pair of trees or the pair of lived bodies does not fuse together. Rather, the distance between them is still perceived. In fact, the distance is what sustains the very activity of the synthesis. A pairing is what distant, distinct things permit.

In the following text from the *Analyses,* Husserl also speaks about a relationship of pairing. Or at least he speaks about the initial stages of pairing, most notably that of similarity:

> Let us regard statically the co-existence of two or more objects that are related with respect to content ... Where there has been a coinciding through overlapping [*wo durch Überschiebung die Deckung geworden ist*], the coinciding without conflict [*die Deckung ohne Streit*] (the coinciding of uniformity [*Glecihheitsdeckung*]) does not yield at that moment anything more of duality, of splitting in two with respect to content. A fusion with respect to content is carried out in the synthesis of the two respective consciousnesses, specifically, the fusion forming a singularity of community with regard to content. But while there is also something of fusion here in the

overlapping of similarity [*Ähnlichkeitsüberschiebung*], there is not a pure fusion and formation of unity; rather, there is unity as presupposition, as the ground of concealment [*Verdeckung*], and thereby of repression and eruption. Accordingly, we will say: What is present statically as the uniform connection of discrete contents (or as the merely similar connection of discrete contents) is itself already a mode of the two respective syntheses as coincidence [*einen und andern Deckungssynthese*]. It is coinciding *par distance* [*Deckung par distance*]. (*APAS*, 176–7)

If we combine this passage with the passage about the pair of trees, we see that it is the very act of taking up the distance between the similars, between the trees, that allows their individuality to be concealed (*verdeckt*). First, it must be noted that the distance between the similars is what urges consciousness on, in favour of their similarity. In taking them in, consciousness must move from the one to the other. And as it moves, consciousness strives to make something out of them, out of the distance between them.

I remember a graduate course on Husserl where a friend of mine discussed the relationship of shoes to one another as an illustration of pairing. She wrote that the left shoe, in its appearance by itself, perhaps by the door, immediately gives us over to the right one. We do not see *a* shoe, but *the* left one. I am struck years later by this example when our toddler, holding a left shoe, is upset because she cannot 'find her shoes.'

The very pairing of the shoes, then, indicates that the relation of the shoes to each other is precisely that which makes possible the experience of incompletion, of loss, of concealment. The shoes belong together, and in that belonging, the possibility of not being together is also given. The distance between the shoes is both the motor of their togetherness and the possibility of their falling apart.

In general then, what consciousness notices as it moves is that the objects are already calling out for its regard as already having a claim on each other. The objects' claim, a noematic one, is that of 'overlapping.' In noticing that noematic invitation or pressure, made possible by the distance between them that forces consciousness to act, to bridge them – that is, in noticing the overlapping content – consciousness then feels called to take up the distance between the two similar things, called to take up the overlapping contents and respond to them. And consciousness's response to the overlapping contents is the deployment of its act of recognition – in this case, its noetic, synthetic unity of identification as overlaying.

It is the overlaying that conceals, within the same movement, the individuals as claiming to be overlapping objects. For to be recognized as a pair, which the objects were claiming to be, one shoe or one tree must, in a sense, give up its own sphere in order to be grasped as together with the other.

Wherever there are similars at a distance, wherever there is the experience of pairing, unity is 'presupposed' and concealment and 'repression' and 'eruption' must occur as the very consequence of consciousness's recognition of the noematic pressure of overlapping. For me to perceive the pair of shoes or trees together is to shut down my perception of each one and thus to allow the future of their relationship to each other, and to me, to matter. As I grasp the pair, and only as I do so, I may notice, in attending to the pair, that one of the trees is older than the other, or is hollow, or sick. Or the other shoe might be revealed as scuffed or stained. A 'conflict' between the trees or shoes can, at any moment, reassert itself as simply repressed by the relation of pairing.

If we turn from the description of a pair of trees and shoes, or any relation of similarity, as inaugurating a pairing through the distance between the members, and we turn now towards the relationship between persons in a bodily pairing, we can see, again, how overlaying at a distance recurs explicitly. Again in his third volume of *Intersubjectivity* material, this time in number 29, 'Toward Phenomenological Anthropology,' there is a section titled 'I-You-Overlaying.' There Husserl admits the kind of presupposed unity, concealment, repression, and eruption cited above in the quote from *Analyses*:

> Just as I can come into conflict [*Streit*] with myself, thus can an I in this overlaying [*Deckung*] come into conflict [*Streit*] with that I overlaying it [*mit ihm deckenden*]. (*Husserliana XV*, 476–7; my translation)

Husserl then goes on to talk about this possibility of conflict as also being the possibility of resolution by attempting a most intimate overlaying or '*innigste Deckung*' (*Husserliana XV*, 477; my translation).

If we remember the example of the mannequin/human in the store window from chapter 1, we can now see the necessity of acknowledging that specific conflict. In the experience of the shop window, unable to predicate what was inside the window, the observer was in conflict both with herself (was she seeing a mannequin or a human?) and potentially with the object (which might be the double of her subjectivity and looking back at her). The observer's self-conflict was intimately linked to the possible conflict with another person. And the only way to resolve the situation would be for the observer to deploy her conflict with self with respect to the object in the window.

That is, the observer could press against the glass, stare hard at the mannequin's 'eyes' or 'skin.' In so doing, the observer would open herself up to conflict with the person, if it were one, who might take offence at this act, or laugh at it. In this case, and in every case, predication ('this is a mannequin' or 'no, this is a human') can only happen by moving towards a more intimate overlaying of self and other on the basis of one's own judgment, which pursues evidence as a kind of self-overlaying.

To predicate is to take a stand. It is utter a sentence and thereby to open oneself up to the other. It is to take one's own unity and bring it forward to the other subjectivity who could take up one's sentence as her or his own. It is to deploy one's unity in a relationship of co-existence.

To predicate is also to conceal the individuality of oneself and the other, who can disagree, who can point out variations that do not fit the predication I utter. And the conflict that may well ensue over the description of an experience cannot help but insert itself within my experience, separating the phases or parts of my process of making sense of the world.

In this short quote above, then, we see Husserl as moving towards the claim that one's own process of self-overlaying is made for the overlaying with the other person, and vice versa. We also see him acknowledging that whatever the I or the ego is, as the overlaying of self with self, it incorporates difference, distance, and conflict, such that concealment, repression, and eruption are always possible.[3]

If we return briefly to the example of listening to jazz music, which we have used throughout the book, we can see this structure enacted. Playing jazz does not simply mean the playing of harmonious, melodic, regular music. The structure of call and response is not always 'nice.' It can be jarring. I can hear the clash of the piano with the bass or saxophone as given for a particular reason, to indicate, say, anger or fear. And I can hear the way the pianist struggles against the theme or against herself as she played previously within the same song. All of this can occur by means of an important 'lesson' to the listener, according to a unitary and effective purpose within the music itself. In short, within an experience of listening to jazz I can hear conflict occurring within a basic structure of pairing, of togetherness. I can hear conflict and resolution as the very mechanism by which the piece sounds itself.

For Husserl, though, the unity of conflict, of strife, is possible only within the givenness of pairing, of togetherness. We struggle, we fight, because we are given together, because our anonymity matches, because our personhoods matter to one another. Our essential structures cannot help but be like the ancient Greek myth of Philemon and Baucis. We grow together even as we remain apart. Like the myth, what we can move on to see from Husserl's description of overlaying and awakening is how this very structure supports a kind of attentiveness, of hospitality, such that the tendency to grow together is developed well, not as a kind of intended fusion but as a negotiated play of differences within an overarching attention to the things themselves.

II. Merleau-Ponty and *Recouvrement*

If Husserl's use of the term *Deckung* and its cognates shifts at all across his works, it shifts towards the recognition of the overlaying-at-a-distance that is operative within the phenomenon of pairing. 'Coincidence' as a translation of the verb *decken* thoroughly misses the way that the unity of identification occurs at a gap, at a distance, through conflict, and so on. Indeed, the German verb *decken* has connotations of a sexual encounter, of the overlaying of bodies that never quite fuse in their intertwining. What I will now go on to show is how later thinkers, Merleau-Ponty and Levinas in particular, take up this notion of overlaying-at-a-distance and oppose it to the notion of coincidence, thereby attempting to take Husserl's thought in the direction of an authentic description of ethics, of alterity, and of exteriority.

Maurice Merleau-Ponty, at least to my reading of him, consistently claims an important kinship with Husserl. For some commentators, however, this claim appears largely false.[4] Nevertheless, in this section I argue that Merleau-Ponty indeed is quite Husserlian, especially when he speaks against coincidence (*coincidence*) in favour of flesh (*chair*), distance (*ecart*) and overlaying (*recouvrement*) in portions of *The Visible and the Invisible*.

In this claim, I follow Dan Zahavi, who makes the point that Merleau-Ponty followed up the issues surrounding Husserl's identification of notions like overlaying and awakening in Merleau-Ponty's own further developments of the phenomenology of intersubjectivity:

[W]hat is crucial is [Merleau-Ponty's] emphasis on the importance that the rupture in *self-coincidence* [*Selbstkoinzidenz*] has for the possibility of intersubjectivity: I can only encounter the other if I am beyond myself from the very beginning; thus I can only experience the other if I am already a possible other in relation to myself, and could always appear to myself as an other. Although one can already find inceptions along these lines in Husserl, Merleau-Ponty pursued these key ideas with unsurpassable emphasis. (Zahavi 2000, 159)[5]

A first piece of evidence to support Zahavi's position and my own is the following: while not including a specific mention of the German word *Deckung* in the texts cited below, Merleau-Ponty does consistently use in them the term *recouvrement* to indicate an overlaying. And *recouvrement* is the term that Emmanuel Levinas used to render *Deckung* into French in his translation of the *Cartesian Meditations*, which Merleau-Ponty would have read.

Further evidence is available within Merleau-Ponty's descriptions that follow. First, however, by way of contrast, I would like to point out the decisiveness with which Merleau-Ponty rejects coincidence as a description of philosophy or of accurate description of the relationship one bears with the world or oneself. The following comes from his essay 'Interrogation and Dialectic' within *The Visible and the Invisible*:

> Philosophy is not a rupture with the world, nor a coinciding [*coincidence*] with it, but it is not the alternation of rupture and coincidence either ... Philosophy does not decompose our relationship with the world into real elements, or even into ideal references which would make of it an ideal object, but it discerns articulations in the world, it awakens in it [*elle y reveille*] regular relations of prepossession, of recapitulation, of overlapping [*d'enjambement*], which are as dormant in our ontological landscape, subsist there only in the form of traces, and nevertheless continue to function there, continue to institute the new there. (Merleau-Ponty 1968, 99–101)

If we return to our first chapter, and the discussion of reflection there, the choice to reflect as a way of awakening to one's involvement comes again to mind. Overlapping relations, as in those of the noematic, affective pressure of *Überschiebung*, as in more than a simple coincidence of self-same states, is what phenomenology pursues. And as it pursues these 'regular relations,' it acknowledges the distance of these 'traces' from the life that reflection lives. Meanings are articulations that function on their own, that welcome new layers of interpretation, that indeed compel those reinterpretations based on the distance they bear from even the sharpest eidetic reflection.

When Merleau-Ponty turns from describing phenomenological description and reflection to describing intentionality, or the subject's relations to objects, he echoes the distrust of coincidence. And in the following passage, he states the preferred manner of describing one's relation to objects as 'overlaying' [*recouvrement*]. This rather long but extremely crucial passage stands in his essay 'Interrogation and Intuition,' also in *The Visible and the Invisible,* where he notices that having a thing in view and having one's consciousness of that thing in view are not simultaneous possibilities:

> We never have at the same time the thing and the consciousness of the thing, we never have at the same time the past and the consciousness of the past, and for the same reason: in an intuition by coincidence [*coincidence*] and fusion [*fusion*], everything one gives to Being is taken from experience, everything one gives to experience is taken from Being. The truth of the matter is that the experience of a coincidence can be, as Bergson often says, only a 'partial coincidence [*coincidence partielle*].' But what is a coincidence that is only partial? It is a coincidence always past or always future, an experience that remembers an impossible past, anticipates an impossible future ... and therefore is not a coincidence, a real fusion, as of two positive terms or two elements of an alloyage [*alliage*], but an **overlaying** [*recouvrement*], as of a hollow [*creux*] and a relief which remain distinct. (Merleau-Ponty 1968, 122–3; my emphasis)

Let us now take some time to draw out what is implicit in this text.

To intend a thing, to experience it, is to conceal either the thing or one's own reflection on having the thing in view. At least concealment seems to be necessary, since the thing and one's consciousness of it are not given, simply, together. If they are given together, then there is no difference, as Merleau-Ponty says, between 'being' and 'experience,' no distance by which we can constitute or make sense of what is given, as Christopher Macann has argued in his previous study of *Deckung* in Husserl.

However, Merleau-Ponty says, the fact that I and the thing do not fully coincide with eacn other, the fact that we are not simply given as paired together in the same moment, should not cause us to do away with the descriptive concept of layers. If full coincidence would make Being mute and experience deaf, the intimacy with which the thing is given to consciousness, and vice versa, can still support a description of that unity as a 'partial coincidence.'

The thing and one's body, for example, are layers of a single unity, and they need to be if transcendental phenomenology is to work at all, is to show meaning and being to be coordinated. As Merleau-Ponty argues in "The Body as Expression and Speech" in *The Phenomenology of Perception*, the object gestured to by the other person 'is genuinely present and fully comprehended when the powers of my body adjust themselves to it and overlap it [*le recouvrent*]' (Merleau-Ponty 1994, 215E/216F). But the thing and the subject, the thing and the lived body, overlay each other, or coincide *partially*, in the way that 'an impossible future' coincides with one's own. The thing and I partially coincide or overlay each other, then, in the way that I relate to the alien other person, whose future breaks into my own present as both mine and not-mine, as never-mine.

I and the world are given together, Merleau-Ponty argues, as a hollow and a relief, always at a distance from each other, even in their erotic striving towards each other. The thin sheaf of distance between us, between hollow and relief, does not undo the shape of our being made for each other. The intimacy proceeds by means of the friction, of the distance, of the overlaying that is never total. The membranes move and strive, and in their moving provide moments of being lost and moments of being concealed – along with moments of coming back to oneself and coming back to the thing.

One must, then, move back and forth from thing to consciousness of it. And one must move this way, in a zigzag, as Husserl puts it, *because* one is united with it as having more to offer, as not simply being oneself. Experience *must* work according to this limitation. The limitation is the very possibility of the thing mattering. And the concealment of reflection in favour of answering to the thing directly (or vice versa) is what enables reflection to draw out meaning and therefore to keep the relation to the thing from collapsing into a simple index of self.

Immediately after the former description cited above from 'Interrogation and Intuition' in *The Visible and the Invisible*, Merleau-Ponty moves to consider more explicitly the body's self-relation as making possible the overlaying-at-a-distance of consciousness to things:

> When I find again the actual world such as it is, under my hands, under my eyes, up against my body, I find much more than an object: a Being of which my vision is a part, a visibility older than my operations or my acts. But this does not mean that there was a fusion or coinciding of me with it:

on the contrary this occurs because a sort of dehiscence [*dehiscence*] opens my body in two, and because between my body touched and my body touching, there is an overlapping [*recouvrement*] or encroachment [*empiete-ment*], so that we must say that the things pass into us as well as we into the things. (Merleau-Ponty 1968, 123)

Chapter 3 of this book made the same point in terms of Husserl's own terminology. Here Merleau-Ponty echoes that. The painting whose apples appear to move one another, and me; the soloist who passes into the background and by doing so affects the group and her listeners – these are possibilities because of the human body, which essentially is a distance or self-opening or 'dehiscence' upon itself. The body 'over-laps' and 'encroaches' upon itself. And by doing so, the body allows itself to unite with the things, with the world, in the same manner as its self-relation. The world forms a hollow or a relief for my body in the same way that a hand makes way for another hand, as in a clasp, or a shake, or a caress, or a slap.

The fusion of the body with itself only happens by means of its inser-tion of distance and encroachment. The belonging together of the world and of consciousness happens by means of that same insertion: 'It is therefore necessary that the deflection (*ecart*), without which the experi-ence of the thing or of the past would fall to zero, be also an openness upon the thing itself, to the past itself, that it enter into their definition' (124). Distance or deflection is the opening of the body to itself, of the body onto the thing. Distance defines us both.[6]

In addition to discussing the relation of the thing to consciousness, and the body to itself, in terms of overlaying (*recouvrement*), Merleau-Ponty also speaks of intercorporeality, the relation of lived body to lived body, of flesh to flesh (*chair*), as overlaying as well. He does this most prominently in 'The Intertwining, The Chiasm' in *The Visible and the Invisible*. There he describes how, just as one's own two hands can be experienced together within a touching–touched relation that is re-versible, as Husserl admits, so too he lived body of the other and of myself can also be experienced together within their touching–touched reversibility – in a handshake, in a landscape that passes from one into the other, in an action or passion:

The handshake too is reversible; I can feel myself touched as well and at the same time as touching ... Why would not the synergy exist among different organisms, if it is possible within each? Their landscapes inter-weave, their actions and their passions fit together [*s'ajustent*] exactly: this is possible ... as soon as we rather understand it as the return of the visible upon itself, a carnal adherence of the sentient to the sensed and of sensed to the sentient. For as *overlapping* [*recouvrement*] and fission, identity and difference, it brings to birth a ray of natural light that illuminates all flesh (*chair*) and not only my own. (Merleau-Ponty 1968, 142)

The way of all flesh is, as it were, to enact an 'overlapping' and that at a distance. The way of all flesh is internally and externally 'adjusting' to self and to one another. The structure 'within each' makes possible the interweaving and overlaying of both, and vice versa, since the visible coils upon itself.[7] It is noteworthy, to say the least, that this notion of 'overlapping' here is the unity of 'identity and difference' and that, as such a unity, it illuminates more than it can substantiate by itself.[8]

There is much more to say about how Merleau-Ponty carries out Husserl's description of overlaying at a distance. In *The Visible and the Invisible*, which includes some of his working notes, Merleau-Ponty explicitly mentions a number of terms of Husserl's in German – performance (*Leistung*) and transfer (*Übertragung*) are important ones from the *Cartesian Meditations*, a work which Merleau-Ponty also cites explicitly at the end of 'Interrogation and Intuition,' immediately after he has discussed the necessity of surpassing 'coincidence' with 'overlaying.'

However, Merleau-Ponty may, according to Claude Lefort, shift in his description of the flesh, and he in doing so he may move away from overlaying (*recouvrement*) towards 'depossession': 'Thus what was first announced in terms of *overlapping*, homogeneity, and reversibility seems later to have to be qualified in terms of s*egregation*, fission, and alterity. Finally, the original incorporation of the sensible and the incorporation into the sensible comes to be connected with an original "depossession."'[9]

Even to himself, then, perhaps Merleau-Ponty's working through of Husserl's description of overlaying was insufficient to account for the phenomena of human experience. Nevertheless, even if this is true, it seems that Merleau-Ponty proceeds by taking Husserl seriously and by moving carefully from the description of pairing to a description of ethics.

III. Levinas, Coincidence, and Ethics

Like Derrida, who explored what he perceived as Husserl's reliance on coincidence in *Speech and Phenomena*, and like Merleau-Ponty, Emmanuel Levinas also takes up Husserl and the notion of coincidence in one of his major works, *Totality and Infinity*. In turning now to look at this book, we will see how Levinas, too, takes seriously the notion of overlaying and distance together, and how, for him, Husserl allowed for Continental Philosophy to pursue ethics in a new way.

In the very first sentence of the preface to *Totality and Infinity*, Levinas states his intention to clarify a kind of phenomenological ethics. Such an ethics maintains a link to Husserl, but it may also move beyond him. The crux of the position that Levinas maintains is that 'the essential of ethics is in its transcendent intention and ... not every transcendent intention has the noesis-noema structure. Already of itself ethics is an "optics."'[10] The route to the Other, and to responsibility to that Other, is not within the realm of consciousness. Instead, ethics is a way of seeing, not simply a way of knowing or constituting.

This move of Levinas, to construe the relationship to the Other as non-intentional – that does seem different from Husserl's description of pairing. And Levinas in fact criticizes Husserl's account in the Fifth Cartesian Meditation as a description that 'dissimulates, in each of its stages which are taken as a description of constitution, mutations of object constitution into a relation with the Other.'[11] (67). Nevertheless, his disagreement with Husserl is not total. For Levinas, Husserl is the route to the Other. And he explicitly maintains in his preface, immediately after stating ethics as an optics, that 'Husserlian phenomenology has made possible this passage from ethics to metaphysical exteriority.' But given his disagreement with Husserl, how could that statement be true in a meaningful way?

A full answer to that question, an exhaustive account of the way that Husserl assists Levinas in Levinas's turn to the absolute Other, would present another chapter or another book. However, I would like to attempt a brief answer here, hoping that by doing so I can enable this book to achieve its end, which is to encourage the rereading of Husserl as anticipating (and furthering a review of) Continental Philosophy's later occupation with alterity, absence, and difference.

Briefly, then, I would argue, at least from the point of view of *Totality and Infinity*, that Levinas takes seriously the notion of coincidence and also demonstrates how coincidence becomes something like overlaying-at-a-distance. For Levinas, the Other comes from on high, as a revelation. She coincides with what she says. In doing so, she throws into relief the very notion of coincidence. I recognize my own coincidence in her shadow, and, I recognize mine as disrupted, as ruptured.

In her coincidence, she opens me to ethics as a non-totalizing, non-*a priori* practice of intersubjective teaching and learning.

Let me say this slightly differently: I am the Same; I am self-coincident. When the Other is revealed, he is not revealed as a noematic object, and he is not a doubling of my ownness or my lived body. Rather, his self-coincidence interrupts mine in order to coincide *with* me while remaining absolutely distant and disturbingly absent. Levinas states this most clearly for our purposes in his discussion of fecundity, in his section of *Totality and Infinity*'The Subjectivity in Eros':

> Voluptuosity, as the coinciding [*coincidence*] of the lover and the beloved, is charged by their duality: it is simultaneously fusion and distinction ... Voluptuosity transfigures the subject himself, who henceforth owes his identity not to his initiative of power, but to the passivity of the love received. (Levinas 1998, 270)

Whether or not Husserl used *Deckung* as a way to channel the connotations of erotic life, it certainly seems that Levinas does here in his use of '*coincidence.*' The coincidence, as the overlaying of bodies, preserves their distinction, their difference. And in doing so, this coinciding undoes the relationship of each subject with itself, it decentres, as Husserl might have described *Fremderfahrung*. The erotic experience undoes the structure of 'initiative' and allows for something to issue forth that redefines, by its passivity, the intersubjectivity that is begun in voluptuosity.

In Eros, Levinas goes on to argue, self-coincidence becomes broken open to a third, to the establishment of what Levinas calls the child, and to paternity. In the progress to fecundity and paternity, two moves are involved. First, the undoing of self-coincidence: 'The coinciding of freedom with responsibility constitutes the I, doubled with itself, encumbered with itself. Eros delivers from this encumberment, arrests the return of the I to itself' (271). This move, the undoing or arresting of the way I overlay myself without a distance, inserts a distinction not just of myself to myself but also of freedom to responsibility. I may be responsible for things I am not yet free for (a child, a lover). I may be free for things I am not yet responsible for (a future self not defined by its initiative and power). The deliverance from encumberment, in other words, is the insertion of a future and a past that are, as Merleau-Ponty said, impossible.

In the second move, after interrupting the self-coincidence of the I, the I participates within a project that it does not initiate – that of fecundity and of paternity. Sexuality, erotic relationship engenders something, creates something: 'Fecundity is part of the very drama of the I. The intersubjective reached across the notion of fecundity opens up a plane where the I is divested of its tragic egoity, which turns back to itself, and yet is not purely and simply dissolved into the collective' (273). To be bound up with the other in the linking of eros is to be an I without being an ego, without being a constituting, reflective function. To be erotic is to be outside of, or prior to, the distinction between one and many, to be prior to the distinction between involvement and reflection.

I would claim that these two moves, the interruption of self-coincidence and the involvement of self in an intersubjectivity that is still a coincidence that preserves difference and distance – these two moves are ones Husserl recognizes within the process of *Fremderfahrung*. At least, they are surely moves that Husserl *could* recognize if he recognizes the Other as occurring not by my own will but by means of a pre-givenness that involves both of us within a non-totality.

As Levinas concludes *Totality and Infinity,* he claims that the relationship of eros as fecundity 'breaks up reality into relations irreducible to the relations of genus and species, part and whole, action and passion, truth and error; that in sexuality the subject enters into relation with what is absolutely other, with an alterity of a type unforeseeable in formal logic' (276). If my argument in chapter 4 is sound, and if the logic of the relationship with the Other is in fact the guarantee of all logic – if, as I have argued, the relationship with the other person is the most sophisticated logical relation – then this may also be a point of contact between Levinas and Husserl. It is the involvement of one's whole being, one's whole body, one's whole self-overlaying in a coincidence that is not coincident that guarantees and propels the relationships of part–whole and of *noesis–noema*. It is the future of the Other, together with oneself, that engenders the possibility of meaning at all.

I will end this section with a final citation from Levinas. It should bring back before us the ongoing discussion of a jazz group and listening to a performance. It should also help situate our discussion in terms of Husserl's assertion that the community of intersubjectivity is an *open* one, even if one guided by a kind of *telos* of meaningful, reflective, shared knowing.

For Levinas, the coinciding in voluptuosity and the issuing of both into a lived relationship with a third does not present a form to be known, dominated, or eidetically reduced:

> The I's form no totality; there exists no privileged plane where these I's could be grasped in their principle. There is an anarchy essential to multiplicity. In the absence of a plane common to the totality (which one persists in seeking, so as to relate the multiplicity to it) one will never know which will, in the free play of wills, pulls the strings of the game; one will not know who is playing with whom. But a principle breaks through all this trembling and vertigo when the face presents itself, and demands justice. (294)

Husserl, Merleau-Ponty, and Levinas are no totality, certainly. There are real differences and real thematic emphases that operate in different directions. Perhaps the differences, in this last chapter at least, have been concealed too quickly in favour of their coincidences, in favour of their shared project. But perhaps 'a principle' has broken through, from the Fifth Cartesian Meditation onwards, of overlaying at a distance, of the way in which distance and absence matter, as standing at the heart of presence. Perhaps the face of Husserl reappears as the teacher who can engender in those who read him something that is not simply his own initiative, that is a theme on which we might improvise.

As Bob Sandemeyer put it well in his excellent, recent book on Husserl's corpus, Husserl 'understands a system of philosophy to be an ethos and a community of striving toward clarification of endless, open-ended problems. This ethos and this striving have a history and a teleology, and he [Husserl] sees himself a participant in this intra-historical striving.'[12] Within the texts of Levinas and Merleau-Ponty, as within the hearing of the call and response of a jazz performance, it is difficult to sift through who is playing and to whom. The view that could narrate once and for all the exact contributions of each author, the exact and self-sufficient reading of each text, would be quite a view, and we feel 'trembling and vertigo.' Are we engaged in something that can never be summed up? Is there no sense of a way through the problems related to alterity? Are we doomed to striving and never to reaching?

Yet, as Levinas has said, a face breaks through and demands justice, a question erupts and Husserl returns again with his insistence on the pairing of concealing, discovering, and overlaying. To read Husserl is to read the ethics of caring about meaning. And to do justice to him is to have to reread his work, and those who read him, on behalf of all those who do or might come to read him well.

It is certainly hard to say who is playing and to whom. But there is a reason why almost every major Continental philosopher in the twentieth Century cut his or her teeth on Husserl. His face comes as if from on high, as if a revelation. And at the same time, he submits himself to the intra-historical, ethical process of answering 'to the things themselves.'

Notes

Introduction

1 This experience occurred several months after I reread Merleau-Ponty's essays on Cezanne, and the description obviously owes much to 'Cezanne's Doubt' and 'Eye and Mind.' One crucial passage from 'Cezanne's Doubt': 'The lived object is not rediscovered or constructed on the basis of the contributions of the senses; rather it presents itself to us from the start as the center from which these contributions radiate.' Maurice Merleau-Ponty, *Sense and Non-Sense* (Evanston: Northeastern University Press, 1964), 15.

2 Donn Welton, *The Other Husserl: The Horizons of Transcendental Phenomenology* (Bloomington and Indianapolis: Indiana University Press, 2000), 9.

3 Edmund Husserl, *Ideas Pertaining to a Pure Phenomenology and to a Phenomenological Philosophy. First Book. General Introduction to a Pure Phenomenology*, trans. Fred Kersten (The Hague: Martinus Nijhoff, 1982), 297.

4 Martin Heidegger, *Sein und Zeit* (Tübingen: Max Niemeyer, 1972). English translation: *Being and Time*, trans. Joan Stambaugh (Albany: SUNY Press, 1996). See section 7: 'There are various ways phenomena can be covered up [*Die Art der mooglichen Verdecktheit*]. In the first place, a phenomenon can be covered up [*verdeckt*] in the sense that it is still completely undiscovered [*unentdeckt*] ... In the second place, a phenomenon can be buried over. This means it was once discovered [*entdeckt*] but then got covered up again [*der Verdeckung*]. This covering up can be total, but more commonly, what was once discovered [*das zuvor Entdeckte*] may still be visible, though only as semblance' (32).

5 Cairns lists both 'coincidence' and 'overlapping' as synonyms for *Deckung*, though 'coincidence' is definitely the primary one. He also sees no real distinction between the meaning of *Überschiebung* and that of *Deckung*. He

reserves 'overlaying' as a translation of *Überdeckung*. Dorion Cairns, *Guide for Translating Husserl* (The Hague: Martinus Nijhoff Publishers, 1973).

6 Under *Husserliana VI: Husserl, The Crisis of the European Sciences and Transcendental Phenomenology: An Introduction to Phenomenological Philosophy*, trans. David Carr (Evanston: Northwestern University Press, 1970), 52–3.

7 Derrida writes that he would have liked to have integrated Husserl's notion of 'covering (*Verdeckung*) and fusion (*Verschmelzung*) as "originary phenomena" (*Urphänomen*) in the genesis of a "being in itself" in the sphere of immanence.' Jacques Derrida, *The Problem of Genesis in Husserl's Philosophy* (Chicago: University of Chicago Press, 2003), 149.

8 See also *Analyses Concerning Passive and Active Synthesis* (hereafter *APAS*), 192ff. There, in section 28, Husserl speaks of the different syntheses of overlaying and their connection to concealment and discovery: 'In comparing matters with similar characteristics [*Ähnlichen*] we find two things that stand out, (i) the synthetic coinciding in a commonality [*synthetische Deckung in einem Gemeinsamen*], that is in sameness, and yet (ii) the synthetic conflict [*synthetischen Widerstreit*] of particular matters of this commonality that repress one another reciprocally in the process of overlapping [*Überdeckung*]. Repressing means that one conceals [*verdeckt*] the other, that the concealed element [*Verdeckte*] tends toward unconcealment [*Aufdeckung*], then breaking through conceals [*verdeckt*] the previously unconcealed element [*Aufgedeckte*], etc.' (*APAS*, 192).

9 Dan Zahavi, *Self-Awareness and Alterity: A Phenomenological Investigation* (Evanston: Northwestern University Press, 1999), 201.

Chapter 1

1 Two very important works on the phenomenology of reflection, both of which refer directly to Husserl, are Merleau-Ponty's preface to his own *Phenomenology of Perception* and his 'Reflection and Interrogation' in *The Visible and the Invisible*. Important to my own account of reflection within phenomenology – namely, as a kind of reflection that is not opposed to involvement but that occurs *with* it – is the following: 'Reflection does not withdraw from the world towards the unity of consciousness as the world's basis; it steps back to watch the forms of transcendence fly up like sparks from a fire; it slackens the intentional threads which attach us to the world and thus brings them to our notice; it alone is consciousness of the world because it reveals the world as strange and paradoxical.' Merleau-Ponty, *Phenomenology of Perception*, trans. Colin Smith (London: Routledge, 1994), xv. See also Merleau-Ponty, *The Visible and the Invisible* (Evanston: Northwestern University Press, 1968).

2 Maurice Natanson in *Edmund Husserl: Philosopher of Infinite Tasks* (Evanston: Northeastern University Press, 1973) argues that the natural attitude is itself responsible for the crises that occur. He says that the natural attitude is 'the ongoing nature of mundane experience' in which 'the context of any event is open and undecided in any strict way' (25). This description occurs in a passage in which he is describing how it is possible in the natural attitude to make mistakes about someone's wincing, whether it occurs because of pain or pleasure or a facial tic. This indeterminacy of the natural attitude's insights is what allows it to continue to hypnotize consciousness into believing that the world determines the meaning of a situation.

3 Simone de Beauvoir in *The Ethics of Ambiguity* (New York: Citadel Press, 2000) details the position of the 'serious person,' who loses himself or herself in an object or project in order to avoid taking an authentic stance towards human freedom. Something like this is what I am arguing here – that the natural attitude fosters a kind of lostness in the world and its objects that leads ultimately to a crisis for which there is no answer: 'There then blazes forth the absurdity of a life which has sought outside itself the justifications which it alone could give itself' (de Beauvoir, 52). Moving into transcendental subjectivity is one way of moving towards an authentic recognition of freedom by means of exploring the relationship between subject and world, between the subject and the others with whom we are always already intertwined as *the* transcendental ego. For Husserl's similar view, see his 'Philosophy as Mankind's Self-Reflection,' in *The Crisis of the European Sciences and Transcendental Phenomenology: An Introduction to Phenomenological Philosophy,* trans. David Carr (Evanston: Northwestern University Press, 1970).

4 Husserl actually refers to levels of transcendental reflection in *The Crisis* (*Husserliana VI*) as he moves from considering intentionality to considering intersubjectivity: 'we held fast to the correlation belonging to the first level of reflection [*der ersten Reflexionsstufe*].' The highest level, for him, is the layer of reflection on the transcendental ego as transcendental intersubjectivity.

5 For a Husserlian account of reflection and for the novel description on its own terms, see Dan Zahavi's *Self-Awareness and Alterity: A Phenomenological Investigation* (Evanston: Northwestern University Press, 1999). In that work, Zahavi argues convincingly for 'different forms of reflection' as all involving a process of 'self-othering' that brought them into contact with intersubjectivity. For Zahavi, the way in which I overlay myself in reflection as such cannot be a matter of 'coincidence': 'it if had in fact been characterized by a radical self-coincidence, and distinguished by the solid-

ity of its simple, tight, and closed self-presence, it would have been very difficult to comprehend how we could ever have attained the necessary self-detachment and self-distance that permits us to reflect, and eventually even to adopt, a mundane perspective on ourselves' (200).

6 See Stapleton: 'From the standpoint of the natural attitude, it is the world in its bestowing of worldliness upon entities which prevents the collapse of the "in itself" into the "for us."' Timothy Stapleton, 'The "Logic" of Husserl's Transcendental Reduction,' *Man and World* 15 (1982): 369–82 at 378.

7 Under *Husserliana VI*, see *The Crisis of the European Sciences and Transcendental Phenomenology: An Introduction to Phenomenological Philosophy*, trans. David Carr (Evanston: Northwestern University Press, 1970). See in particular Part II, where he discusses the essential scientist, Galileo, who 'did not reflect closely on all this: how the free imaginative variation of this world and its shapes results only in possible empirically intuitable shapes and *not* in exact shapes; on what sort of motivation and what new achievement was required for genuinely geometric idealization' (49). Compare this with Husserl's 'Origin of Geometry' essay, too, in Appendix VI to the *Crisis of the European Sciences*.

8 In *Formal and Transcendental Logic (Husserliana XVII)*, Husserl claims that the sciences are not sufficient to account for a full description of human experience, of intentionality, 'until they lay aside the blinders imposed by their method … until they relate their combined researches to the universality of being and its fundamental essential unity' (Husserl 1969, 4). The move to phenomenology is thus not a move outside of being but *within* being, within being as a *whole*, as the whole of consciousness with its objects, with its world, with its others.

9 O'Murchadha posits the motivation for the reduction to be a similar world or cultural conflict: 'What motivates the reduction is the insight that the self-evident meaning of something in our world has quite another meaning, or none at all, in another world. The philosophical turn is then to ask what can be the basis of meaning that is not simply relative to our world or their world.' Felix O'Murchadha, 'Reduction, Externalism, and Immanence in Husserl and Heidegger,' *Synthese* 160, no. 3 (2008): 375–95 at 379–80.

10 I am thus clearly suggesting here that there can be a motivation within the natural attitude for taking up phenomenology. I am sadly aware, however, that even crises do not *force* people to perform the phenomenological reduction. Like Fink, I would argue that phenomenology is something that must have already been reaching out within my own transcendental life in order to pursue it. Nevertheless, I do not agree with Fink that 'compel-

ling motivation for the phenomenological reduction is not there in the natural attitude – and for reasons of principle' Given that phenomenology enworlds itself *back* into the human world, as a project others can witness, I would argue that there must be sufficient motivation to turn towards oneself 'down to the innermost ground' within the world. See Eugen Fink, *Sixth Cartesian Meditation: The Idea of a Transcendental Theory of Method*, trans. Ronald Bruzina (Bloomington: Indiana University Press, 1995), 32.

11 Adorno believes that Husserl is thoroughly idealistic, in the simple sense. In fact, Adorno argues, 'in phenomenology, the bourgeois spirit strives mightily to break out of the prison of the immanence of consciousness ... Much can be learned from both the attempt and the failure.' Theodor W. Adorno, *Against Epistemology: A Metacritique: Studies in Husserl and the Phenomenological Antinomies*, trans. Willis Domingo (Oxford: Basil Blackwell, 1982), 189–90.

12 See Poul Lübcke's claim to reframe the debate about Husserl's epoche and phenomenology. He claims it is not obvious whether Husserl's work (which he separates into the young Husserl and the old) can actually be said to lead to realism, idealism, or some point beyond these. At stake is whether Husserl's method requires a kind of verificationism or not. Poul Lübcke, 'A Semantic Interpretation of Husserl's *Epoche*,' *Synthese* 118 (1999): 1–12.

13 Dan Zahavi follows Gadamer in articulating this thesis that Husserlian phenomenology is neither realist nor idealist. For Zahavi, it is clear in Husserl's texts that 'Being and consciousness are essentially interdependent, and ultimately one in the absolute concretion: the transcendental subjectivity' (Zahavi 1994, 44). Fink argues that the transcendental reduction compels us to reduce the Idea of being in order to form 'a new transcendental concept of being.' Fink, *Sixth*, 75.

14 Merleau-Ponty argues this in the following way: 'To reflect is *not to coincide* with the flux from its source unto its last ramifications; it is to *disengage* from the things ... by submitting them to a systematic variation ... In recognizing that every reflection is eidetic and, as such, leaves untouched the problem of our unreflected being and that of the world, Husserl simply *agrees to take up the problem* which the reflective attitude ordinarily avoids – the discordance between its initial situation and its ends' (1968, 45–6; my emphasis).

15 Fink argues that 'the unfruitfulness of the dispute between idealism and realism ultimately consists in this, that both are held fast in a common *naivete* that neither one has ever itself made thematic, namely, they remain

held fast in the horizon of the world.' Fink, *Sixth*, 158. Husserl's transcendental idealism, Fink goes on to say, 'can have no counterconcept' because it shows the intertwining of the world and consciousness in a new way, the way of constitution (159). See also Merleau-Ponty's 'Other Selves and the Human World,' n8, in his *Phenomenology of Perception*.

16 See Hopkins, in which he defends Husserl from the charge that Husserl's notion of reflection involves him in four paradoxes. One of the chief paradoxes that Hopkins defends Husserl from is the paradox of difference: 'I think that even the most ardent follower of Derrida *would not want to maintain* that the two words "transcendental Ego" are for Husserl signs that function to take the place of, to represent, or otherwise point to something which, while "presently" absent, nevertheless is conceived of in terms of a fulfilled presence or *coincidence* with itself.' Burt C. Hopkins, 'Husserl's Account of Phenomenological Reflection and Four Paradoxes of Reflexivity,' *Research in Phenomenology* 19 (1989): 180–94 at 192; my emphasis.

17 Zahavi also claims that 'the phenomenological reduction does not require neutrality on existential questions.' Dan Zahavi, 'Beyond Realism and Idealism: Husserl's Late Concept of Constitution,' *Danish Yearbook of Philosophy* 29 (1994): 44–62 at 50. This is true especially in light of the Fifth Cartesian Meditation, where it is clear that the other person's existence does not fall under the reduction.

18 Husserl in the Second Cartesian Meditation already articulates this as the very possibility of phenomenology as a science of consciousness: 'Accordingly, not only in respect of particulars but also *universally* [*Universalität*], the phenomenologically meditating Ego can become the "non-participant onlooker" at himself' (*CM*, 37). I am arguing that the origin of this 'universal' viewpoint lies in *Fremderfahrung* and that the layer of the onlooker remains bound to the layer of the involved participant.

19 Fink notices an awakening that occurs with the enactment of the reduction: 'This signifies a primal event in the life of transcendental subjectivity, it comes to itself, it "awakens [*erwacht*]" – to speak in a metaphor [*Gleichnis*] – out of the age-old sleep of being-outside-itself' (Fink, *Sixth*, 113).

20 In section 24 of *Ideas I*, titled 'The Principle of All Principles,' Husserl claims that the transcendental reduction requires a description of experience that obeys the following principle: 'every originary presentive intuition is a legitimizing source of cognition, that everything originarily … offered us in "intuition" is to be accepted simply as what it is presented as being, but also within the limits in which it is presented there' (Husserl 2001, 44). In other words, phenomenology describes the *manner* in which each noema is offered, the manner of its givenness.

21 Fink argues that 'by performing the reduction we achieve transcendental un-captivation and openness to everything that, in an ultimate sense, "is."' Fink, *Sixth*, 42.

22 'Synthesis' is one of the most important concepts in Husserlian phenomenology. He defines it in the Second Cartesian Meditation as 'the sort of combination uniting consciousness with consciousness … a mode of combination exclusively peculiar to consciousness.' *CM*, 39. In his example of the die flowing away in manners of appearance as it (possibly or actually) rolls on a gambling table, for example, Husserl says that the given manners of appearing that I am conscious of do not occur as fragments that are accumulating the one after the other. It is not induction, in other words, that lets me grasp the die as a die through time or as it rolls. On the contrary, the different moments of appearance of the moving die 'flow away in the unity of a synthesis, such that in them "one and the same" is intended as appearing. The one identical die appears, now in near appearances, now in far appearances' (39). The synthesis of the object depends on that of the subject: 'the whole of conscious life is unified synthetically' (42). And in order to identify any object at all – the die, for example – I have to be self-unifying.

   Kockelmans characterizes the importance of synthesis for Husserl's transcendental phenomenology as follows: 'It becomes obvious that in the transcendental sphere, the different objects are not found in the thoughts as are matches in a box but rather are constituted in different types of syntheses. One of the major tasks of phenomenology consists precisely in analyzing and describing these different forms of syntheses from a noematic as well as a noetic point of view.' Joseph J. Kockelmans, *Edmund Husserl's Phenomenological Psychology: A Historico-Critical Study* (Atlantic Highlands: Humanities Press, 1978), 19.

23 In *The Crisis*, Husserl defends the transcendental ego from the claim that it is unknowable before the reduction: 'In truth of course I am a transcendental ego but I am not conscious of this; being in a particular attitude, the natural attitude, I am completely given over to the object-poles, completely bound by interests and tasks which are exclusively directed toward them.' *Crisis*, 205.

24 Luft shows convincingly how Husserl moved from the language of the transcendental ego to that of the 'transcendental person' in later descriptions. In so doing, Luft argues, Husserl intended to describe the transcendental subjectivity as 'not an abstract or "theoretical" moment of the human person, but the person viewed in its fullest concretion.' Sebastian Luft, 'Husserl's Concept of the Transcendental Person: Another Look at the

Husserl–Heidegger Relationship,' *International Journal of Philosophical Studies* 13, no. 2 (2005): 141–77 at 155).

25 See Drummond: 'The temporal structure of the perceptual act, then, grounds the distinction between the genuinely and non-genuinely appearing sides or aspects of the object, and the temporal duration of the act is filled also by bodily activities motivating the emptying of filled intentions and the filling of empty ones.' John Drummond, 'The Structure of Intentionality,' in *The New Husserl: A Critical Reader*, ed. Donn Welton (Bloomington: Indiana University Press, 2003), 65–92 at 77. Drummond also argues for association as bridging the gap between formality and materiality of what is at stake in the intentional act's grasp of its objects.

26 Husserl focuses on the character of the object of experience as given or self-given [*selbstgeben*]. See the Third Cartesian Meditation, in which Husserl says that evidence is 'the quite preeminent mode consciousness that consists in the self-appearance [*Selbstercheinung*],the self-exhibiting [*Sich-selbst-Darstellens*], the self-giving [*Sich-selbst-Gebens*], of an affair, an affair-complex (or state of affairs), a universality, a value, or other objectivity, in the final mode: "itself there" ['*Selbst da*'], "immediately intuited," "given originaliter"' (*CM*, 57). See also Kockelmans's discussion of evidence: '[W]hat is adequately self-given can and must be taken as an absolute beginning. It is assumed further that everything that is given in consciousness in an immediate act of seeing is adequately self-given' (Kockelmans 1994, 83). The notion of self-givenness may very well be a concealing, as well as a revealing, of any further (divine) giver.

27 This process of verification of what is emptily intended in the original noetic grasp of the thing, this process of verifying the co-given profiles or meanings of the noema, is what Husserl defines as 'evidence.' In *Analyses Concerning Passive and Active Synthesis* (hereafter *APAS*), Husserl defines evidence *as* overlaying: '[W]hat is evidence other than seeing the self of what is meant, that is, the fulfilling effective realization in possessing the self; what is it other than the synthesis of coinciding [*Synthese der Identitätsdeckung*] that forms an identity, a coinciding of a merely anticipatory intending with the fulfilling self?' (*APAS*, 160).

28 Zahavi claims: 'Experiences are not objects; rather they are accesses to objects. These accesses can take different forms; one and the same object … can be given in a number of different modes of givenness, it can for instance be given as perceived, imagined, or recollected. Experiential properties are not properties like red or bitter; rather they are properties pertaining to these different types of access.' Dan Zahavi, 'Intentionality and Phenomenality: A Phenomenological Take on the Hard Problem,' In *The*

Problem of Consciousness: New Essays in Phenomenological Philosophy of Mind,
ed. Evan Thompson (Calgary: University of Calgary Press, 2003), 63–92 at
79.

29 In fact, Sokolowski argues that the correlation between the *noesis* and *noema* allows the noesis to deposit meaning into the noema, thereby ensuring
the activity of both: 'The noesis found in a given type of act will deposit
a corresponding noematic sense in its object, and constitutional analysis
consists in showing how this takes place. For example, acts of imagination deposit a sense of "imaginary" in their noematic correlation.' Robert
Sokolowski, *The Formation of Husserl's Concept of Constitution* (The Hague:
Martinus Nijhoff Publishers, 1964), 144.

30 I envision the relationship between the noema and the noesis as something
like the way Socrates describes his relation to Euthyphro, perhaps ironi-
cally: 'as it is the lover of inquiry must follow his beloved wherever it may
lead him' (Grube 2002, 14c).

31 Jean-Michel Roy works to disentangle Husserlian phenomenology from
some of the less convincing arguments against it made by analytic philosophers. He leaves open the possibility that Husserl's descriptions still have
work to do to avoid all pitfalls, but he correctly claims that 'far from seeing
the idea that an object is passively received by the subject *as opposed* to the
idea that it is constructed by this subject, Husserl contends that givenness
in the sense of passive reception is a form of constitution.' Jean-Michel
Roy, 'Phenomenological Claims and the Myth of the Given,' in *The Problem
of Consciousness: New Essays in Phenomenological Philosophy of Mind,* ed.
Evan Thompson (Calgary: University of Calgary Press, 2003), 1–32 at 25.

32 Dan Zahavi, 'Beyond Realism and Idealism: Husserl's Late Concept of
Constitution,' *Danish Yearbook of Philosophy* 29 (1994): 44–62 at 50.

33 Landgrebe describes the transcendental reduction as an act that does justice to 'the horizon co-posited in every single act [of consciousness].' Ludwig Landgrebe, *The Phenomenology of Edmund Husserl: Six Essays,* ed. Donn
Welton (Ithaca: Cornell University Press, 1981), 125. By reducing one's
consciousness to the consciousness of the object strictly as meant, Landgrebe argues, the phenomenologist clarifies what each act of consciousness
in fact intends as its sense: 'the reduction was first introduced as a general
resolution not to cooperate in any positing that oversteps the meant qua
meant but, on the contrary, to inhibit every such positing' (125).

34 For excellent if competing discussions of the problem of givenness, and
the way it implies, without being able to deliver, a way out of a simple
exchange between subjects or between subject and object, see two works
by Jacques Derrida: *Given Time I: Counterfeit Money,* vol. 1, trans. Peggy

Kamuf (Chicago: University of Chicago Press, 1994); and *The Gift of Death*, trans. David Wills (Chicago: University of Chicago Press, 1996). See also Jean-Luc Marion, *Reduction and Givenness: Investigations of Husserl, Heidegger, and Phenomenology*, trans. Thomas A. Carlson (Evanston: Northwestern University Press, 1998). Marion claims that givenness made Husserl stick to the sphere of presence, where Husserl was bedazzled: 'Husserl, indeed, completely bedazzled by unlimited givenness, seems not to realize the strangeness of such an excessiveness and simply manages its excess without questioning it. That is, unless bedazzlement doesn't betray – by *covering over* – a fear before the broadening of presence by givenness' (38; my emphasis). See Costello (2009) for a rebuttal to this argument.

35 Dan Zahavi, *Husserl's Phenomenology* (Stanford: Stanford University Press, 2003), 89.

36 See Maurice Merleau-Ponty, 'The Spatiality of One's Own Body and Motility,' in *Phenomenology of Perception*, where he argues that the lived body is the third, constitutive term between figure and ground (115). Also, Fink argues that 'not the "members" of the correlation but the *correlation* is the prior thing. It is not that subjectivity is here and the world there and between both the constitutive relationship is in play but that the genesis of constitution is the self-actualization of constituting subjectivity in world-actualization.' Fink, *Sixth*, 45.

37 Zahavi, *Husserl's Phenomenology*, 54.

38 *EJ*, 92–3.

39 Ibid., 95.

40 See Jacques Derrida, *The Problem of Genesis in Husserl's Philosophy* (Chicago: University of Chicago Press, 2003), where he addresses this issue of the origin of possibility and negation in Husserl's *EAJ*. There, Derrida argues that the development of Husserl's phenomenology from a static to a genetic phenomenology, one concerned with the becoming of meanings prior to their givenness, entails this goal: it 'proposes to retrace the absolute itinerary that leads from antepredicative evidence to predicative evidence. In that, it supposes that the broader transcendental reduction has been carried out, which no longer leaves us facing eidetic structures, even were they those of consciousness, but facing the purity of experience itself' (106). The reason I am including here the example of the mannequin/ human is that the issue for Husserl is how the possibility of the other person is what ante-predicatively grounds logical concepts. As Derrida himself notices, Husserl may have had the other person as the origin of antepredicative experience in mind for a while: 'the objectivity of knowledge, of which transcendental phenomenology is the "theory," is only possible

– and Husserl insists on this himself – through the passive synthesis of the temporal and sensible hyle and through the originarity of transcendental intersubjectivity. The common root of these three themes is again brought to light by Husserl, who defines the original hyle (*Urhyle*) as the kernel of the alter ego (*ichfremde Kern*)' (147–8).

41 Husserl acknowledges the role of pre-predicative experience explicitly in *CM:* 'Predicative includes pre-predicative experience. That which is meant or, perchance, evidently viewed receives predicative expression; and science always intends to judge expressly and keep the judgment or the truth fixed ... But the expression as such has its own comparatively good or bad way of fitting what is meant or itself given; and therefore it has its own evidence or non-evidence which also goes into the predicating. Consequently evidence of the expression is also a determining part of the idea of scientific truth, as predicative complexes that are, or can be, grounded absolutely' (11). What Husserl is emphasizing here is that a science needs to ground both what appears and the manner in which what appears is taken up as a 'predicative complex.' If the concept of possibility appears within the pre-predicative experience of doubt, then this origin must be reflected within the way one acts upon it, uses it, and talks about it. Otherwise, science separates the things that it says and does from the phenomena that give rise to it, and this is precisely what science does not want to do.

42 Adorno writes about Husserl's use of a similar example – that of being tricked by a waxwork figure, in *Against Epistemology:* 'He finds his peace in the world of things in intercourse not with women but with puppets. The embarrassment, however, is of one who does not know whether to take the internal as external or vice versa. And now he concedes himself the original wish to escape in no other way than in the distorted figure of dread' (Adorno 1982, 219). Obviously, I find this argument to miss the entire point of phenomenology, particularly regarding the relevance of the alien for logic and perception. However, Adorno in this very example does help point out how the visibility of logic preoccupied Husserl for some time in this very example.

43 For an excellent treatment of *Fremdheit* or alienness in Husserl's work, see Waldenfels, who writes that central to Husserl's definition of alienness is that it is not a property: 'Alienness is not a property of things and persons in the world, but an aspect of the world in whose horizon they meet up with us in any number of ways.' Bernhard Waldenfels, 'Experience of the Alien in Husserl's Phenomenology,' *Research in Phenomenology* (1990): 19–33 at 21. Alienness is 'how' individuals show themselves to be inaccessible, and alienness is not a property they own (23). But this manner of

appearing is something one can make sense of because one participates in it; one is also self-alienating: 'To say that the structuring of the alien occurs by means of the own is to say that alienness arises from a process of self-alienation similar to the way in which the past comes about through the process of de-presentation' (26).

44 See Waksler's description of how the establishment of co-presence and reciprocity requires an important discussion of conflict within the synthesis of identity. Frances Chaput Waksler, 'Analogues of Ourselves: Who Counts as an Other?' *Human Studies* 28, no. 4 (2005): 417–29.

45 See also *EJ*, 111 ff. In these pages, Husserl distinguishes the acts of explication and contemplation. Peculiar to explication is a certain kind of overlaying or *Deckung*. Explication is the passage, for example, from the grasp of a substrate 'S' to an aspect or quality 'a' of that S. First, Husserl says, there comes to notice the fact that there is 'a certain mental overlapping [*eine gewisse geistige Überschiebung*] of the two apprehensions [of S and its determination a]' (115). This *noematic* overlapping, however, is insufficient to account for the unity of the substrate and determination in its particular manner of unity: 'even if wholly dissimilar objects are contemplated as a unity, an overlapping takes place [*vollzieht sich eine Überschiebung*]' (115). The ego can be in two places at once, be attentive to some degree to more than one thing at a time. The difference between holding different things in grasp as a plurality and moving from substrate to properties first comes here: 'there is an essential difference, depending on whether, in this synthetic activity, it is *according to the objective sense* that a synthetic coincidence [*eine Synthesis der D e c k u n g*] is produced, thus in an entirely special identity-synthesis, or whether such a thing does not take place' (115; my emphasis).

If the overlaying synthesis happens 'according to the objective sense' or to the 'rule' of the object itself, then the overlaying can be of substrate and properties; if the overlaying does not happen according to the 'rule' or principle of an object but according to a rule the ego imposes on different phenomena, then the overlaying is the product of my interest only: 'If we pass from a color over to a sound, then this is not the case. But if we pass, always synthetically, from one color to another, there is already a synthesis of coincidence [*Deckungssynthese*]; the moments which overlap [*die Überschobenen*] one another coincide [*decken sich*] according to likeness or similarity' (115–16). This passage serves to emphasize that 'overlapping' is a *noematic* sense and that 'overlaying' is a *noetic* one.

46 When discussing the method of phenomenology in *Formal and Transcendental Logic*, Husserl notes that the move towards an *eidos* is also a move

towards synthesis on the basis of conflict, and he does so through the terminology under consideration in this book: 'all the variants … stand in relationship of synthetic interrelatedness and integral connectedness; more particularly, they stand in a continuous and all-inclusive synthesis of "coincidence in conflict [*Deckung in Widerstreit*]." But precisely with this coinciding [*Deckung*], what necessarily persists throughout this free and always-repeatable variation comes to the fore: the invariant' (*Husserliana XVII*, 248). It is through conflict, then, that identity is produced even at the level of categorial or essential intuition.

47 This is Zahavi's claim as well: 'A relation to a foreign subjectivity seems to be in play whenever there is talk of a multiplicity of coexisting profiles! It is through the foreign I that the incompatibility of the coexisting profiles becomes compatible.' Dan Zahavi, *Husserl and Transcendental Intersubjectivity: A Response to the Linguistic-Pragmatic Critique*, trans. Elizabeth A. Behnke (Athens: Ohio University Press, 2001), 49.

48 If, as Kym Maclaren does, we wish to continue to pursue the genetic phenomenology of infant development, we might also see that it is not just that the self's particular powers of recognition develop *in tandem* with the body's power of movement (the feet or the object as such). Rather, there is evidence to support the claim that one's grasp of the *entire* self and *all* its cognitive and self-aware functions develop *only within* the intercorporeal, intersubjective nexus: 'it is through our embodied, motor-perceptual implication in others that we first develop a sense of actual selfhood.' Kym Maclaren, 'Embodied Perceptions of Others as a Condition of Selfhood? Empirical and Phenomenological Considerations,' *Journal of Consciousness Studies* 15 (2008): 63–93 at 65. We will return to this argument below.

49 It is important to distinguish here among 'subjectivity,' 'consciousness,' 'cogito,' and 'ego.' See Douglas Heinsen, 'Husserl's Theory of the Pure Ego,' in *Husserl: Intentionality and Cognitive Science*, ed. Hubert L. Dreyfus (Cambridge, MA: MIT Press, 1984), 147–68. Basically, as Heinsen states, the ego is what Husserl calls the 'pole' of consciousness – the fact that thinking, intuiting, and willing centre in a unity that transcends and unites each act with each other act. The *cogito* is each particular act of thinking, willing, and intuiting – it is the act of intending each noema or *cogitatum*. Consciousness is the name Husserl gives for the unity that the objects and intentional acts have with one another – it is the name for the connection between *cogito* and *cogitatum*. Subjectivity is, then, the name for the relation between the ego, the *cogito*, and the *cogitatum*. It is the fact that the ego becomes more sophisticated, gaining habitualities and characteristics by its very act of uniting one *cogito*; subjectivity, in other words, is the name

for the entire *life* of consciousness that the ego lives. If Husserl speaks of the *transcendental ego* in distinction from transcendental subjectivity, I believe that that is only because he wants to emphasize that it is the fact that the existence of consciousness within subjectivity, within a life, causes the pole, the ego, to take on a certain reflective awareness of its life, to *own* the structure *ego–cogito–cogitatum.*

50   Husserl uses the Greek term *eidos* or *eidetic* to signify the essence or the invariant structures of an object under any of the possible manners of givenness or appearance of this object to a subjectivity. Such invariant structures serve as the laws whereby subjectivity can apprehend a thing as what the thing is. See David Michael Levin, *Reason and Evidence in Husserl's Phenomenology* (Evanston: Northwestern University Press, 1970), esp. chapter 7, 'Apodicticity in the Eidetic Mode of Consciousness.' Levin calls attention to the fact that an *eidos* has both a noematic and a noetic character by emphasizing the way in which the *eidos* appears as a structure of the object and as a law for consciousness: '[F]rom the noematic point of view, an essence is a structure, an object of signification. But from the noetic point of view, it is an a priori law of necessity, prescribing that without which an object of this sort cannot be thought' (161).

51   Emmanuel Levinas in chapter 6 of his *Theory of Intuition in Husserl's Phenomenology* (trans. Andre Orianne [Evanston: Northwestern University Press, 1973]) explores the intuition of essences (what Husserl calls *Wesensschau*). He examines the intuition of essences as an operation founding (and thus distinct from) deduction and induction. He also notes that *eide* are 'essences of the objects we find around us, considered in all their concreteness. They have neither the exactness nor the perfect determination of geometric concepts' (117). He emphasizes that for Husserl, exact or pure essences are merely 'idealizations of inexact ones' (118).

52   David Levin (1970) in this note seems to agree with the force, if not the conclusion, of Aron Gurwitsch's famous challenge to the existence of the transcendental ego in that he, too, wonders whether the *eidos'* 'transcendental ego' is apodictic: 'of especial importance here is the apodicticity of the *eidos* "transcendental ego." Husserl chooses to ignore altogether with what toil and casting about he finally arrived, in the *Meditations*, at his insights into the basic structures of consciousness' (175). Levin considers it the most fundamental essence for Husserl (180); yet if all Husserl can claim for its apodictic content is the fact of its existence, if the historical project of achieving the *eidos* is not reflected in the *eidos* itself, then Levin agrees with Quentin Lauer that 'insofar as Husserl succeeds in winning apodicticity, he has an "empty," merely formal achievement' (200).

53 The previous section, with its discussion of the mannequin/human, should be borne in mind while reading this one. The distinction between *Körper* and *Leib* is roughly the distinction between mannequin and human. The unified layers of the body of a subject were separate and conflicting in the example from *EJ* because they were the possible body of another. In oneself, and in the actual other person, these two layers form a single unity, mostly non-problematic in normal living – except in disease. In fact, Husserl also uses the term *Leibkörper* to describe a person's body.

54 One way of understanding this description from within psychology, performed in the natural attitude, would be to take up the work of Bowlby and Ainesworth on attachment theory. Inge Bretherton, who writes on the history of attachment theory, cites Bowlby in a crucial passage here: 'If growth is to proceed smoothly, the tissues must he exposed to the influence of the appropriate organizer at certain critical periods' (Bretherton 1992, 765).

55 While not focusing on the organ–object–organ movement, Smith in his commentary on the *Cartesian Meditations* does notice that 'when I perceive a material object as similar to my own body … the sense that pertains to my own body over and above its physical appearance – being a sensitive organ that is the null-centre of perceptual orientation and action – will be transferred to the similar material thing' (Smith 2003, 221). I would argue that the body as a whole organ, as that which is transferred, is an experience not given and not transferred until the experience of the other has already done its work to explode the sphere of ownness.

56 Husserl claims that 'apperception is not an inference, not a thinking act' (*CM*, 111). It is an immediate and perceptual grasp of a co-perceiving act. It is not an analogy. I feel her perception of me overlaying unproblematically or conflicting with my own.

Chapter 2

1 An earlier version of this chapter appears as 'Essential Intuition: A Communal Act' in *ALEA: Revista Internacional de Fenomenología y Hermenéutica* 7 (2009): 57–84.

2 What follows might be contested by Marianne Sawicki. In her article 'Empathy Before and After Husserl' (*Philosophy Today* [Spring 1997]: 123–7), she pursues Husserl's use and exploration after 1910 of the term 'in-feeling' of *Einfuhlung*. She argues that Husserl's discovery 'that the structure of one's in-feeling of the experiences of other people is similar to the structure of entertaining a memory or a hope' allowed Husserl to forget about

the problem of other people: 'Henceforward, Husserl no longer regarded *Fremderfahrung*, the experience of other people, as an interesting or provocative problem. His focus shifted to "constitution," the egoic autonomic function of assembling unified identities out of the seriated appearings of objects in consciousness' (126). I hope to show that Husserl, in his writings in the 1920s in which he used and explored the term *Deckung*, still took *Fremderfahrung* to be a problem and that constitution was not only 'egoic' but also passive and shared, involving a kind of synthesis of overlaying across and by means of gaps.

3 Merleau-Ponty's discussion of the way in which we intend one another sexually is an important reminder of how similarity works: 'There is an erotic comprehension not of the order of understanding, since understanding subsumes an experience, once perceived, under some idea while desire comprehends blindly by linking body to body.' Merleau-Ponty, *Phenomenology of Perception* (1994, 181). The notion of 'erotic comprehension' as a concrete synthesis is, I believe, etymologically included within Husserl's use of the verb *decken*, which has sexual connotations in German.

4 For the notion of community as occurring by means of discontinuities, see Jean-Luc Nancy, *The Inoperative Community*, ed. Peter Connor, trans. Peter Connor, Lisa Garbus, Michael Holland, and Simona Sawhney (Minneapolis: University of Minnesota Press, 1991).

5 In fact, in the third volume of intersubjectivity material, Husserl describes the overreaching proper to intersubjectivity as occurring in a similar manner to that of the layers of sense of body and psyche: 'Both layers reach into [*greifen*] one another [*ineinander*], or the first appresented layer, the corporeal, appresents the psychic continuously. In its turn, the psychic appresents in reverse the corporeal' (*Husserliana XV*, 85; my translation).

6 For an excellent discussion of the phenomenology of the family, see David Ciavatta's *Spirit, the Family, and the Unconscious in Hegel's Philosophy* (Albany: SUNY Press, 2010).

7 Christopher Macann in his study of the term *Deckung* titled *Presence and Coincidence: The Transformation of Transcendental into Ontological Phenomenology* (Dordrecht: Kluwer Academic Publishers, 1991), argues that Husserl's phenomenology fails to describe bodily life and hence intersubjectivity adequately. The reason for this failure, according to Macann, is that Husserl's phenomenology 'collapses into an alternative "doctrine of coincidence." Insofar as the self *is* its ego, *is* its body, or in other words insofar as the self *coincides* with that which it seeks to constitute, the task of constitution is rendered invalid by the failure to appreciate the implications of the principle of coincidence' (4). Overall, however, I think Macann is wrong in his

characterization of the course of Husserlian phenomenology and that his error stems largely from the way he reads the meaning of the word *Deckung* apart from its cognates and from Macann's own lack of consideration of Husserl's descriptions of conflict and abnormality. Husserl's use of the term *Deckung* is not a doctrinaire insistence on the absolute seamlessness of the self with its ego, body, or alien other. Rather, Husserl's use of that term demonstrates quite the opposite – that the overlaying brings to prominence the gaps that also appear between the self and its own experiences.

8 Cairns's translation of the next sentence is strange in that it forces the issue of coincidence where none is warranted. Here is his translation: 'This overlaying can bring a total or a partial coincidence, which in any particular instance has its degree, the limiting case being that of complete "likeness"' (*CM*, 113). Here is the German: '*Diese Deckung kann total oder partiell sein; sie hat jeweils ihre Gradualität, mit dem Grenzfall der "Gleichheit"*' (142). Here is a more direct translation: 'This overlaying can be total or partial. It has in any case its degree, with the limit-case being likeness' (my translation).

9 See Lohmar, where he argues that 'it is decisive for the understanding of the "synthesis of coincidence" that what is brought into coincidence are the intentional moments of the respective acts. The fulfilling coincidence is not based on equal or similar hyletic data.' Dieter Lohmar, 'Husserl's Concept of Categorial Intuition,' in *One Hundred Years of Phenomenology: Husserl's Logical Investigations Revisited*, ed. Dan Zahavi and Frederik Stjernfelt (Dordrecht: Kluwer Academic Publishers, 2002), 125–47 at 134).

10 In *Husserliana XV*, in his discussion of phenomenological anthropology, Husserl describes the overlaying between oneself and another as the 'taking-over' or 'taking-part-in' another's acts and life: 'If no counter-motives are in play, I co-perform without any further ado, in the overlaying [*Deckung*] of my I with that of the other ... his manners of acting, his position-takings, his validities: I take over [*übernehme*] so to say his validities as really belonging to him as my own, his judgments as mine' (462–3, my translation). This passage shows a very concrete understanding of overlaying in terms of relationships even within the generality of *Fremderfahrung*. And Husserl also notes that the 'taking-over' of another person's judgments or projects 'awakens' a communal world (463–4).

11 This is at least one reason why Descartes, in his *Meditations*, wanted to assume subjectivity to be completely separable from the body.

12 See Emmanuel Levinas's 'Philosophy and Awakening' in *Discovering Existence with Husserl*, trans. Richard A. Cohen and Michael B. Smith (Evanston: Northwestern University Press, 1998). There, Levinas argues that Husserl's phenomenology has gone far beyond clarifying experience as reality:

'drowsy intentions awakened to life will reopen vanished horizons, ever new, disturbing the theme in its identity qua result, awakening subjectivity from the identity in which it rests in its experience' (174). Such an awakening results for Levinas, perhaps, in a style that can 'call attention to what is discovered *behind* the consciousness that is subject to its ontic destiny in the thought of the Same' (174). Levinas goes on to say that it is the other person who calls me to wakefulness in Husserl's phenomenology (178).

13 Kathleen M. Haney, in *Intersubjectivity Revisited: Phenomenology and the Other* (Athens: Ohio University Press, 1994), also emphasizes the pairing of oneself and the alien other as an overlaying and not a coinciding in the following: 'eventually the primal constituting originary ego can separate herself from the pair because of the *reciprocal spatial difference* concomitant with her temporal connection to the other' (54; my emphasis). And in her description of the mother–child pairing, she again emphasizes the notion of overlaying as the mother's 'covering' of the child's needs but still preserving distinctions: 'the mother–child pair … involves each member in a fulfilling pairing with the other *not* because they are the same but precisely because they are complementarily *different*' (56; my emphasis).

14 For Zahavi, the ability I have as transcendental ego to constitute the sense of objects occurs in the shared space with others, or even more narrowly, the space between us: 'It is only in inter-subjectivity that this I is a constitutively functioning I, i.e., a transcendental I … The constitutive foundation, the "place" that allows for appearances, would thus seem to be precisely this *inter-space* (*Zwischenraum*) of interrelationship' (2001, 65; my emphasis).

15 Derrida in *On Touching – Jean-Luc Nancy* (Stanford: Stanford University Press, 2005) addresses briefly the notion of *Deckung* in Husserl. Indeed, I would argue that he suggests there that it is the gap between self and other that makes intuition possible: 'a spacing that dislocates, a non-coincidence (which also yields the chance *effects* of full intuition, the fortune of immediacy effects), wherever Husserl speaks of "overlapping" and "coincidence" (*Deckung*)' (181).

16 See Natalie Depraz, 'Empathy and Compassion as Experiential Praxis: Confronting Phenomenological Analysis and Buddhist Teachings,' in *Space, Time, and Culture*, ed. David Carr and C.-F. Cheung (Netherlands: Kluwer Academic Publishers, 2004), 189–200. The particular stance of Buddhism is interrogated by means of Husserlian pairing.

17 I see James Mensch as making a similar point in his discussion of the second solution to the problem of intersubjectivity in *Intersubjectivity and Transcendental Idealism* (Albany: SUNY Press, 1988). There, he emphasizes that the phenomenological reduction has given the phenomenologist the

opportunity to recognize her relationship with her ground, with her temporality, and with other egos. Intersubjectivity, for Mensch also, is not primarily an epistemological problem but rather a call to action: 'The problem of intersubjectivity is transformed into that of caring for the factually given (and hence fragile) web of human relations. It is a web, a nexus, into which we are born and which we ourselves must maintain and expand' (393).

18 Husserl's use here of the grammatical structure 'as-if' strikes me as a parallel to Kant's in his *Critique of Judgment*. There, especially in Section 6, Kant argues that we must act as if beauty were a predicate of the object when talking about it, in order to account for the universal presentation of beauty within the particular experience of this object. The subjunctive character of the experience and the necessary attribution of beauty to the object, which we know to be false, is a product of the way we form community within perception as such.

19 For a discussion of enworlding, see Eugen Fink, *Sixth Cartesian Meditation: The Idea of a Transcendental Theory of Method*, trans. Ronald Bruzina (Bloomington: Indiana University Press, 1995).

20 Husserl has also used these terms in *Formal and Transcendental Logic* when detailing the ways that three kinds of evidence (and presumably the three kinds of judgments correlated to them) relate to one another as the phenomenologist passes from one to the other: 'the change is at the same time an overlapping [*Überschiebung*] and a coinciding [*Deckung*] – the latter because the judgment-unity of the lower level [*Stufe*] enters at the same time into the higher level by identification, in such a fashion that the novelty belonging to the higher level (the distinctness, or properness of the judgment; or else the filledness of the evidence) must be taken as a predicate in its own right' (Husserl 1969, 178). In other words, the kind of overlaying and overlapping that appears within the relation of judgments to one another preserves distinctions while pressing towards a unity of act, purpose, and object.

21 Professor John Russon once gave an example of the time he first understood what a party was. As a child, he had been to a number of places where a group of people were present alongside him. What stood out on one important occasion was the fact that there was a purpose running through this gathering that set it off from the others, a kind of immediate grasp of the essence within that experience that allowed him to draw together both retroactively and proactively (a) the kind of variations that a party entailed and that he had witnessed; and (b) which gatherings would not participate in a fluid process of variation of the essence 'party' – for example, a board or department meeting. Of course, this is an example

within the natural attitude. But Husserl is claiming that, even within the project of transcendental phenomenology, essences appear as arising in a similar way, as correlates to the activity of consciousness that sustain the experience of 'belonging' together.

22 Sawicki claims an opposing view. She attributes to Edith Stein and not to Husserl the idea that intuition of essences – in fact all necessity – occurs because of 'the human person's direct access to other persons.' Sawicki, 'Empathy Before and After Husserl,' 125. She sees Husserl as saying this only 'at first blush' and argues that Husserl always maintained that 'the world must and does appear to me just as it would to anyone else who might stand where I stand; for my own unique individuality is irrelevant to my observations' (125). I think that this is false, and I try to argue why even the notion of possibility is something Husserl understands within the process of actual others overlaying my ownness.

23 Husserl, *Analyses Concerning Passive and Active Synthesis: Lectures on Transcendental Logic* (*Husserliana 11*), trans. Anthony J. Steinbock (Dordrecht: Kluwer Academic Publishers, 2001), 349–50.

24 Ibid., 350.

25 Ibid., 351.

26 Ibid.

Chapter 3

1 'Within the unity of logical thinking, unities belonging to all levels exercise their functions for thinking and cognition; therefore the focus can change and, with it, the sense of the unity that pervades the coinciding [*Deckung*], yet changes from level to level' (*Formal and Transcendental Logic*, 1969, 178–9). The sense of the unity is at once single and multiple. The sense changes from level to level insofar as one's ego can take a stand on one or another layer.

2 See Lingis's assertion in *Phenomenological Explanations* (Dordrecht: Martinus Nijhoff Publishers, 1986), particularly in 'The Mind's Body,' about how Husserl discovered that 'corporeity appears impossible to conjure and reappears in a totally denaturalized and deobjectified incidence after all the reductions, within the absolute sphere itself, as the incarnation of absolute consciousness' (23). I would argue that it is overlaying that marks, as Lingis would say, 'how corporeity is *implicated in the internal structure of consciousness*' (23; my emphasis).

3 In the third of his intersubjectivity volumes, Husserl further suggests that one's own structure emulates that of the encounter: 'Here is an apodictic

universal structure sketched out – in my ego, in each ego generally – an egological intersubjectivity as sketched out in each ego in *its own structure'* (*Husserliana XV*, 192; my emphasis and translation).

4 James Dodd, in *Idealism and Corporeity: An Essay on the Problem of the Body in Husserl's Phenomenology* (Dordrecht: Kluwer Academic Publishers, 1997), explains the relation between perception and sensation: 'Perception, for Husserl, is always more than sensation; it is an apprehension, therefore something noetic, that moves beyond sensation … Sensation is a moment of perceiving and not of that which is perceived' (40). I agree, but sensation nevertheless evinces the same kind of overlaying with perception that tends to lead to a kind of identifiable union in other cases. When Dodd claims then that sensation 'is a part of subjectivity … that remains *marginalized'* and even that 'paradoxically, it is the marginalized dimension of subjective life that is *extended,'* I would explain this as the necessary freedom and concealment that overlaying brings to the life of the ego (40–1). The previous layers of the synthesis of overlaying conceal themselves, sediment themselves, alienate themselves. But in so doing they ensure the possibility of one's return to them.

5 See Alia Al-Saji, 'The Site of Affect in Husserl's Phenomenology: Sensations and the Constitution of the Lived Body,' *Philosophy Today – SPEP Supplement* (2000): 51–9. Al-Saji makes the case for sensations and other 'structures of affect' in Husserlian phenomenology as conceived neither 'on the model of intentional lived experiences, explicitly related to objects' nor 'as neutral hyletic contents awaiting interpretation' (51). Instead, Husserl's alternative is to give 'an account of affect as preintentional and yet essential to the development of intentionalities' (51). By being preintentional, sensations are never fully able to be constituted and described phenomenologically. Yet these same sensations, unable to be fully described and determined in their relations with one another, *yield* a full perception sense of one's body because they are overlaying at a *distance*. As Al-Saji says, 'the reflexivity of the senses is performed *across a gap*. For the very doubling of sensation means that, while sensations may *overlap* (e.g., 'smoothness'-sensation and pressure-sensation), they are never identical or fused into one. The Body is thus a provisional unity, and the synthesis of the senses is an open-ended communication' (55; my emphasis).

6 Macann argues that 'the double-sidedness of the body (as physical body and as sensational field) is *not* something that can be phenomenologically constituted. Rather, this two-sidedness attests to a fundamental *coincidence* which, precisely because it can not be phenomenologically constituted, can, and must be, ontologically affirmed' Christopher Macann, *Pres-*

ence and Coincidence: The Transformation of Transcendental into Ontological Phenomenology (Dordrecht: Kluwer Academic Publishers, 1991), 96; my emphasis). By asserting their perceived 'coincidence,' Macann wants to say here that Husserlian phenomenology only legitimately asserts that the two sides of the lived body just *happen* to be experienced together, without any necessary and experiential connection being experienced between them, without providing any evidence of their mutual founding of the higher-level experience of the 'I can' or the intentionality reaching *through* the body. I disagree for two reasons. First, in the encounter with the other person there arises the distance from one's lived body requisite for the self-constitution of it in term of pre-intentional and intentional layers. Second, in the encounter with the other, given the experience of the other person's gaze or perception of oneself, it is possible to maintain both sides of one's own lived body within an experience, such as the experience of becoming quite uncomfortable telling a joke that is obviously going very badly with one's audience.

7 See Natalie Depraz, 'Can I Anticipate Myself? Self-Affection and Temporality,' in which she argues with Husserl that 'it is possible to develop an attention to one's own affections that does not abolish them but makes them become that much more effective' (1998, 83). I think that this is true because the structure of self-affection, like the affection of sensation, engages that of *Fremderfahrung*. More on that below in chapter 4.

8 In *APAS*, Husserl claims the following: 'Insofar as this [i.e. the way similarity works] is the case, awakening can certainly transgress the sense-fields' (229). One field can awaken the other. A smell can awaken a colour. A sight of a billboard can awaken a sound of a friend's voice. The reason I include this here is that, despite the fact that Husserl does not mention overlaying explicitly in this reference, the relationship of awakening for Husserl presupposes a relationship of overlaying.

9 See Alphonso Lingis, *Phenomenological Explanations* (Dordrecht: Martinus Nijhoff Publishers, 1986), particularly the fourth chapter, 'Involution in the Sensuous.' Here he argues, following Merleau-Ponty, that the corporal schema synthesizes the fields of sensation prior to intentionality proper, while still being a kind of intentionality: 'the synthesizing agency is not the spontaneity of the mind, but the corporal schema, which does not engender or posit the ideal term of their unity, but focuses upon a thing as upon a transversal unity of the different sensorial tones and textures concording, fitting together, expressing one another' (62). Lingis immediately goes on to talk of the synthesis of 'the monocular images' into a binocular one as well as of sight with touch in ways that Husserl does in *Ideas II (Husserliana IV)*.

10 Husserl makes a similar point in *Ideas II (Husserliana IV)*: 'there lies in the sensations an order which "coincides" [*'deckende' Ordnung*] with the appearing extension; but that is *already implicit* in the apprehension from the outset, in such a way that the stimulation-effects do not appear as something alien [*Fremdes*] and as just an effect, but rather as something *pertaining* to the appearing Corporeal body [*Leibeskörper*] *and* to the extensive order, and as something ordered in a *coincident* order [*in sich deckender Ordnung Geördnetes*]' (162, my emphasis).

11 Husserl claims this explicitly in *Ideas II*: 'if ultimately the eye as organ, and along with it, the visual sensations, are in fact attributed to the Body, then that happens indirectly by means of the properly localized sensations [i.e., touch]' (156). The increased *freedom* of vision (they overlay at a distance) arises only by way of *concealing* their dependence on the motion of touch. This concealment is made evident through the medical means to address experiences of perceptual conflict or abnormality – for example, contact lenses.

12 For an important discussion of the erotic structure of perception, see John Russon, *Bearing Witness to Epiphany: Persons, Things, and the Nature of Erotic Life* (Albany: SUNY Press, 2009): 'Erotic life is witnessing to the emergence of the call of the other. In our burgeoning sexuality we experience the birth of humanity within us as the epiphany of sharing, that is, *freedom* as co-definition' (75).

13 Husserl describes the psyche or soul of a cat playing in terms of an excess or surplus. Although he does not explicitly talk about an ego here, I believe that the description has to be the same for the ego as well: 'The excess of reality beyond the mere physical thing is not something that can be separated off by itself, not something juxtaposed, but something *in* the physical thing; thus it moves "along with" the thing and acquires its spatial determination by its being in something which is itself spatial' (*Ideas II*, 186).

14 Two extremely important essays on the role of the ego within Husserlian phenomenology are Jean-Paul Sartre, *The Transcendence of the Ego: An Existentialist Theory of Consciousness*, trans. Forrest Williams and Robert Kirkpatrick (New York: Noonday Press, 1962); and Aron Gurwitsch, 'A Non-Egological Conception of Consciousness,' *Philosophy and Phenomenological Research* 1 (1941): 325–38. Neither Sartre nor Gurwitsch tend to recognize the qualitative transcendence of the ego to its lived experiences in the way that Husserl does – namely, as the institution of the life to which all the acts and unities of conscious life matter and which, on its own and for itself, develops habitualities.

15 Kathleen M. Haney, in her fine book *Intersubjectivity Revisited: Phenom-
    enology and the Other* (Athens: Ohio University Press, 1994), makes a
    similar claim about the relationship between the ego and the body: 'The
    experience of Husserl's transcendental ego originates in active, conscious
    "turning toward" what attracts it and reflects on its original, necessary
    possibilities which it *derives not abstracts* from its embodiment' (159; my
    emphasis).

16 For this notion of objects serving as the place and source of our own
    memory, see John Russon, *Human Experience: Philosophy, Neurosis, and the
    Elements of Everyday Life* (Albany: SUNY Press, 2003): 'Our memory, most
    fundamentally, is what we experience *as* the determinateness of objects
    that communicates to us what we can and cannot do. Our objects, rather
    than our brain cells, are the "files" that retain our past' (41). What Husserl
    would offer as a supplement to Russon's claim is that particular objects
    could appear to us as the sedimentations of our particular experiences *only
    if* the entirety of our memory, our historicity as such, were already experi-
    enced as a function of the total flesh of the life-world. Memory is not 'most
    fundamentally' an experience of standing aloof from the world in order to
    remain locked within oneself. Rather, memory is acknowledging the world
    as one's self, as sustaining the very connections between, for example, the
    present picture of a lyre and the thought of one's absent friend that follows
    in an instant. The life-world is the network of paths we have carved out
    from object to object in response to their claims to similarity or difference.
    And we have left those paths there where we found them, namely in the
    objects, since it has become clear to us that the world is close enough to
    us that it will continue to carry us forth from one object to another. This
    is why, if the objects wear down, and the picture fades, and the neighbor-
    hood changes, the memories are gone. In such an experience of loss, we
    have made explicit the fact that we have always already attributed the
    force of our memory to the world, that we have implicitly agreed that our
    subjectivity is not simply inside this body but is in all that we grasp. Such
    a life-world is not simply an indifferent container. It is the very life by
    which memory works its way, its organizational features that make asso-
    ciations possible.

17 An earlier version of this chapter appeared previously as 'Towards a Phe-
    nomenology of Objects: Husserl and the Life-World' in *Gramma: Journal of
    Theory and Criticism* 14 (2006).

18 Donn Welton, *The Other Husserl: The Horizons of Transcendental Phenomenol-
    ogy* (Bloomington: Indiana University Press, 2000), 340.

19 Ibid., 343.

20 Ibid., 372.

21 It seems to me that Welton tries to articulate the experience of the world in a very similar way: 'We have the world not as a single whole but as nexus of significance, and our approach to it is always from within' (2000, 346). I agree that we have the world from within. However, I also argue that we must experience the world at least in a certain manner as a single whole and *not* simply as a nexus. We must experience the life-world in a way that makes possible the manner in which we experience our body as a whole – that is, apodictically but inadequately, and as the condition for our allowing certain organs or members or particular worlds to surface and recede. I am grateful to Professor Welton for also sharing with me some of his more recent thoughts on the life-world, particularly those on affectivity and how we share the flesh of the world through the experience of affection.

22 Again, I find the parallel to the self-constituting flux of internal time interesting. The life-world is experienced as one's own flux that nevertheless has a style, a life that one can trust as sustaining one's own life as transcendental consciousness. A flux that is self-constituting stability – this is what we experience as the life-world, I would argue.

23 The 'ontology' that Husserl mentions here is not, I think, a claim that the life-world itself does not appear. Rather, the life-world is able to sustain ontological claims as to its structures because it does not fall under the reduction, just as my transcendental ego and the alien other person do not. The life-world does not fall under the reduction because it quite simply is our own. Just as in the Fifth Cartesian Meditation, the transcendental ego discovers itself to be united with its body, its fields of sensation, and so forth, so too here the transcendental intersubjectivity finds itself to be united with its life-world.

For a competing description of the life-world, see Aron Gurwitsch, 'The Last Work of Edmund Husserl' where he claims that 'in bringing out the idea of an ontology of the *Lebenswelt*, Husserl hardly goes beyond formulating it. His main interest lies in a different direction' (426). For Gurwitsch, getting clear on the overarching *Lebenswelt* as embracing all particular life-worlds is not a significant project, and this explains Husserl's silence. However, I would argue that it is Merleau-Ponty who continues this Husserlian project and who shows in a more convincing way (through implication at least) why Husserl's *Crisis* moves in the ways that it does towards a re-emphasis on transcendental intersubjectivity, thus linking the *Crisis* to the *Cartesian Meditations*.

Chapter 4

1 Zahavi argues that 'one has to avoid the idea of an instantaneous non-temporal self-awareness, but one must also stay clear of the notion of a completely fractured time-consciousness, which makes both consciousness of the present, and of the unity of the stream unintelligible' Dan Zahavi, 'Inner Time-Consciousness and Pre-reflective Self-Awareness,' in *The New Husserl: A Critical Reader,* ed. Donn Welton (Bloomington: Indiana University Press, 2003), 157–80 at 173.

2 See the 'Temporality' chapter in Maurice Merleau-Ponty, *Phenomenology of Perception,* trans. Colin Smith (London: Routledge, 1994): 'We are saying that time *is* someone, or that temporal dimensions, in so far as they perpetually overlap [*se recouvrent perpetuellement*], bear each other out [*se confirment l'une l'autre*] and ever confine themselves to making explicit what was implied in each, being collectively expressive of that one single explosion or thrust which is subjectivity itself' (482).

3 This is not to say that recollection cannot appear or feel forced upon me. But my active participation is still required. Even in the repetition of a similar, traumatic event that appears to me to force me to dwell in the recollection of the two events together, as if they were the whole of my life, I am more active than in retention. And it is precisely by engaging recollection in a more active way, remembering the life between the traumas, that I can emerge as the person who can take a stand on different 'successions' of recollection, without thereby overcoming the automatic preservation of all lived experiences within the process of retention as such.

4 The marker for Husserl that separates phantasy from recollection is this: 'In mere phantasy no positing of the reproduced now and no *coinciding* [*keine Deckung*] of this now with a past now is given. Recollection on the other hand posits what is reproduced and in this positing gives it a position in relation to the actually present now and to the sphere of the original temporal field to which the recollection itself belongs' (*Husserliana X,* (53E/51G).

5 Merleau-Ponty describes the Husserlian constitution of objective time in terms of *recouvrement,* the French translation of *Deckung:* 'The origin of objective time ... is not to be sought in any eternal synthesis, but in the mutual harmonizing and overlapping [*recouvrement*] of past and future through the present, and in the very passing of time.' *Phenomenology of Perception* (488E/480F).

6 The title of Section 23 of *Husserlian X* is 'Coinciding [*Deckung*] of the Reproduced Now with a Past. Distinction between Phantasy and Recollection.'

7 Important work on the broadening of Husserl's time-consciousness material to protentions and to intersubjectivity has been published by Rodemeyer: 'We find the other subject already there in our own subjectivity,
as an open possibility that exceeds our own temporal consciousness.'
Lanei Rodemeyer, 'Developments in the Theory of Time-Consciousness:
An Analysis of Protention,' in *The New Husserl: A Critical Reader*, ed. Donn
Welton (Bloomington: Indiana University Press, 2003), 125–56 at 147. Rodemeyer sees the discussion of protention and of futurity as moving beyond the *Cartesian Meditations*, however.

8 Rodemeyer, in her later book, uses Zahavi to argue that, 'noting a certain
relation between temporalizing consciousness and intersubjectivity in
these arguments, we see how they might *overlap* as foundations, rather
than compete, and this is precisely Zahavi's point. The indicated intersubjective horizons, in order to be recognized, seem to require a temporalizing
consciousness which it itself open to such horizons. Thus the appresentation of the absent side of the cupboard could rest upon *two* structures: that
of my subjective temporalizing consciousness and that of my intersubjective horizons. Further, such appresentations might act as the *link* between
these two structures.' Lanei Rodemeyer, *Intersubjective Temporality: It's
About Time* (Dordrecht: Kluwer Academic Publishers, 2006), 52.

9 Bouckaert claims that the *Logical Investigations* present 'an intersubjective
structure in which suprasubjectivity grounds intersubjectivity. The later
texts, *Cartesian Meditations* for example, present a structure which is a
reverse of the earlier one, since there it is the transcendental intersubjectivity which grounds suprasubjectivity.' Bertrand Bouckaert, 'The Puzzling
Case of Alterity in Husserl's *Logical Investigations*,' in *One Hundred Years of
Phenomenology: Husserl's Logical Investigations Revisited*, ed. Dan Zahavi and
Frederik Stjernfelt (Dordrecht: Kluwer Academic Publishers, 2002), 185–98
at 196.

10 For an important work on the *Logical Investigation*, which explores the way
in which Husserl's terms and descriptions function, see Jay Lampert, *Synthesis and Backwards Reference in Husserl's Logical Investigations* (Dordrecht:
Kluwer Academic Publishers, 1995).

11 See especially Section 25 of the First Investigation, titled 'Relations of Coincidence [*Deckungsverhältnisse*] Among the Contents of Intimation and
Naming.'

12 Stapleton claims that 'the concept of foundation is precisely that which
supplies the noematic basis for the method of eidetic intuition … Imaginative variation is the vehicle through which we discover that certain objects
can be only in interconnectedness with others' Timothy Stapleton, 'The

"Logic" of Husserl's Transcendental Reduction,' *Man and World* 15 (1982): 369–82 at 373.

13   Husserl's logic of wholes and parts from the Third Investigation is something he held consistently within *Experience And Judgment:* 'We understand from the subjective side what has already been established in the Third Investigation from a *purely noematic point of view* namely that dependent parts "interpenetrate," contrary to independent parts which are "exterior to one another."' Husserl, *EJ*, 143; my emphasis. As Husserl goes on in his work, he thus begins to see the *noetic* or subjective participation in the whole/part logic.

14   In *EJ*, Husserl clarifies the difference between piece and moment as a difference in the kinds of overlaying or *Deckung* at work in each case: 'To begin with, only one of the pieces is apprehended on the basis of the contemplated whole. It is in coincidence [*Deckung*] with the whole, but in a wholly unique way, which *differs from the coincidence* [*Deckung*] between a substrate and a dependent moment. In both cases – thus, in *every* explicative coincidence [*Deckung*] – with the dissociation of a part on the basis of a whole … something is dissociated and something is left over which is not dissociated. This means that the congruence is only partial. But the *way in which* the nonexplicated remainder is present to consciousness is completely different in explication by pieces than in explication by dependent moments' (143; my emphasis).

15   Two quick points. Notice, first, how the translation of *Deckungszusammenhänge* veers from 'coincidence' to 'covering.' The word just simply does not consistently mean coincidence. And second, within this quote exist many of the terms with which Husserl later goes on to describe *Fremderfahrung*. The notion of 'progress' or transition, *Übergang*, the notion of distance, *Abstand*, and the notion of 'covering' as *überdeckende* or *Deckung* all figure prominently in both descriptions.

16   Drummond argues that Husserl may have moved to understand his own theory of wholes and parts in just this way – that is, in terms of using the distinction between kinds of parts to apply to consciousness itself: 'I want to suggest, however, that in the second edition of the *Investigations* Husserl manifests a more complete understanding of the import of his own discussion of parts and wholes … It is not until the Fifth Investigation of the second edition that Husserl fully exploits the possibility of establishing wholes via intentional as well as real reflations. To put the matter another way, I want to isolate what I take to be a shift in Husserl's understanding of the whole that is the object of phenomenological reflection.' John Drummond, 'The *Logical Investigations*: Paving the Way to a Transcendental

Logic,' in *One Hundred Years of Phenomenology: Husserl's Logical Investigations Revisited*, ed. Dan Zahavi and Frederik Stjernfelt (Dordrecht: Kluwer
Academic Publishers, 2002), 31–40 at 37–8.

17 This text goes on to say, however, that 'on the other hand, we cannot at
all conclude from the content of our basic definition [of wholes and parts]
that it is impossible that pieces should enter into foundational relationships in regard to *a more comprehensive whole* in which they all count as
non-independent moments' (*LI volume 2*, 42; my emphasis). Husserl does
show here, I think, that it might be possible to encounter unities in which
the same part could play a role as a piece and as a moment. But he does
not seem to acknowledge that possibility within the *same whole*, nor could
he outside of intersubjectivity.

18 This is not to say that books or poems or music do not engage the duplication of intersubjectivity. They do. But these objects also are able to be
experienced as alien other persons, too. A philosopher once asked Derrida
whether he thought the text was 'alive.' He responded that it was certainly
'a lie.' She clarified, saying that she had asked about whether the text was
'alive.' That too, he replied. We encounter products of intersubjectivity as
themselves others. They conceal and reveal just as our own unity does.

19 Stapleton, in 'The "Logic,"' almost argues this here: 'Consciousness, when
purified of all worldly interpretations, embraces both the "for us" and the
"in itself" as *momenta* of the one, only, concrete whole: transcendental subjectivity' (379).

20 Husserl describes this situation as follows: 'It is also clear that men become apperceivable only as finding Others and still more Others, not just
in the realm of actuality but likewise in the realm of possibility … To this
community there naturally corresponds, in transcendental concreteness, a
similarly open community of monads, which we designate as transcendental intersubjectivity' (*CM*, 130). It is the openness of the community that
is emphasized. Even though 'for each man, every other is implicit' in the
world's horizon, still 'in fact most other men remain horizontal' (*CM*, 131).

21 See Husserl's description of teleology in the essay within the third volume of intersubjectivity material titled 'Teleology: The Implication of the
Eidos Transcendental Intersubjectivity in the Eidos Transcendental I; Fact
and Eidos.' There Husserl speaks of how transcendental intersubjectivity makes clear within itself 'the universal absolute will, which lives in all
transcendental subjects and which makes possible the individual concrete
being of all transcendental subjects is the god-like will. But the collected
intersubjectivity presupposes this *absolute* will not as something preceding that intersubjectivity, as something possible without it, but *as its own*

structural layer, without which this absolute will cannot be concrete' (*Husserlianaa XV*, 381; my translation and emphasis). In each particular situation or human relationship, the perspective of the relationship is a possible phenomenon, a possible facet of experience because persons essentially produce through their particularity a layer of their relations that is universal, eidetic.

Conclusion

1 Albert Johnstone, 'The Relevance of Nonsymbolic Cognition to Husserl's Fifth Meditation,' *Philosophy Today* 43, no. 4 (1999): 88–98.
2 As Haney describes, the fusion of paired lived bodies is immediately sundered and made a task of recovery: 'Primal associations may unite paired egos in mutual fusion but the inevitable splintering of such moments only points to differences ... Empathic processes overcome these differences between human persons through "filling in" the actual contents of otherness of the other, thereby providing the means for a kind of reunification of the self and others.' Kathleen M. Haney, *Intersubjectivity Revisited: Phenomenology and the Other* (Athens: Ohio University Press, 1994), 135–6.
3 'Repressing means that the one conceals [*verdeckt*] the other, that the concealed element [*Verdeckte*] tends toward unconcealment [*Aufdeckung*], then breaking through conceals the previously unconcealed element' (*APAS*, 176).
4 See Taylor Carman, 'The Body in Husserl and Merleau-Ponty,' *Philosophical Topics* 27, no. 2 (1999): 205–24. Carman argues the more standard interpretation, to the contrary, that Husserl's conception of the body is *opposed* to that of Merleau-Ponty. For Carman, Husserl sees the lived, bodily intentionality as 'a kind of intermediary phenomenon bridging what remains, in his eyes, a conceptual "abyss" separating consciousness from reality ... The body is not itself constitutive of intentionality, for Husserl, but is instead a noetic achievement of transcendental subjectivity' (224). For Carman, Merleau-Ponty contrasts to this 'noetic' and 'intermediary' account of the body an account of the body as 'a primitive constituent of perceptual awareness as such, which in turn forms the permanent background of intentionality at large ... The body in its perceptual capacity just *is* the I in its most primordial aspect' (224.). Of course, it is my contention that what Carman says about Merleau-Ponty's description of the lived body is also something that Husserl evinces in the notion of overlaying.
5 See Dan Zahavi's *Husserl and Transcendental Intersubjectivity* (Athens: Ohio University Press, 2001).
6 Merleau-Ponty says this even more directly: 'That every being presents

itself at a distance, which does not prevent us from knowing it, which is on the contrary the guarantee for knowing it: this is what is not considered' (Merleau-Ponty 1968, 127).

7 See David Morris, 'The Fold and the Body Schema in Merleau-Ponty and Dynamic Systems Theory,' *Chiasmi International* 1 (1999): 275–86. Morris works to show how phenomenology, in particular that of Merleau-Ponty, can identify one's lived experience of one's body as an experience that folds in on itself, that operates schematically in a kind of a priori manner quite different from the normal *a priori:* 'The body schema is, in other words, the principle of the natural perceptual dialogue in which the world and body permeate and separate from one another – enmesh and "give birth" to one another's perceptual identities – through their interpermeation ... The body schema, then, is a new sort of *a priori*, it is a pre-personal past of embodiment, and when radical reflection seeks this new *a priori*, it seeks the unreflective fund of its own experience' (281). In Morris's words, the new *a priori* that Merleau-Ponty's work reveals is 'self-conceptual' (282) and is 'an *a priori* that belongs to living existence itself, prior to scientific reflection, prior to all reflection' (283).

8 Burke implies that Merleau-Ponty is exploiting the notion of *Deckung par distance*: 'Merleau-Ponty argues that this intuition is not a return to the immediate; it is not the effective fusion or *perfect coincidence* with Being in its original integrity ... rather than as coincidence and fusion, Merleau-Ponty defines intuition as *proximity through distance*.' Patrick Burke, 'Listening at the Abyss,' in *Ontology and Alterity in Merleau-Ponty*, ed. Galen Johnson and Michael B. Smith (Evanston: Northwestern University Press, 1990), 81–97; my emphasis. One listens to the voice or feels the reversibility of the other's flesh 'within the abyss of *noncoincidence* between the touching and the touched, the seeing and the seen, which *institutes* these reversible domains and is, paradoxically, the secret of their bond' (87). For Husserl, too, the overlayings that are most perfect still have the distance of a passed-over distinction between them, just as the eidetic intuition has, at its foundation, the separation of perspectives from one another.

9 Claude Lefort, 'Flesh and Otherness,' in *Ontology and Alterity in Merleau-Ponty*, ed. Galen Johnson and Michael B. Smith (Evanston: Northwestern University Press, 1990), 3–13.

10 Emmanuel Levinas, *Totality and Infinity: An Essay on Exteriority*, trans. Alphonso Lingis (Pittsburgh: Duquesne University Press, 1998), 29.

11 Ibid.

12 Bob Sandmeyer, *Husserl's Constitutive Phenomenology: Its Problem and Promise* (New York: Routledge, 2009), 33.

Bibliography

APAS   Refers to *Husserliana XI*. English: *Analyses Concerning Passive and Active Synthesis: Lectures on Transcendental Logic*. Trans. Anthony J. Steinbock. Dordrecht: Kluwer Academic Publishers, 2001.

CM   Refers to *Husserliana I*. English: *Cartesian Meditations: An Introduction to Phenomenology*. Trans. Dorion Cairns. The Hague: Martinus Nijhoff Publishers, 1960.

EJ   *Experience and Judgment: Investigations in a Genealogy of Logic*. Trans. James S. Churchill and Karl Ameriks. Evanston: Northwestern University Press, 1973.

Husserliana

Ideas I   *Husserliana III*

Ideas II   *Husserliana IV*

LI   *Logical Investigations*. Refers to *Husserliana XVIII* and *XIX*.

PCIT   Refers to *Husserliana X*. English: *On the Phenomenology of the Consciousness of Internal Time (1893–1917)*. Trans. John Barnett Brough. Dordrecht: Kluwer Academic Publishers, 1991.

Texts by Husserl in the *Husserliana* series, including English translations

Husserliana I. Cartesianische Meditationen und Pariser Vorträge. Ed. Stephen Strasser. Den Haag: Martinus Nijhoff Publishers, 1950, rpt. 1973. *Cartesian Meditations: An Introduction to Phenomenology*. Trans. Dorion Cairns. The Hague: Martinus Nijhoff Publishers, 1960.

Husserliana III, 1–2. Ideen zu einer reinen Phänomenologie und phänomenologischen Philosophie. Erstes Buch. Allgemeine Einführung in die reine Phänomenologie. Ed. Karl Schuhmann. Den Haag: Martinus Nijhoff Publishers, 1976. *Ideas Pertaining to a Pure Phenomenology and to a Phenomenological Philosophy. First*

Book. General Introduction to a Pure Phenomenology. Trans. Fred Kersten. The Hague: Martinus Nijhoff Publishers, 1982.

Husserliana IV. Ideen zu einer reinen Phänomenologie und phänomenologischen Philosophie. Zweites Buch. Phänomenologische Untersuchungen zur Konstitution. Ed. Marly Biemel. Den Haag: Martinus Nijhoff Publishers, 1952. *Ideas Pertaining to a Pure Phenomenology and to a Phenomenological Philosophy. Second Book. Studies in the Phenomenology of Constitution.* Trans. Richard Rojcewicz and Andre Schuwer. Dordrecht: Kluwer Academic Publishers, 1989.

Husserliana VI. Die Krisis der europäischen Wissenschaften und die transzendentale Phänomenologie. Eine Einleitung in die phänomenologische Philosophie. Ed. Walter Biemel. Den Haag: Martinus Nijhoff Publishers, 1954, rpt. 1962. *The Crisis of the European Sciences and Transcendental Phenomenology: An Introduction to Phenomenological Philosophy.* Trans. David Carr. Evanston: Northwestern University Press, 1970.

Husserliana X. Zur Phänomenologie des inneren Zeitbewusstseins (1893–1917). Ed. Rudolf Boehm. Den Haag: Martinus Nijhoff Publishers, 1966. *On the Phenomenology of the Consciousness of Internal Time (1893–1917).* Trans. John Barnett Brough. Dordrecht: Kluwer Academic Publishers, 1991.

Husserliana XI. Analysen zur passiven Synthesis. Aus Vorlesungs- und Forschungsmanuskripten 1918–1926. Ed. Margot Fleischer. Den Haag: Martinus Nijhoff Publishers, 1966. *Analyses Concerning Passive and Active Synthesis: Lectures on Transcendental Logic.* Trans. Anthony J. Steinbock. Dordrecht: Kluwer Academic Publishers, 2001.

Husserliana XIII. Zur Phänomenologie der Intersubjektivität. Texte aus dem Nachlass. Erster Teil: 1905–1920. Ed. Iso Kern. Den Haag: Martinus Nijhoff Publishers, 1973.

Husserliana XIV. Zur Phänomenologie der Intersubjektivität. Texte aus dem Nachlass. Zweiter Teil: 1921–1928. Ed. Iso Kern. Den Haag: Martinus Nijhoff Publishers, 1973.

Husserliana XV. Zur Phänomenologie der Intersubjektivität. Texte aus dem Nachlass. Dritter Teil: 1929-1935. Ed. Iso Kern. Den Haag: Martinus Nijhoff Publishers, 1973.

Husserliana XVII. Formale und transzendentale Logik. Versuch einer Kritik der logischen Vernunft. Ed. Paul Janssen. Den Haag: Martinus Nijhoff Publishers, 1974. *Formal and Transcendental Logic.* Trans. Dorion Cairns. The Hague: Martinus Nijhoff Publishers, 1969.

Husserliana XVIII. Logische Untersuchungen. Erster Band. Prolegomena zur reinen Logik. Ed. Elmar Holenstein. Den Haag: Martinus Nijhoff Publishers, 1975. *Logical Investigations.* 2 vols. Trans. J.N. Findlay. Edited by Dermot Moran. London: Routledge 2001.

Husserliana XIX, 1–2. Logische Untersuchungen. Zweiter Band. Untersuchungen zur Phänomenologie und Theorie der Erkenntnis. Ed. Ursula Panzer. Den Haag: Martinus Nijhoff Publishers, 1984. *Logical Investigations.* 2 vols. Trans. J.N. Findlay. Edited by Dermot Moran London: Routledge & Kegan Paul, 2001.

Texts by Husserl outside the *Husserliana* series, including English translations

Fink, Eugen. *VI. Cartesianische Meditation: Teil I. Die Idee einer transzendentalen Methodenlehre. Texte aus dem Nachlass Eugen Finks (1932) mit Anmerkungen und Beilagen aus dem Nachlass Edmund Husserls (1933/34).* Ed. Hans Ebeling, Jann Holl, and Guy von Kerckhoven. Dordrecht: Kluwer Academic Publishers, 1988. *Sixth Cartesian Meditation: The Idea of a Transcendental Theory of Method.* Trans. Ronald Bruzina. Bloomington: Indiana University Press, 1995.

– *VI. Cartesianische Meditation: Teil II: Ergänzungsband. Texte aus dem Nachlass Eugen Finks (1932) mit Anmerkungen und Beilagen aus dem Nachlass Edmund Husserls (1933/34).* Ed. Guy von Kerckhoven. Dordrecht: Kluwer Academic Publishers, 1988.

Husserl, Edmund. *Aktive Synthesen: Aus der Vorlesung 'Transzendentale Logik' 1920/21.* Dordrecht: Kluwer Academic Publishers, 2000.

– *Ergänzungsband zu 'Analysen zur Passiven Synthesis.'* Ed. Roland Breeur. Dordrecht: Kluwer Academic Publishers, 2000.

– *Analysen zur Passiven Synthesis. Aus Vorlesungs- und Forschungsmanuskripten 1918–1926.* In *Gesammelte Werke,* Band IX. Den Haag: Martinus Nijhoff Publishers, 1966.

– *Shorter Works.* Ed. Peter McCormick and Frederick A. Elliston. Notre Dame: University of Notre Dame Press, The Harvester Press, 1981.

– *Phänomenologische Psychologie. Vorlesungen Sommersemester 1925.* Ed. Walter Biemel. Den Haag: Martinus Nijhoff Publishers, 1962. *Phenomenological Psychology. Lectures, Summer Semester, 1925.* Trans. John Scanlon. The Hague: Martinus Nijhoff Publishers, 1977.

– *Erfahrung und Urteil. Untersuchungen zur Genealogie der Logik.* Ed. Ludwig Landgrebe. Hamburg: Felix Meiner, 1972, rpt. 1985. *Experience and Judgment: Investigations in a Genealogy of Logic.* Trans. James S. Churchill and Karl Ameriks. Evanston: Northwestern University Press, 1973.

Secondary Sources on Husserl and Phenomenology

Adorno, Theodor W. *Against Epistemology: A Metacritique: Studies in Husserl and the Phenomenological Antinomies.* Trans. Willis Domingo. Oxford: Basil Blackwell, 1982.

Al-Saji, Alia. 'The Site of Affect in Husserl's Phenomenology – Sensations and the Constitution of the Lived Body.' *Philosophy Today – SPEP Supplement* (2000): 51–9.

Behnke, Elizabeth. 'Edmund Husserl's Contribution to Phenomenology of the Body in *Ideas II*.' In Nenon and Embree 1996: 135–60.

Berger, Gaston. *The* Cogito *in Husserl's Philosophy*. Trans. Kathleen McLaughlin. Evanston: Northwestern University Press, 1972.

Bernet, Rudolf, Iso Kern, and Eduard Marbach. *An Introduction to Husserlian Phenomenology*. Evanston: Northwestern University Press, 1989.

Bredlau, Susan. 'A Respectful World: Merleau-Ponty and the Experience of Depth.' *Human Studies* 33, no. 4: 411–23.

Bretherton, Inge. 'The Origins of Attachment Theory: John Bowlby and Mary Ainesworth.' *Developmental Psychology* 28, no. 5 (1992): 759–75.

Bouckaert, Bertrand. 'The Puzzling Case of Alterity in Husserl's *Logical Investigations*.' In Zahavi and Stjernfelt 2002: 185–98.

Burke, Patrick. 'Listening at the Abyss.' In Johnson and Smith 1990: 81–97.

Cairns, Dorion. *Guide for Translating Husserl*. The Hague: Martinus Nijhoff Publishers, 1973.

Carman, Taylor. 'The Body in Husserl and Merleau-Ponty.' *Philosophical Topics* 27, no. 2 (1999): 205–24.

Carr, David. *Phenomenology and the Problem of History: A Study of Husserl's Transcendental Philosophy*. Evanston: Northwestern University Press, 1974.

Carr, David, and C.-F. Cheung, eds. *Space, Time, and Culture*. Netherlands: Kluwer Academic Publishers, 2004.

– 'Transcendental and Empirical Subjectivity: The Self in the Transcendental Tradition.' In Welton 2003: 181–98.

Ciavatta, David. *Spirit, the Family, and the Unconscious in Hegel's Philosophy*. Albany: SUNY Press, 2010.

Cobb-Stevens, Richard. 'James and Husserl: Time-Consciousness and the Intentionality of Presence and Absence.' In Zahavi 1998: 41–58.

Costello, Peter. 'Essential Intuition: A Communal Act.' *ALEA: International Journal of Phenomenology and Hermeneutics* 7 (2009): 57–84.

– 'Towards a Phenomenology of Gratitude – A Response on Behalf of Heidegger to Jean-Luc Marion.' *Balkan Journal of Philosophy* 1, no. 2 (2009): 77–83.

Crowell, Steven Galt. 'Husserl, Derrida, and the Phenomenology of Expression.' *Philosophy Today* 40, no. 1 (Spring 1996): 61–70.

Dauenhauer, Bernard P. 'The Teleology of Consciousness: Husserl and Merleau-Ponty.' *Analecta Husserliana* 9, ed. Anna Tymieniecka. Dordrecht: D. Reidel Publishing, 1979. 149–68.

de Beauvoir, Simone. *Ethics of Ambiguity.* New York: Citadel Press, 2000.

DeBoer, Theodore. *The Development of Husserl's Thought.* The Hague: Martinus Nijhoff Publishers, 1978.

Depraz, Natalie, and Dan Zahavi, eds. *Alterity and Facticity.* Dordrecht: Kluwer Academic Publishers, 1998.

– 'Can I Anticipate Myself? Self-Affection and Temporality.' In Zahavi 1998.

– 'Empathy and Compassion as Experiential Praxis: Confronting Phenomenological Analysis and Buddhist Teachings.' In Carr and Cheung 2004: 189–200.

– and Diego Cosmelli. 'Empathy and Openness: Practices of Intersubjectivity at the Core of the Science of Consciousness.' In Thompson 2003: 163–204.

– 'The Husserlian Theory of Intersubjectivity as Alterology: Emergent Theories and Wisdom Traditions in Light of Genetic Phenomenology.' *Journal of Consciousness Studies* 8, nos. 5–7 (2001): 169–78.

– 'The Phenomenological Reduction as Praxis.' *Journal of Consciousness Studies* 6, nos. 2–3 (1999): 95–110.

Derrida, Jacques. *Edmund Husserl's Origin of Geometry. An Introduction.* Trans. John P. Leavey, Jr. Lincoln: University of Nebraska Press, 1989.

– *Given Time I: Counterfeit Money,* vol. 1. Trans. Peggy Kamuf. Chicago: University of Chicago Press, 1994.

– *On Touching – Jean-Luc Nancy.* Stanford: Stanford University Press, 2005.

– *Speech and Phenomena.* Trans. David Allison. Evanston: Northwestern University Press, 1973.

– *The Gift of Death.* Trans. David Wills. Chicago: University of Chicago Press, 1996.

– *The Problem of Genesis in Husserl's Philosophy.* Chicago: University of Chicago Press, 2003.

Desanti, Jean T. *Fenomenologia e prassi.* Milano: Lampugnani Nigri Editore, 1971.

Dodd, James. *Idealism and Corporeity: An Essay on the Problem of the Body in Husserl's Phenomenology.* Dordrecht: Kluwer Academic Publishers, 1997.

Dreyfus, Hubert L., ed. *Husserl: Intentionality and Cognitive Science.* Cambridge, MA: MIT Press, 1984.

Drabinski, John E. 'The Hither-Side of the Living-Present in Levinas and Husserl.' *Philosophy Today* 40 (Spring 1996): 142–50.

Drummond, John. 'The *Logical Investigations*: Paving the Way to a Transcendental Logic.' In Zahavi and Stjernfelt 2002: 31–40.

– 'The Structure of Intentionality.' In Welton 2003: 65–92.

Elkin, Henry. 'Towards a Developmental Phenomenology: Transcendental-*Ego* and Body-*Ego*.' *Analecta Husserliana,* vol. 2. Ed. Anna Tymieniecka. Dordrecht: D. Reidel Publishing, 1972. 258–66.

Farber, Marvin. *The Foundation of Phenomenology. Edmund Husserl and the Quest for a Rigorous Science of Philosophy.* Albany: SUNY Press, 1968.

Fillion, Réal. *Multicultural Dynamics and the Ends of History: Exploring Kant, Hegel, and Marx.* Ottawa: University of Ottawa Press, 2008.

Fink, Eugen. *Sixth Cartesian Meditation. The Idea of a Transcendental Theory of Method.* Trans. Ronald Bruzina. Bloomington: Indiana University Press, 1995.

Gurwitsch, Aron. *The Field of Consciousness.* Pittsburgh: Duquesne University Press, 1964.

– 'A Non-Egological Conception of Consciousness.' *Philosophy and Phenomenological Research* 1 (1941): 325–38.

– 'The Last Work of Edmund Husserl.' *Philosophy and Phenomenological Research* 17 (March 1957): 370–98.

Haney, Kathleen M. *Intersubjectivity Revisited: Phenomenology and the Other.* Athens: Ohio University Press, 1994.

Heidegger, Martin. *Sein und Zeit.* Tübingen: Max Niemeyer, 1972. English translation: *Being and Time.* Trans. Joan Stambaugh. Albany: SUNY Press, 1996.

Heinsen, Douglas. 'Husserl's Theory of the Pure Ego.' In Dreyfus 1984: 147–68.

Held, Klaus. 'Husserl's Phenomenological Method.' In Welton 2003: 3–31.

Holenstein, Elmar. *Phänomenologie der Assoziation.* Den Haag: Martinus Nijhoff Publishers, 1972.

Hopkins, Burt C. 'Husserl's Account of Phenomenological Reflection and Four Paradoxes of Reflexivity.' *Research in Phenomenology* 19 (1989): 180–94.

Hume, David. *A Treatise of Human Nature. Analytical Index by L.A. Selby-Bigge.* Ed. L.A. Selby-Bigge. Oxford: Clarendon Press, 1978.

Jacobson, Kirsten. 'Agoraphobia and Hypochondria as Disorders of Dwelling.' *International Studies in Philosophy* 36 (2004): 31–44.

– 'A Developed Nature: A Phenomenological Account of the Experience of Home.' *Continental Philosophy Review* 42 (2009): 355–73.

James, William. *The Moral Philosophy of William James.* Ed. John K. Roth. New York: Thomas Y. Crowell Company, 1969.

Johnson, Galen, and Michael B. Smith, eds. *Ontology and Alterity in Merleau-Ponty.* Evanston: Northwestern University Press, 1990.

Johnstone, Albert. 'The Relevance of Nonsymbolic Cognition to Husserl's Fifth Meditation.' *Philosophy Today* 43, no. 4 (1999): 88–98.

Kersten, Fred. 'On Understanding Idea and Essence in Husserl and Ingarden.' *Analecta Husserliana,* vol. 2. Ed. Anna Tymieniecka. Dordrecht: D. Reidel Publishing, 1972. 55–63.

Kersten, Fred, and Richard Zaner, eds. *Phenomenology: Continuation and Criticism.* The Hague: Martinus Nijhoff Publishers, 1973.

Kockelmans, Joseph J. *Edmund Husserl's Phenomenological Psychology: A Historico-Critical Study.* Atlantic Highlands: Humanities Press, 1978.

– *Edmund Husserl's Phenomenology.* West Lafayette: Purdue University Press, 1994.

– ed. *Phenomenology: The Philosophy of Edmund Husserl and Its Interpretation.* New York: Doubleday, 1967.

Kohák, Erazim. *Idea and Experience: Edmund Husserl's Project of Phenomenology in Ideas I.* Chicago: University of Chicago Press, 1978.

Kozlowski, Richard. *Die Aporien der Intersubjektivität. Eine Auseinandersetzung mit Edmund Husserls Intersubjektivitätstheorie.* Würzburg: Königshausen & Neumann, 1991.

Lampert, Jay. *Synthesis and Backwards Reference in Husserl's Logical Investigations.* Dordrecht: Kluwer Academic Publishers, 1995.

Landen, Laura. 'Of Forests and Trees: Wholes and Parts.' *Proceedings of the American Catholic Philosophical Association* 69 (1995): 81–89.

Landgrebe, Ludwig. *The Phenomenology of Edmund Husserl: Six Essays.* Ed. Donn Welton. Ithaca: Cornell University Press, 1981.

Levin, David Michael. *Reason and Evidence in Husserl's Phenomenology.* Evanston: Northwestern University Press, 1970.

– 'Tracework: Myself and Others in the Moral Phenomenology of Merleau-Ponty and Levinas.' *International Journal of Philosophical Studies* 6, no. 3 (1998): 345–92.

Levinas, Emmanuel. *Autrement qu'etre ou au-dela de l'essence.* The Hague: Martinus Nijhoff Publishers, 1978.

– *Discovering Existence with Husserl.* Trans. Richard A. Cohen and Michael B. Smith. Evanston: Northwestern University Press, 1998.

– *Otherwise Than Being or Beyond Essence.* Trans. Alphonso Lingis. Dordrecht: Martinus Nijhoff Publishers, 1974.

– *The Theory of Intuition in Husserl's Phenomenology.* Trans. Andre Orianne. Evanston: Northwestern University Press, 1973.

– *Totalite et infini: Essai sur l'exteriorite.* The Hague: Martinus Nijhoff Publishers, 1974.

– *Totality and Infinity: An Essay on Exteriority.* Trans. Alphonso Lingis. Pittsburgh: Duquesne University Press, 1998.

Lingis, Alphonso. *Phenomenological Explanations.* Dordrecht: Martinus Nijhoff Publishers, 1986.

Lohmar, Dieter. 'Husserl's Concept of Categorial Intuition.' In Zahavi and Stjernfelt 2002: 125–47.

Lübcke, Poul. 'A Semantic Interpretation of Husserl's *Epoche.*' *Synthese* 118 (1999): 1–12.

Luft, Sebastian. 'Husserl's Concept of the Transcendental Person: Another Look at the Husserl–Heidegger Relationship.' *International Journal of Philosophical Studies* 13, no. 2 (2005): 141–77.

Maclaren, Kym. 'Embodied Perceptions of Others as a Condition of Selfhood? Empirical and Phenomenological Considerations.' *Journal of Consciousness Studies* 15 (2008): 63–93.

Macann, Christopher. *Presence and Coincidence: The Transformation of Transcendental into Ontological Phenomenology.* Dordrecht: Kluwer Academic Publishers, 1991.

Mahoney, Timothy A. 'Socrates' Loyalty to Athens and His Radical Critique of the Athenians.' *History of Philosophy Quarterly* 15, no. 1: 1–22.

Marion, Jean-Luc. *Reduction and Givenness: Investigations of Husserl, Heidegger, and Phenomenology.* Trans. Thomas A. Carlson. Evanston: Northwestern University Press, 1998.

Marratto, Scott. *The Intercorporeal Self: Merleau-Ponty on Subjectivity.* Albany: SUNY Press, 2012.

McKenna, William. *Husserl's 'Introduction to Phenomenology.'* The Hague: Martinus Nijhoff Publishers, 1982.

– ed. *Derrida and Phenomenology.* Dordrecht: Kluwer Academic Publishers, 1995.

Mensch, James Richard. *After Modernity: Husserlian Reflections on a Philosophical Tradition.* Albany: SUNY Press, 1996.

– *Intersubjectivity and Transcendental Idealism.* Albany: SUNY Press, 1988.

– *Postfoundational Phenomenology: Husserlian Reflections on Presence and Embodiment.* University Park: Penn State University Press, 2000.

– *The Question of Being in Husserl's Logical Investigations.* The Hague: Martin Nijhoff Publishers, 1981.

Merleau-Ponty, Maurice. *Consciousness and the Acquisition of Language.* Trans. Hugh J. Silverman. Evanston: Northwestern University Press, 1973.

– *Phenomenologie de la Perception.* Paris: Gallimard, 1945.

– *Phenomenology of Perception.* Trans. Colin Smith. London: Routledge, 1994.

– *The Primacy of Perception and Other Essays on Phenomenological Psychology, the Philosophy of Art, History, and Politics.* Ed. James M. Edie. Evanston: Northwestern University Press, 1964.

– *Le Visible et l'Invisible. Suivi de notes de travail par Maurice Merleau-Ponty.* Paris: Gallimard, 1964.

– *Sense and Non-Sense.* Evanston: Northwestern University Press, 1964.

– *The Visible and the Invisible.* Evanston: Northwestern University Press, 1968.

Mohanty, J.N. *Edmund Husserl's Theory of Meaning.* The Hague: Martinus Nijhoff Publishers, 1969.

Morris, David. 'The Fold and the Body Schema in Merleau-Ponty and Dynamic Systems Theory.' *Chiasmi International* 1 (1999): 275–85.

Nancy, Jean-Luc. *The Inoperative Community*. Ed. Peter Connor. Trans. Peter Connor, Lisa Garbus, Michael Holland, and Simona Sawhney. Minneapolis: University of Minnesota Press, 1991.

Natanson, Maurice. *Edmund Husserl. Philosopher of Infinite Tasks*. Evanston: Northwestern University Press, 1973.

Nenon, Thomas, and Lester Embree, eds. *Issues in Husserl's* Ideas II. Dordrecht: Kluwer Academic Publishers, 1996.

O'Murchadha, Felix. 'Reduction, Externalism, and Immanence in Husserl and Heidegger.' *Synthese* 160, no. 3 (2008): 375–95.

Patocka, Jan. *An Introduction to Husserl's Phenomenology*. Trans. Erazim Kohák. Ed. James Dodd. Chicago: Open Court, 1996.

Plato. *Euthyphro*. In *Five Dialogues*. Trans. G.M.A. Grube. Indianapolis: Hackett Publishing, 2002.

Rabanaque, Luis. 'Percept, Concept, and the Stratification of Ideality.' In *Advancing Phenomenology: Essays in Honor of Lester Embree*, ed. Thomas Nenon and Philip Blosser. Dordrecht: Springer-Verlag, 2010.

Recco, Greg. *Athens Victorious: Democracy in Plato's Republic*. Lanham: Lexington Books, 2007.

Ricoeur, Paul. *Husserl. An Analysis of His Phenomenology*. Trans. Edward G. Ballard and Lester E. Embree. Evanston: Northwestern University Press, 1967.

Römpp, Georg. *Husserls Phänomenologie der Intersubjektivität. Und ihre Bedeutung für eine Theorie intersubjektiver Objektivität und die Konzeption einer phänomenologischen Philosophie*. Dordrecht: Kluwer Academic Publishers, 1992.

Rodemeyer, Lanei. 'Developments in the Theory of Time-Consciousness: An Analysis of Protention.' In Welton 2003: 125–56.

– *Intersubjective Temporality: It's About Time*. Dordrecht: Kluwer Academic Publishers, 2006.

Roy, Jean-Michel. 'Phenomenological Claims and the Myth of the Given.' In Thompson 2003: 1–32.

Russon, John. *Bearing Witness to Epiphany: Persons, Things, and the Nature of Erotic Life*. Albany: SUNY Press, 2009.

– *Human Experience: Philosophy, Neurosis and the Elements of Everyday Life*. Albany: SUNY Press, 2003.

– 'The Self as Resolution: Heidegger, Derrida, and the Intimacy of the Question of the Meaning of Being.' *Research in Phenomenology* 38 (2008): 90–110.

– 'The Spatiality of Self-Consciousness: Originary Passivity in Kant, Merleau-Ponty, and Derrida.' *Chiasmi International* 9 (2007): 219–32.

Sanday, Eric. 'Challenging the Established Order: Socrates' Perversion of Callicles' Position in Plato's *Gorgias*,' *Epoché* (forthcoming).

Sandmeyer, Bob. *Husserl's Constitutive Phenomenology: Its Problem and Promise.* New York: Routledge, 2009.

Sartre, Jean-Paul. *Being and Nothingness: A Phenomenological Essay on Ontology.* Trans. Hazel E. Barnes. New York: Washington Square Press, 1992.

– *The Transcendence of the Ego: An Existentialist Theory of Consciousness.* Trans. Forrest Williams and Robert Kirkpatrick. New York: Noonday Press, 1962.

Sawicki, Marianne. 'Empathy Before and After Husserl.' *Philosophy Today* 40, no. 1 (Spring 1997): 123–7.

Schües, Christina. 'Conflicting Apprehensions and the Question of Sensations.' In Depraz 1998: 139–62.

Schutz, Alfred. *Collected Papers I. The Problem of Social Reality.* Ed. Maurice Natanson. The Hague: Martinus Nijhoff Publishers, 1962.

– *The Phenomenology of the Social World.* Trans. George Walsh and Frederick Lehnert. Evanston: Northwestern University Press, 1967.

– 'The Problem of Transcendental Intersubjectivity in Husserl.' *Collected Papers III.* Ed. I. Schutz. *Phänomenologica* 22. The Hague: Martinus Nijhoff Publishers. 84–91.

Searle, John R. *Intentionality. An Essay in the Philosophy of Mind.* Cambridge: Cambridge University Press, 1983.

Sheets-Johnstone, Maxine. 'Re-thinking Husserl's Fifth Meditation.' *Philosophy Today* 43 (1999 Supplemental): 99–106.

– 'Phenomenology and Agency: Methodological and Theoretical Issues in Strawson's "The Self."' *Journal of Consciousness Studies* 6, no. 4 (1999): 48–69.

Smith, A.D. *Routledge Philosophy Guidebook to Husserl and the Cartesian Meditations.* London: Routledge, 2003.

Soffer, Gail. 'Perception and Its Causes.' In Nenon and Embree 1996: 37–56.

– 'The Other As Alter Ego: A Genetic Approach.' *Husserl Studies* 15, no. 3 (1999): 151–66.

Sokolowski, Robert. *The Formation of Husserl's Concept of Constitution.* The Hague: Martinus Nijhoff Publishers, 1964.

– *Husserlian Meditations: How Words Present Things.* Evanston: Northwestern University Press, 1974.

Stapleton, Timothy. 'The "Logic" of Husserl's Transcendental Reduction.' *Man and World* 15 (1982): 369–82.

Steinbock, Anthony J. *Home and Beyond. Generative Phenomenology after Husserl.* Evanston: Northwestern University Press, 1995.

Ströker, Elisabeth. *Husserl's Transcendental Phenomenology.* Stanford: Stanford University Press, 1993.

Talero, Maria L. 'Joint Attention and Expressivity: A Heideggerean Guide to the Limits of Empirical Investigation.' In *Heidegger and Cognitive Science*, ed. Julian Kiverstein and Michael Wheeler. London: Palgrave-Macmillan, 2011.

Thompson, Evan, ed. *The Problem of Consciousness: New Essays in Phenomenological Philosophy of Mind*. Calgary: University of Calgary Press, 2003.

Waksler, Frances Chaput. 'Analogues of Ourselves: Who Counts as an Other?' *Human Studies* 28, no. 4 (2005): 417–29.

Waldenfels, Bernhard. 'Experience of the Alien in Husserl's Phenomenology.' *Research in Phenomenology* (1990): 19–33.

Welton, Donn, ed. *The New Husserl: A Critical Reader*. Bloomington: Indiana University Press, 2003.

– *The Origins of Meaning: A Critical Study of the Thresholds of Husserlian Phenomenology*. The Hague: Martinus Nijhoff Publishers, 1983.

– *The Other Husserl: The Horizons of Transcendental Phenomenology*. Bloomington: Indiana University Press, 2000.

Yamagato, Yorihiro. 'The Self or the Cogito in Kinaesthesis.' In Zahavi 1998: 9–20.

Yamaguchi, Ichiro. *Passive Synthesis und Intersubjektivität bei Edmund Husserl*. The Hague: Martinus Nijhoff Publishers, 1982.

Zahavi, Dan. 'Beyond Realism and Idealism: Husserl's Late Concept of Constitution.' *Danish Yearbook of Philosophy* 29 (1994): 44–62.

– *Husserl und die transzendentale Intersubjektivität. Eine Antwort auf die sprachpragmatische Kritik*. Dordrecht: Kluwer Academic Publishers, 1996.

– *Husserl and Transcendental Intersubjectivity: A Response to the Linguistic-Pragmatic Critique*. Trans. Elizabeth A. Behnke. Athens: Ohio University Press, 2001.

– 'Husserl's Intersubjective Transformation of Transcendental Philosophy.' In Welton 2003: 233–54.

– *Husserl's Phenomenology*. Stanford: Stanford University Press, 2003.

– 'Inner Time-Consciousness and Pre-reflective Self-Awareness.' In Welton 2003: 157–80.

– 'Self-Awareness and Affection.' In Depraz and Zahavi 1998: 205–28.

– ed. *Self-Awareness, Temporality, and Alterity: Central Topics in Phenomenology*. Dordrecht: Kluwer Academic Publishers, 1998.

– 'Intentionality and Phenomenality: A Phenomenological Take on the Hard Problem.' In Thompson 2003: 63–92.

– *Self-Awareness and Alterity: A Phenomenological Investigation*. Evanston: Northwestern University Press, 1999.

– *Subjectivity and Selfhood. Investigating the First-Person Perspective*. Cambridge, MA: MIT Press, 2005.

Zahavi, Dan, and Frederik Stjernfelt, eds. *One Hundred Years of Phenomenology: Husserl's Logical Investigations Revisited.* Dordrecht: Kluwer Academic Publishers, 2002.

Zaner, Richard M. *The Problem of Embodiment. Some Contributions to a Phenomenology of the Body.* The Hague: Martinus Nijhoff Publishers, 1971.

Index

New Studies in Phenomenology and Hermeneutics

General Editor: Kenneth Maly